A Young Man's Journey

By the same author
WAI-WAI

NICHOLAS GUPPY

A Young Man's Journey

JOHN MURRAY

© Nicholas Guppy 1973

Printed in Great Britain by
The Camelot Press Ltd.
London and Southampton
0 7195 2852 6

In memory of my mother I dedicate this book to the people, animals, plants and saprophytes of Guyana—may they evolve together into an ecologically mature society where all are mutually esteemed.

Contents

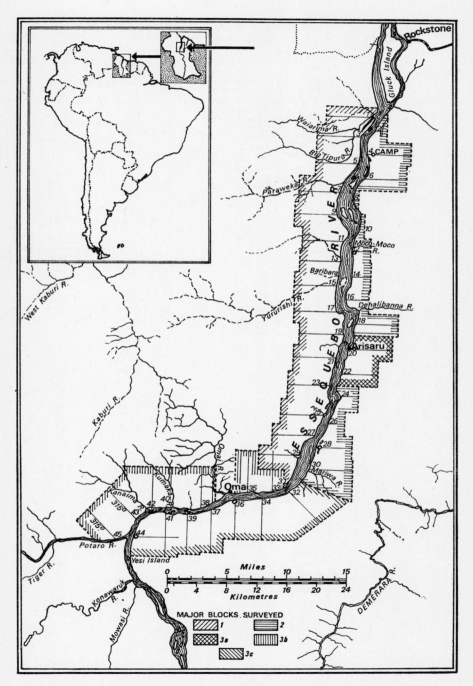

Sketch-map of the Essequebo River showing the expedition camps

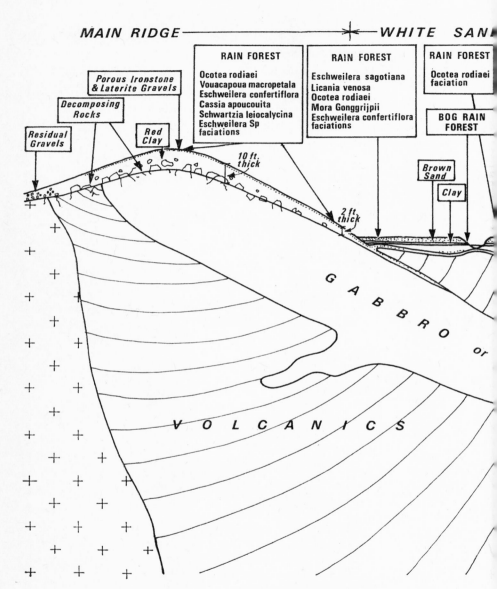

MAIN RIDGE ———————— ✳ ——WHITE SAN

RAIN FOREST

Ocotea rodiaei
Vouacapoua macropetala
Eschweilera confertiflora
Cassia apoucouita
Schwartzia leiocalycina
Eschweilera Sp
faciations

RAIN FOREST

Eschweilera sagotiana
Licania venosa
Ocotea rodiaei
Mora Gonggrijpii
Eschweilera confertiflora
faciations

RAIN FOREST

Ocotea rodiaei
faciation

**BOG RAIN
FOREST**

Porous Ironstone
& Laterite Gravels

Decomposing
Rocks

Residual
Gravels

Red
Clay

10 ft.
thick

2 ft.
thick

Brown
Sand

Clay

G A B B R O   or

V O L C A N I C S

Idealised cross section of the survey area

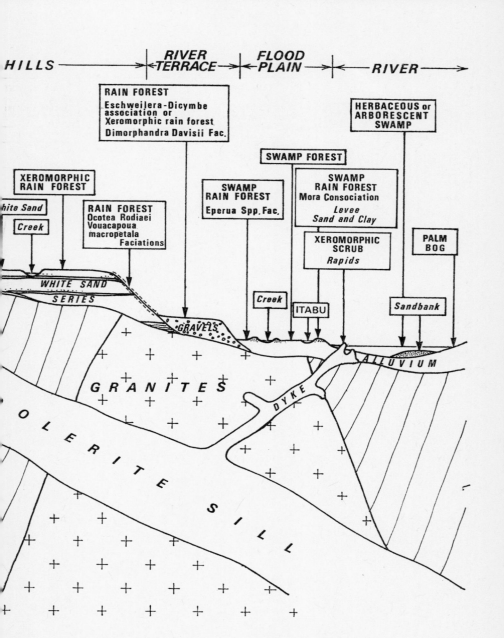

HILLS ──────── RIVER TERRACE ──── FLOOD PLAIN ──── RIVER ──────→

RAIN FOREST
Eschweilera-Dicymbe
association or
Xeromorphic rain forest
Dimorphandra Davisii Fac.

HERBACEOUS or
ARBORESCENT
SWAMP

XEROMORPHIC
RAIN FOREST

SWAMP FOREST

SWAMP
RAIN FOREST
Mora Consociation
Levee
Sand and Clay

RAIN FOREST
Ocotea Rodiaei
Vouacapoua
macropetala
Faciations

SWAMP
RAIN FOREST
Eperua Spp. Fac.

White Sand

Creek

XEROMORPHIC
SCRUB
Rapids

PALM
BOG

WHITE SAND
SERIES

Creek

ITABU

Sandbank

GRAVELS

ALLUVIUM

G R A N I T E S

DYKE

O L E R I T E   S I L L

Illustrations

from the authors' photographs

Introduction

A young man of twenty-three began this book. His metamorphosis, aged forty-six, has completed it. Are we the same person? His troubles have shaped me, his face causes me a pang when I look at old photographs. And for twenty years I have been digging into his memories.

Could I ever have been so innocent as he? A terrible war had just been fought when he went to Guyana—yet that young man believed that humans are naturally motivated by goodwill towards their fellows, and that there was such a thing as 'truth', which could be discovered, and must be made one's guide. From even these few facts the reader will guess that he was a romantic, from a sheltered background. Over-educated by his three years at Cambridge and one at Oxford, he was ignorant of almost everything that today he holds important—of everything beyond a tiny literate world of friends and family. He knew nothing about money except that it was hard to earn, and was still shocked by trivialities like impoliteness and greed. His motivations were idealistic, his hopes old-fashioned. I say all this so that you will not think that I wrote this book—I have merely edited it, and tried to fill in gaps.

In 1949, with an honours degree in Botany, this precursor of mine took his first job and went to British Guiana (as it then was) as Assistant Conservator of Forests, where he remained except for another year at Oxford, until 1953. This book is the story of six of his early months there: three of them spent in exploring, all of them crucial in his growing up. It is a fragment of autobiography, therefore, rather than a travel book in the strict sense. But why was it so long in being completed? Partly because the young man was writing other finished or half-finished books during those slow years while he changed into me, partly because he had little money, or energy, to spare. A sponsor, a rich mistress or wife, and it might have been finished earlier. But perhaps it is well that it was not, for only now am I able to accept him. He was at times embarrassingly naïve and vulnerable. But he was truthful. I could have moulded his material much more, but I want to let him live, not dress him up with false maturity.

The events recorded in these pages shaped our subsequent life. But one thing has remained steady since their time: the desire to perceive clearly and to describe two simultaneous 'realities'—the external, objective world of a little-known region about which no other book has been written; and the internal, subjective experience of a place and time in which 'I' was changing rapidly. To some extent this means that at times I have used what may appear to be the techniques of fiction. But 'I' kept a full diary throughout this period, and most of the directly quoted conversations, as well as almost all of the other material used, have been taken from this. Again, certain personalities have been renamed or reassembled, so as to give me greater freedom in reporting. If they are still apparently identifiable, it is unintentional. Anyone who sees himself in one of the less attractive characters must indeed be suffering from a very guilty conscience.

Most books are written on one level—as detective novels or philosophy, as botany or travel—and aimed at a particular fragment of their readers. Yet in real life the person who is introspective at one moment is laughing at the next; the harassed office worker becomes a lover in the evening or settles down to identify a flower. Here I have assumed the reader to be a normally complex and changeable human. On this particular expedition certain analogies I had noticed between human and plant societies began to take solid form. Among plants, as every gardener knows, there are gangsters, entrepreneurs, solid citizens, successful nonentities. Plant ecologists, studying the relatively objectively observable communities formed by such individuals, have evolved concepts still alien to sociologists, but which to me seem to give remarkable insights into human problems. Only a few years ago anthropomorphism (the ascription of human attributes to animals) was considered the ultimate sin by biologists. Now its obverse, zoomorphism, has become their delight—scarcely a day passes without some animal trait being upheld as revealing a truth about ourselves. So let me now, to give pleasure to speculatives, toss in the new intellectual vice of phytomorphism. For not only are plants the real (and often fashionably bisexual) heroes and heroines of this book, but from observing them I have learned much of what I believe I know about people.

Manaus,
November 1972

NOTE: *Guiana* is a geographical region. It comprises that part of northeastern South America where the rivers flow into the Atlantic or into the lower Orinoco, rather than into the Amazon, but it includes the watershed mountains as a whole.

Guyana is a country which forms part of that region. Its name before independence was British Guiana.

I think that the river
Is a strong brown god—Sullen, untamed and
    intractable

.   .   .   .   .   .

Keeping his seasons and rages, destroyer, reminder
Of what men choose to forget. Unhonoured,
    unpropitiated
By worshippers of the machine, but waiting,
    watching and waiting.

T. S. Eliot: 'The Dry Salvages'

1

Easter at Bartica

I have a strongly analogising brain. I was thinking of the
parallels between human and plant societies as I lay in bed,
sweaty, impatient with inactivity—and puzzled. My sprained
and swollen ankle was wrapped in a wet poultice and rested
on a towel. I had twisted it three days before while swimming.
In escaping from a poisonous water snake my foot had slid
between two submerged rocks, and I had put my weight on
it. I would probably not be able to work in the jungle for
several weeks.

It was mid-morning. I glanced out of the window. Beyond
a few corrugated-iron shacks and an irregular shrub or two,
stretched a rippling plain of blue-black water: the Essequebo
River, four miles wide. Its jungled banks were faintly visible on
either hand; in the distance northwards it simply flowed into
the horizon. Nearer, two islands flew laputa-style, apparently
suspended in mid-air above the polished water.

The sky was glaring. the sun burned on the red dust road.
The only sound was the strumming of the Easter trade winds in
the eaves of the hotel, the flagellation of the palms in the
derelict garden opposite.

I stretched out to the records on the floor beside my bed,
chose Bartok's 6th string quartet played by the Ehrling Bloch
quartet, and lay back to listen. What was he saying? Four
strands of excellent conversation in a strange tongue. I could
catch the gist, but not the meaning of individual words.
Overhead flies circled or perched on the naked bulb hanging
on its length of wire from the wood-strip ceiling. Originally
they had preferred to revolve around my nose or big-toe—
vantage points from which to survey the room: its iron-framed
bed, Morris chair, table, washbasin, and bare wooden floor—
stark, but comfort in a hot, humid, dusty climate. By raising

and lowering the bulb I had discovered their preference for a position about 14 inches away from any of the room's flat surfaces. I have given them what they wanted—a better vantage-point—and now I was able to lie untroubled.

A shout outside: I leaned on my elbow and glanced down on the road. Normally it would have been empty, but this was Easter Saturday, climax of the kite-flying season, and already it was crowded with men and boys. The earliest had been out since 7 a.m. and had obtained the best positions on the waterside. Above them a whole line of tissue spermatozoa—coloured boxes, diamonds, squares with long twisted tails of knotted cloth—darted, wriggled or undulated. Several had loose side-panels, and emitted buzzing sounds.

A clear space among them was occupied evidently by a 'mad-bull'—a kite with razor blades or bits of glass on its tail to enable it to cut the strings of rivals. Following the thread of the kite down from the sky, my eyes came to its owner, a muscular Negro who stood on the grassy road-verge fifty yards away. His face was blissful as he gazed upwards—could his *really* be a mad-bull? Beside him were a rum bottle and a few sticks of sugar-cane. Elsewhere other devotees lolled or stood, similarly prepared for the day.

I lay back and continued reading: sparse statistics about an area some hundred miles further south up the Essequebo—a forgotten, uninhabited stretch of country cut off from the coastlands by tremendous rapids, but reputed to contain amazingly rich forests. In a few months I should be leading an expedition to survey them, an exciting prospect for someone who had hitherto spent only three nights under canvas. But particularly so because I was a botanist who specialised in plant ecology—the relationship between plants and their environment. Such a little-known region would offer many prospects of discovery.

Half an hour later the talking and shouting outside my window had risen to such a pitch that I sat up again and looked out. The hotel's public bar had opened, and Amerindians and Negroes were going in and out with glasses and rum bottles in their hands, while others were standing about, moving, or quarrelling in groups. Many wore long cutlasses, a sign that they were probably wood-cutters or prospectors, who had come in from the bush to spend Easter at Bartica. Right in the middle of the throng two such men were facing each other. They evidently meant business—they were red-eyed with belligerence. 'You done cheat me, man—you take me gold, and wha' you leave me? Eh, man; eh, man? Answer dat!' and slash! The taller man had blood on his forearm, a red patch on his shoulder. Shouts, and the onlookers scattered as the shorter, more aggressive of the protagonists turned and went for them, before returning to tackle his foe again. None of the town's half-dozen policemen could be seen—on public holidays they always vanished. 'Chop 'e, man, chop 'e!' shouted a passer-by, almost casually. No one seemed to take much notice of this conflict—indeed two others were now raging. It was more a question of the soberer staying out of the way of the drunker, of dodging flying cutlass blows and avoiding the fallen, yet of remaining within reach of the bar. Many of these men had probably lived isolated for months, seldom meeting their friends and enemies. Now all the resentment and frustrations they had built up in solitude were being released by drink.

My hotel was owned by one of the barons of the interior diamond and gold fields—what if the mob should invade it? But then, was this a mob? It was still a mass of individuals. It could easily turn into a mob—it only needed focusing. But for the moment our thin front door was a psychological barrier strong enough to separate me, politely eating lunch on a tray, from the uncouth world outside.

Speeded up cine photography shows that plants are violently aggressive: they strangle, poison, and elbow each other out of existence. We must presume that they act as individuals, even when apparently in concert. Their behaviour is direct, purposeful (why not? Though this is not to say conscious), and unaffected by ethics or finer feelings. It leads to the organisation of complex and very stable societies, such as forests, in which roles are apportioned between the plants present, and antagonisms at any given moment appear minimal. Was the sort of interaction that I saw in front of me also a necessary part of society-building—and leading in the same sort of direction? I had been bullied at school, I had been a spectator (several times bombed) in a horrific war: I had

B

seen numerous fights. None of these things had seemed to me likely to produce positive results in building a society, but I had not really thought it out satisfactorily. Might analogies drawn from plants, which apparently behaved so similarly, help us to understand humans? It would be interesting if they could—if only because one could view plant behaviour with detachment.

At one o'clock the bar closed, and by 1.30 the street outside was almost clear, except for half a dozen prostrate dark-stained figures, groaning or horribly still: badly wounded, dead, or drunk, it was hard to tell; I hoped mostly just drunk. I recognised one of them as Julian James, an Amerindian employed by the Forest Department. 'We always take him on expeditions'—my immediate boss, Dennys Fanshawe, had said.

Julian was beginning to stir. He raised himself on one arm, head hanging, and retched. A sticky pool spread in front of him. Feeling better, he looked around. His face was bruised, with a big cut on the cheek. His shirt was torn and soaked with sweat, dust, vomit and blood. He began crawling towards another prone figure, beside whom lay a cutlass. Was he going to attack the man, or just recover his knife?

I watched as he picked up the knife and staggered to his feet. 'Julian!' I shouted. He paused, half looked up, with eyes visibly crimson even thirty yards away, then staggered off down the road shouting drunkenly. Nobody took any notice of him, though he made wild swipes at anybody who came near.

The flyer of the 'mad bull' was still standing unconcernedly by the roadside, the string of his kite in one hand, the other holding a half-chewed stick of sugar-cane. His face rotated dreamily as he gazed up at his powerfully tugging kite.

As he approached him, Julian raised his cutlass. The man turned and a look of amazement came over his face. He jumped back as Julian's arm came down in a tremendous blow, and tumbled over backwards into the ditch, a thin red slice gashed in his biceps. Then scrambling and shaking he got himself out of the way and ran as fast as he could down the street, holding his left hand to the wounded place. His kite fluttered away beyond the roof-tops. Julian paused, then staggered out of sight round the corner.

The last bars of the Bartok died on the air and the record

went round and round with a monotonous knocking. I switched off the gramophone, and lay back.

How could a society be built up round people who behaved like this? Perhaps they were no worse than heavy drinkers anywhere—but drunkards are usually in the minority, whereas in Bartica a large part of the population of the surrounding country had assembled. It was not even as if there had been a carnival spirit, with dancing, singing, lovemaking, as well as fighting—the emotions that I had seen released had all been unpleasant. I did not want to pass judgement—I wanted to understand. Something seemed to be wrong. All this hatred and destructiveness—how could it arise among people living so isolated from each other? Intensity of competition between individuals, I had always assumed, was a product of crowding. Now I saw that it might depend far more on the choices available to each individual. Direct confrontation—over women, jobs, living places, etc.—could arise anywhere, just so long as there were two people wanting the same thing. But this would be less likely to occur if alternatives existed in a more complex society, i.e. with more kinds of jobs, opportunities, places to live, possible mates. In all societies, however, crowding would exacerbate the existing conditions—and crowding in a simple society would be the worst state of all, for it would exhaust options soonest. Men who have no options left have no alternative to fighting.

Bully, then, for a complex society. Furthermore its very complexities would most likely imply a developed system of manners—of rituals for handling difficult and unexpected as well as everyday situations. Clearly these people I had been watching had not evolved any adequate code for handling the stresses to which they were subjected. Their flashpoint was low and their choices were few. All commonplaces perhaps, but at the age of twenty-two one must begin to make one's own generalisations.

But how do you achieve a complex, as distinct from a merely crowded, society? I had always assumed that the natural (as distinct from the supernatural) basis for any morality lay in not hurting others. Now I began to see that mere restraint was not enough for building up a society, even in such a scattered community as this, where contacts with enemies could be avoided, and that a second basis for a natural morality lay in the need for co-operation. It was also clear that individual and social morality were such separate things that they might lead in different directions. Perhaps the value of religions was that they imposed a social morality upon people who would otherwise have had only a personal morality? If so, the possibilities of a society must be based directly upon the possibilities allowed by its religion: no religion, no society.

It was an odd thought, particularly to an ecologist. For plants, without either morality or religion, had built up societies of incredible complexity—richer than those of any other living things except man—upon a laissez faire basis. And the jungles around me at Bartica, and which I would be exploring on my expedition, were among the most complex known of such plant societies. Of course in jungles different species fill different roles, while in human societies different men do. But this did not weaken the analogy—the similarity between interactions in both cases seemed close. The question was—if plants could do it, why not men? Why could not we, with only a personal morality, build societies as complicated (in terms of numbers of different life-styles involved) as those that plants achieved with no morality at all? Logically, once one removed the preconceptions imposed by religion and tradition, any failure to do so seemed only attributable to our distinctively human differences, such as mobility or powers of communication, or the varied needs of different human psychological types. Could these in themselves make morality necessary? Or should morality be regarded as merely an imposed factor that acted as a brake upon our possibilities, above all in keeping our societies comparatively simple? If so, then perhaps simple societies had competitive advantages, which in themselves led, albeit unconsciously, to the development of moralities. It was a question I would have to think of further.

At this time racial antagonisms were largely dormant in Guyana—they had not yet been magnified for political ends. It was hard to imagine *any* of the people I had met here being capable of producing a self-enriching, continually evolving society such as that of Western Europe. But of course that was asking a good deal anywhere, at any time in history.

Besides, here the rules were still imposed from 4,000 miles away. The surface was usually smooth, but if all restraints from outside were removed, what would happen? Would these people acquire soon enough the necessary restraints to create a developing society? Morality, I had begun to suspect, was what first gives a society shape, and then limits its further possibilities of growth.

Perhaps these questions troubled me because Guyana was so different from what I had expected: I had been born in Trinidad and brought up there until the age of twelve, among relatives who were very much part of the old-style English and French planter society—but with the extra repute of eccentrics. My great-grandfather had first come to Trinidad to look at one of his relatives' properties. He had fallen in love with the island and the life, returned on behalf of the British Government to advise on the settlement of liberated slaves, and had stayed on—abandoning a promising career at the bar and reducing his wife to misery and flower-painting—as a planter and member of the Colonial legislature. His son, my grandfather, who became a distinguished palaeontologist (his works are still in print because he described many of the foraminifera which indicate oil-bearing rock strata), was only aged twenty-three when, in 1859, Dr. Günther of the British Museum named after him what has become since his death the world's most popular aquarium fish, the 'Guppy'. He died in 1919, too soon to know that his name had passed into the language.

He organised the island's school system, and rates a favourable mention by Dr. Eric Williams in his *History of the Peoples of Trinidad and Tobago*. My father had been a more humble colonial administrator, and in turn had elected to stay in the island he loved rather than seek promotion elsewhere.

So the West Indies were a strong part of my background—and the people who typified them for me were a series of kindly old gentlemen in white suits and panama hats, full of disappearing knowledge ('Eh, boy, where can you get a cup of *real* chocolate today—the drink that drove Montezuma mad? Made from crushed cocoa beans, vanilla pod, cane sugar and cream? Or a cook who knows how to boil turtle eggs, or the different kinds of mango and avocado? It's unheard of.') They were victims of the economic stagnation of the colonial system,

exacerbated by world-wide depression. They hearkened back
to better times because none seemed to lie ahead; but they all
loved their land, and would think of living nowhere else; and
their style still contributes to the very different West Indian
culture of today.

After spending the war educating myself, either alone in
Perthshire or at school in England, and acquiring a degree at
Cambridge and some post-graduate experience at Oxford in
botany and tropical forestry, I had chosen to work in Guyana so
as to return to my remembered childhood world of rich jungles,
strange animals, beautiful butterflies—and of such people.

But in Guyana they had no equivalent. Love, understanding,
indentification with the country and its history seemed not to
exist among its European population. The country's history
was a story of blood, oppression, rebellion, unhappiness, and
disease—it was unbelievable the weight of sorrow the place
seemed to carry.

In Bartica, and among the Amerindians, I had begun to
find something different. But the initial shock had made me
notice and question people and try to analyse what I saw with
the means that I knew.

Fortunately, my professional interest was in plants, not
people—and plants are much more straightforward. They have
no morals only behaviour, stay in one place, and grow
slowly. Their societies can be measured with detachment. So
plant ecologists have been able to reach more definite ideas
than sociologists about the stages through which plants reach
the ultimate stability known as a 'climax' society, the nature
of which differs from place to place, according to climate,
constituent species, and soil. The relationship between these
factors is often illustrated graphically by means of a triangle,
with arrows between the corners whose thicknesses indicate
the strength with which each factor acts upon the others. Do
human societies go through similar phases of development,
and also reach climax stages? I began to wonder whether if
I treated the beliefs held in a society (including its knowledge,
religion, and economic system) as equivalent in human terms
to climate, the sum of its resources as equivalent to geology and
soil, I could use such an ecological scheme in beginning to
analyse the human world.

Among plants the society produced by the interactions of all these factors would consist of species, among humans of individuals, with differing potentialities and requirements. As each factor changed, so the social point of equilibrium—'the climax' society possible—would itself change, but at each moment a hypothetical social equilibrium would be calculable. If the discrepancy between the calculable and the actual society were great, the society would either be changing rapidly or in danger of revolution.

As I lay in bed wondering about this, I saw the possibility of deriving from these interactions a simple system of social analysis more natural than any of which I was aware proposed by Marx or other social scientists. I decided that I would test the idea against what I saw in Guyana.

At seven o'clock in the evening dinner was brought up to me and I awoke. The streets had cleared; the drunk and wounded had recovered, been dragged away, or had made their own ways back to their homes, or 'loggias'—the open-sided mud-and-thatch lodging houses where bushmen slung their hammocks for a few pence a day when in Bartica.

More dozing until ten, when a low sound disturbed me. The palm plumage outside the window glittered like aluminium, brilliantly moon-rayed against a sky deepening from ultra-marine to black. Far and near, motorboat-toads raced their engines, insects chirruped from bush and grass.

'Neek!' came a low call. Beneath me under the window a dark form was crouched against the wall, having leapt the ditch from the street. It was Aggie!

'Neek, drop down something, man, and I go climb up. Loose de sheet, eh, man?'

'Aggie, it's no good, I got fever. . . . Come and see me tomorrow. I really feel bad.'

'Oh, Neek.'

'I mean it, Aggie. I feel really bad.'

'All right. OK, man.' And springing back across the ditch she picked up her gun, turned round, flashed her teeth at me, and was gone into the darkness.

I had met Aggie only a few weeks before, on my arrival in Bartica. I had been in high spirits, because the friendly pilot of the small seven-passenger Grumman amphibian had allowed me to take the controls until a few seconds from landing. Roaring low over the coconut grove at the far end of the town, scattering nuts and swishing the palms, we had dropped down to the river in a steep curve, striking and bouncing along in a cascade of spray; then stopped, flung open the hatch, anchored, and waited for the boat to come out and take us ashore. In it had been this handsome flashing-eyed girl, carrying a 12-bore shotgun, come to greet her uncle, a huge old man who had sat opposite me. Her surname was Spanish, her uncle Scots; and her bone-structure and complexion suggested a strong mixture of Amerindian—an exciting blend of bloods and temperaments.

The whole party of us had gone to have a drink together in the Bartica hotel before scattering to our various destinations up and down river. Aggie, I learned, lived a few miles up the nearby Mazaruni. By the time we had finished our drink she had told me about herself—she was bursting with eagerness to do so. I recognised the eagerness of someone who led a solitary life—but there was also a touch of predation about the way she took me over, something lazy, casual, and intriguing. She sprawled beside me, her gun on the floor by the chair, completely savage. Her figure, brown from living in the sun, was strong and beautiful, her movements sinewy and catlike. I felt over-civilised under her black-eyed scrutiny: like a *Tournedos à la Béarnaise* set before a female jaguar who really wanted raw meat.

Although I had been extremely lonely since coming to Guyana, because there was almost no one of my own age with whom I could share my experiences, I liked tiny Bartica much more than Georgetown, the capital. I enjoyed my work here, with its frequent trips into the surrounding forests, as much as I disliked the routine of the head office, the conventions of Government officialdom, and the boredom of Georgetown social life. There were fewer people, but they were simpler, and I felt freer. Indeed, I was almost happy.

Bartica styled itself rather grandly—for a place of some six streets—as 'The Gateway to the Interior of British Guiana'. For it was really hardly even a town, only a large jungle village on a cleared point where Guyana's three mightiest rivers, the Essequebo, the Mazaruni, and the Cuyuni, merged into one

enormous stream. Most of its houses were weatherboard shacks
with battered tin roofs, raised above the ground on wooden or
brick posts; its streets were earthen and weed-run, yet it was
full of casual charm—its people were friendly, happy-go-
lucky, and everyone lived as much as possible out of doors in
the abundant sunshine, except during the hours of siesta. First
Avenue, the main shopping street, seethed with ceaselessly
active traders, with gaily dressed men and women of different
races—East Indians, Amerindians, Negroes, Chinese, Europeans, Levantines—with donkeys, goats, dogs, and chickens.
Radios blared calypsos out of open doors and windows, strange
smells wafted to and fro, saw-mills hummed and snarled, and
an extraordinary archaic electric-lighting plant produced
clouds of black smoke from its chimney. All around there was
the coming and going of the rivers: speedboats racing to and
from the riverside houses; steady chug-chugging trading
launches crowded with gold and diamond miners, prostitutes
and balata bleeders, bunches of bananas, crates of salt fish,
and canned goods; and slowly drifting timber-rafts, floating
their logs down from faraway concessions, on which whole
families lived, a-sway in hammocks under little palm-thatch
roofs. In the shallows, amid forests of mooring poles, naked
brown and black babies splashed delightedly, washerwomen
sang, scrubbing their lathery clothes on monstrous half-
submerged greenheart logs, and old grizzled fishermen dried
and mended their nets.

The forest was all around at Bartica: on the hill above the
town, a tremendous rampart; on the far encircling shores, a
low irregular line. Often in the afternoons, when I had finished
work, I would walk down to the point where the two vast rivers
Mazaruni and Essequebo met (the Cuyuni entered the
Mazaruni a little way upstream), just to gaze across at it, far
away over the water.

Then I would walk upstream along the Mazaruni shore.
Away from the noise of the shopping streets there was a sense
of peace and happiness. The buildings became fewer, the red
lateritic roads dwindled into grassy paths banked high on
either side with caladiums and arums, great heart-shaped leaves
spilling dew-drops as one passed. Here boat builders fashioned
extraordinary river craft: boats with flat bottoms, square ends,

spoon-shaped bows, often so weird looking that one could hardly believe them capable of floating or manœuvring—yet perfectly designed for the turbulent inland waters. Then came a group of saw-pits, where superb bronze bodies bent and straightened, dripping sweat, following without pause a plucked string's line along the logs. The air here was filled with the smell of fresh wood from new planks, and one trod softly on piles of yellow sawdust overrun with little purple-flowered convolvulus vines. Beyond, I might meet an old man swinging in his hammock beneath the trees, or one of the Amerindian men who worked for the Forest Department, sitting weaving a basket on his doorstep, surrounded by his children.

Along this shore were several small beaches of soft white sand, lined with palm trees and round-leaved vegetation. It was probably because of them that I liked Bartica so much, for beaches mean freedom, journeys, cleanliness, messages. Strange blackened or whitened water-worn fruit, branches, leaves, and twigs lay strewn on these sands, tidings from the mysterious forests up river. It was hard to believe that this great expanse of water was not the sea. Yet at my feet, where a bean the size of a lady's handbag had come to rest and purple-hued bignonia flowers were piling into a drift, it lapped not clear and fizzing, but strangely quiet and the colour of tea. Each angle of the sun or veer of wind, each passing cloud, produced a play of colours and effects extraordinary to an eye used to northern monotones. The water might be smooth and opalescent at one moment— then suddenly it would grow choppy, a dark steely blue where waves sprang lightly, reflecting the sky. Then a tint of un-believable murky grey would appear, changing to dark amethyst as heavy storm-clouds rolled swiftly up from the sea, 40 miles away down river. The men asleep on a battered old barge leaning on its side among mangroves and tangled roots would leap to their feet at the sudden chill, and run for their homes before the rain came—while over at Kaow Island, 3 miles away, a shaft of sunlight might suddenly pick out an ocean-going ship loading timber, and set the green trees behind it into an incandescent blaze.

Bartica was a town with a history. From being a quiet mission station a hundred years before (on Baro-tika, 'Axe-rust', point), it had burgeoned in the early years of the century amid the excitement of a series of alluvial diamond and gold rushes, which had continued until the late 1920s. Although on nothing like the scale of the Californian, Alaskan, Australian, or South African rushes, there had been the same almost legendary atmosphere. Thousands of 'pork-knockers' (casual prospectors) had set out from here for the further interior, their batelles (gravel-washing pans), food, and equipment on their backs, to live in the depths of the forests, panning each stream they came to. Many died of starvation or fever, many were lost in the bush, many killed in fights, or drowned when boats upset in the rapids. But still they poured through. Even quite large streams would be diverted to expose the bed, and primitive jigs set up to separate diamonds and gold from sand or gravel. Wherever a 'shout' was made, hundreds would rush to stake claims nearby. Fortunes were made overnight, but few were kept.

Endless stories were told of excitement-crazed prospectors rushing into town after their months in the bush, and spending everything they had in a senseless orgy of roistering, drinking and wild generosity. In fleets of continuously hooting taxis (brought by boat from Georgetown), surrounded by whores and highly-dressed henchmen, they would drive around the town until the taxi-meters had rung up all their money. A former circus rider had forcibly fed a donkey with five-dollar notes—only to see it killed by the spectators to recover them. There were fights, murders, robberies—yet an atmosphere of light-hearted vagabondage, of easy high-spirited companion-ship. The great thing was to have the wildest splash while the money lasted. Afterwards? Why, back into the interior for another few months, or even years.

'What can you expect, man?' asked a friend, a half Portu-guese, half East Indian shopkeeper, with whom I was sitting on the river wall one day. 'I'll tell you what's wrong wi' dis country. Nobody but madmen, like dese people you see las' Saturday, will go in de interior. Pork-knockers—a bunch of fools. Dey get de name because dey would come into a store an' knock on de counter, and call out, "Pork, man, pork!" For dat is what dey live on in de bush. Salt pork. But dey is tricky, I telling you. I was a river trader and I get rich. But it was because I work an' kill myself. I used to have to grub-stake dose

men. I would get de receipt from dem, sign—but it's worth
nothing! Sometimes they die. Sometimes they pay—sometimes
they owe me for a whole year! When dey strike rich, next thing
dey go pas' me at night and t'row de money away somewhere
else and back here for mo' food! Sorry, Mr. Gouveia, sorry!
So dat's why dey has to pay more because each time I jus' have
to take a chance. I tell you, it's only a few people get rich,
mostly traders, and gleaners—de ones who come *after* the pork-
knockers leave, and *really* work out de streams with a lot of
men.' He named a few of the colony's families, none very rich
by European or American standards. 'Dose are de men dat do
de real work—yet some of de pork-knockers strike over
$10,000 in one time! They say that there is only *one* of them all
who stay rich! Mostly they spend de money in a few weeks and
go back again, until dey is worn out and die.'

At the height of the gold and diamond fever a railway had
been constructed from the Demerara River to Rockstone on
the Essequebo, to circumvent the miles of dangerous rapids
above Bartica. A hotel had been built at Rockstone, and
regular launch services had been run by several companies—
Hamiltons, Garnetts, Sprostons, the Real Daylight Balata
Company—into areas today scarcely accessible. For by the
1920s most of the easy gold and diamonds had been panned.
The railway line was abandoned to rust, and Rockstone had
crumbled until only the brick pillars of its hotel were reputed
still to stand. To get to the middle Essequebo today I would
have to go through the Essequebo rapids—and where would
I find one of the old river captains to guide me?

'You'll never find one,' my friend said. 'Dey's all dead. Dey
had to know every stone in dat river, I'm telling you, in de dry
season *as well* as de rainy season an' in between. It's like ten
different rivers . . . hundreds of lives lost in dose rivers.'
Bartica had not declined after the railway was built, because
it still remained the base for the Mazaruni and the Cuyuni—
there was no way round the much worse rapids on those rivers.
Even so, at the height of the boom there had been 10,000
prospectors in the Mazaruni region, where today there were
only some 2,000.

At one time the pork-knockers of the Cuyuni had organised
themselves into what they had called the 'Republic'. They had

elected a president, and made their own laws and had posted
guards with guns on two large rocks on either side of the river.
Nobody could enter the Republic without permission on pain
of death. For three years several hundred people had lived in
it, sending emissaries out every now and again to sell gold and
buy provisions. Finally Vincent Roth, working for the Lands
and Mines Department, had won the republicans' confidence
and persuaded them to disarm and allow a police station to be
established.

But the pork-knockers had only touched the gold in the
smaller streams. After World War II British Guiana Consolidated and other enterprises had started dredging the deep
gravels of the larger rivers—and at once met with such success
that gold became again an important item in the country's
balance sheet. And now, for the first time, attempts were being
made to establish reef mining of the type carried out in South
Africa and Australia, and shafts had been sunk as much as
300 feet deep. Nor was gold the only mineral that attracted
people again into the interior. Valuable deposits of bauxite,
manganese, titanium, and columbium had been found, and
there was even a hope of oil. There was limitless hydro-electric
potential—while there remained the riches of tens of thousands
of square miles of almost unexplored and unexploited forests.
Those of the middle Essequebo were reputed to be among the
finest still remaining that were relatively accessible.

So the fabled riches of Guyana were at last to be revealed.
The interior was to be opened up and peopled, industries
developed. But it was a dream that had been dreamed many
times before—ever since Raleigh had dreamed of El Dorado.

'How fertile must the lowlands be,' the enthusiastic Charles
Waterton had written in 1810, 'from the accumulation of
fallen leaves and trees for centuries. How propitious the
swamps and slimy beds of the rivers, heated by a downward
sun, to the amazing growth of alligators, serpents, and innumerable insects. How inviting the forests to the feathered
tribes, where you see buds, blossoms, green and ripe fruit, full
grown and fading leaves, all on the same tree! How secure the
wild beasts may rove in endless mazes! Perhaps those mountains too, which appear so bleak and naked, as if quite
neglected, are, like Potosi, full of precious metal.' Guyana was

like a sleeper who stirs every now and then, wondering whether to wake up—or to doze off again for another half-century.

On the night of our first meeting Aggie had asked me to a party. Wandering along an earth path into which, near the outskirts of the town, one of its tiny streets dwindled, we came to a wooden hut beside the river, hidden in a bank of candle-bushes. It consisted of a single room, with a verandah in front on which three hammocks were slung. There were also two low stools, on one of which stood a bottle of rum and a glass.

The 'party' consisted of a young married couple (he was a clerk in a timber-exporting firm), Aggie's small sister aged ten (with long knobbly knees, bare feet, and wispy hair coiled into two pigtails), a young coffee-coloured bachelor spark, who was evidently after Aggie, but was contenting himself with the sister meanwhile; and ourselves. There was no light, only the rising moon. There was no conversation either, but the bottle was passed round, and we drank neat from it in the semi-darkness.

This was no ordinary rum, I realised, gasping for breath, but 'High Wine', straight from the distillery, and rendered non-poisonous by having a beefsteak hung in it for a few days, to absorb the acetone and fusel oil. Each mouthful that I gulped passed like a red-hot bullet down my oesophagus and lingered, small, round and fiery, when it reached the stomach, where it set up an area of inflammation.

Half an hour after the party had begun, weary and un-willing to continue leaning against the earth wall much longer, I flopped into a hammock—the married couple were already engaged with each other in another. Aggie laid her gun aside and sat down beside me. We did not kiss, but moving around to get comfortable, I felt something soft; a shudder ran through her, and I slid my hand into her blouse opening and over an enormous, beautifully rounded breast. The nipple stuck into the palm of my hand like a cork.

Aggie breathed like a whale, ran her hand up my leg, sank her teeth into my neck and then withdrew them, whispering fiercely: 'Wait, man—don't do nothin'. De boy is studying for mystery. *NO. Wait.*'

'Studying for mystery' puzzled me; then I realised that the youth was going into the Church, and must not be unhinged by libertine behaviour. (That of the married couple—which had evidently reached a climax, judging from the puffing and blowing from the nearby darkness—was sanctified and harmless.) So we lay, locked in an unconsummated embrace, motionless, while the bottle, and then another one, was circulated from hammock to hammock.

This was quite fun, after my six months in the colony, but not enough. However, each time I so much as twitched, Aggie bit deeply into my neck to show me that there was nothing doing, at the same time whispering reassurances for the future. Somewhat unwillingly I accepted the situation and we lay still for a while, listening to the frogs and nightjars outside.

Suddenly there was a thud, as the minister-to-be rolled out of his hammock and hit the floor. He groaned, lay still and began to snore.

'Look, Aggie, he's passed out!' I whispered.

But there was no response from her. I shook her gently. She was fast asleep also, a beautiful, slender, muscular form in the moonlight.

The couple had disappeared into the room, locking the door. Stealthily I got up, lifted Aggie's legs into the hammock in case she tumbled to the ground, and crept back to the hotel.

2

Aggie's River

To begin with, most of my work was done around an abandoned penal settlement a few miles up the Mazaruni. Here—beyond an attractive eighteenth-century wooden 'Colony House', the home of the former Dutch governors of Essequebo—extensive paths had been cut through the jungle leading to various trees whose growth habits, times of flowering, fruition, and leafing, were being studied by Dennys Fanshawe, Deputy Conservator of Forests.

Dennys, an erudite and dedicated man, was a wonderful person to have as boss, instructor, and friend. For despite my botanical qualifications, when I first arrived I could hardly recognise a single plant in the jungle. Botanists are trained to distinguish plants mainly by their flowers—but these were invisible in the tree tops, forty feet overhead, if one was lucky, but more often 120.

In any European woodland there are seldom more than half a dozen kinds of trees, and one can nearly always see their leaves or at least their twigs, if not flowers and fruit. But here there were five or six hundred tree species—of which one could only see the trunks. I felt like a mouse in a crowd of humans, with nothing to look at but endless tall, slender columns, varying not very much at first glance, in shape, colour and texture.

At first I was baffled. Then tiny differences began to stand out, as my eye and memory became attuned. Whenever I came to an unfamiliar tree, I would first stop and examine the shape of the trunk, which might be cylindrical or irregular, fluted or pierced by holes, scalloped, ridged, or knobbly, buttressed or unbuttressed. It might rise directly out of the ground, or be borne aloft on a pyramid of stilt-roots, while in boggy ground there might emerge all around it pneumato-phores, or breathing roots. Next, I would look at the bark:

rough or smooth, peeling, scaling, ridged or pitted, with or without lenticels, distinctive perhaps in colour or pattern—and at this stage I might recognise the tree. If not, I would slash the trunk with a cutlass, whereupon the inner layers of the bark and wood, of different consistencies and colours, like a slice through a cake, were revealed. Some layers might strip off (and be useful for cordage or cigarette paper); others might have a strong characteristic smell, or change colour on exposure to air, or exude latex or sap of different colours. Finally, beneath all the bark layers, was the wood itself. At the end of several weeks I could recognise about a hundred of the common trees. Only then could I begin to establish links with the leaves, flowers and fruit scattered on the ground (or in the folders of our herbarium). This was often the hardest work of all—for how could one distinguish one tree's leaves from those of its neighbours' in these thick leaf carpets? As for flowers—the rare fallen flowers seemed even less connected with the sombre stems around. Only from the boat did I ever glimpse a whole tree crown in flower—but I built up a mental picture of fields and banks of scented blossoms overhead. One day I might find a way to ascend and see them close at hand.

With increasing knowledge and interest I began to go further afield to study the different forests found in different places. At first I had found the jungles monotonous and repetitive, but now I began to recognise their extraordinary variety.

Sometimes we sailed past the penal settlement, past Aggie's house, to where the Mazaruni spread enormously as the huge Cuyuni River entered it from the west. At their junction, in the middle of a great lake of waters, was a tiny rocky islet on which stood an arch of beautiful red bricks and a few tumbled walls—all, bar a few ancient broken gin bottles, that remained of the former Dutch fort and trading post of Kyk-over-al ('Look over all'), which between 1742 and 1751 had been the capital of Guiana. Here had reigned Laurens Storm van s' Gravesande, greatest of the Dutch Gouverneurs—for the Dutch had been the original colonisers of this region, and in the seventeenth and eighteenth centuries their plantations had extended for miles up the great rivers, where today only secondary forest covers the banks.

c

The abandonment of their once-thriving plantations, the relegation to savagery of what had been suave and cultivated landscapes, followed the acquisition of the colony by the British after the Napoleonic wars. Yet it cannot be attributed to British misrule—but to the consequences of British energy. For the British did what the Dutch, traditionally, might have been expected to do: they built a sea wall along the coast, and so enabled the richer coastal plains, formerly brackish-water swamps, to be brought under cultivation. As a result, the trend towards developing the interior was reversed, the riverside plantations were abandoned, and many areas of the interior became less known, more primitive, than one hundred years previously. The population became concentrated along the coast, and an unbalanced single-crop economy based on sugar developed, which has been the cause of almost all the country's woes ever since.

A little way up the Cuyuni beyond Kyk-over-al I caught my first glimpse of the rough country that lay hidden all around behind the river banks. I went there first one Sunday morning with Agrippa, a Negro captain who, with his brawny lieutenant, Jubal, ran a supply launch to the pork-knockers up-stream, and to the Bovianders (descendants of escaped Negro slaves, often intermixed with Amerindian and sometimes European blood) who dwelt along the nearer banks. Afterwards, when it was free, I went in the Forest Department launch so that I could view the scenery and study the riverside vegetation in greater detail.

Near the Cuyuni's mouth the shores were clothed in a tangled mass of secondary forest irregular in outline, from which all commercially valuable trees had been removed. Then after a few miles the banks began to grow rocky, higher trees appeared and became more abundant until they consolidated into a high wall, and a delicious coolness came into the air, while the water became covered in flecks of foam. Then one heard the deep booming of the first of a series of cataracts—not dangerous, for there were channels up which the boat could pass. Finally, however, boats could go no further without a pilot. Then we would tie up beside a great cluster of boulders between which water rushed, and I would strike into the forest to collect plants or continue learning to identify trees.

Near the banks here the forest was dense and dark, tangled with snaking lianes, and extremely difficult to penetrate, for during the several months' long rainy season the river rose by 20 or 30 feet and poured through wide regions on either side of its present bed. So the vegetation here consisted of species which could survive such treatment, and as many of them were not found nearer Bartica, it was a most rewarding place for me.

If we arrived early enough we often found a solitary butterfly-hunter at work on a path close to the bank, a Frenchman, an ex-convict from Devil's Island, who had escaped and found refuge in British Guiana. He had built himself a small palm-thatched shelter under which to sling his hammock and shelter his belongings—which consisted only of the rags he wore, a billycan, a cutlass, a spare pair of miner's boots (cheap rubber-soled canvas-sided boots), a cotton blanket, a flashlight and a large and beautiful cedar-wood box with a close-fitting lid, in which he stored his specimens. These were sometimes to be seen around the clearing, pinned down on boards and set out to dry in the sunlight—each board carefully raised above the ground on legs which stood in tins of water, to prevent ants from climbing up and devouring the fresh insects.

Nearly all his butterflies were Morphos, enormous, strong-flying creatures, whose 6- or 8-inch-wide wings had brilliantly flashing blue upper surfaces. These he sold to tourists either as individual specimens in little glass cases at a dollar or two each, or, if they were at all battered, cut up for making into butterfly-wing jewellery. I had experienced catching Morphos as a child in the West Indies, and knew how rapidly they dodged a net, so I wondered how the Frenchman captured so many. One day he showed me, having made sure that I was in no sense a business rival. He explained that each Morpho species has its own very exact habits—a time in the morning for making its courtship flights, a particular kind of locality, a certain flying height. Some favoured riversides, other glades in the forest, others the darkest, most densely tangled places; some flew at shoulder height, others 20 feet up, others above the tree tops. But one thing they all had in common—the males were highly pugnacious, and could never resist an aerial combat. My friend's technique was to lie in wait in the right place at the correct time, holding in his left hand a stick on the end of which he had fastened a dead and dried male of whatever species he was out to capture: while in the other hand he held his wide-mouthed butterfly net of brown muslin. Then, when a male appeared flying along, he would flourish the bewinged stick at it, inducing it to swoop in attack—and sweep it up in his net with the other hand.

'Achilles and Agamemnon are the commonest,' he said, referring to two species, 'and sometimes I get Adonis. Or perhaps, Monsieur, it is just that they live low down, so I see more of them? But Hecuba! Ah, Hecuba. . . .'

And in my imagination I pictured that particularly magnificent Morphos, so unlike the others because its upper wing surfaces are of a rich golden brown with purplish flashes, as it sailed with them held rigid, high, high, overhead. For Hecuba, the most inquisitive, persistent (and thus intelligent-seeming) of butterflies, was a rarely seen dweller of the tree tops.

Besides this, my friend also encouraged butterflies to come into his hunting grounds by leaving loathsome little piles of fruit, moistened with rum, dotted about on the ground. Occasionally he would surprise a big Caligo, or owl-butterfly (even larger than the Morpho, and rarer and more elusive) at one of these. Sometimes the great butterflies would get so drunk that he could walk right up and pick them up by hand.

Once, after we had become friends, we sat and lunched together—I sharing my fruit and sandwiches (made by the hotel at Bartica) with him, he offering me some deliciously sweet Sawarri nuts, each kernel as large as a baby's foot—and he told me something of his life. He was the illegitimate son of a famous marquess. His father had been generous, and on his death had left him wealthy. But, obsessed with gambling and women, he had become increasingly extravagant, and had ruined himself at Monte Carlo. In desperation he had then become a card-sharper, and eventually, after he had organised a gang at one of the casinos, he had been caught and sent to Devil's Island as an habitual criminal. After ten years there as a prisoner he had been released as a 'Liberé', doomed to spend a further ten years as an enforced settler in French Guiana. It had been from this life that he had escaped, not from the penal settlement itself. 'But now you can never go back to France,' I said. 'Don't you regret that?'

'Yes, I do. By now I would almost be free—I've been here seven years. But when I escaped I couldn't stand it—sitting around with all those derelicts at St. Laurent du Maroni, weaving baskets and getting drunk when we could. A journalist once came down here and wrote a book about me and other Devil's Island escapees, but he cheated me and took all the money. That's when I gave up. I'm too old for the cheating game, and that's all I know how to do apart from this.'

A few months later he was in jail—for misappropriating money lent to help him set up a shop for selling trinkets to tourists. 'He was only a snob,' he was supposed to have said about his benefactor. 'He was impressed by my antecedents.'

My companion on most of my trips was Jonah Boyan, an old Amerindian from Lake Tapacooma in the Pomeroon River district: a tiny, gnarled man with a wrinkled, toothy face, and kindly eyes full of intelligence behind large, round glasses. As we walked through the forests he told me about his life. At Tapacooma Mission School he had learned to read and write. At fourteen he had left to become a balata bleeder, and for the next twenty years had lived in the forests, tapping the remote balata trees for their latex, which is used in making golf balls and submarine-sheathing. All the while his interest had grown in the animals and plants around him, and he had become not only a skilled hunter and tree climber, but a marvellous field naturalist. From the old men and women of his tribe he had learned the names and properties of the different plants and animals, and he had eventually become the sole repository for a vast lore, all of which without him would have been lost for ever. Then he had started working for the Forest Department, and Dennys Fanshawe had recognised his genius. With his help at last it had become possible to describe and identify in the field large numbers of Guianian plants whose characteristics, when alive and growing, had been previously totally unknown.

Now Jonah was permanently on the Forest Department payroll as a plant collector and namer, a preparer of botanical specimens, and a trustworthy and competent foreman. He had even learned the Latin names of many plants (he would smile shyly at the larger words, and write them down so that I could pronounce them first), as well as something of their relationship, so that often he could guess accurately to which family, or even genus, a new or unknown species might belong. Our friendship became firm when I lent him my battered childhood copy of Bates' *The Naturalist on the River Amazon.* For about a month he lived with it, reading slowly, totally absorbed. I was a little worried lest Bates' high-handed Victorian dismissal of 'the natives' as childlike savages might offend him, but far from it—he seemed to like Bates enormously *as a man* (and he reveals little enough of himself), and found objection only to his occasional use of Portuguese names. For, as he explained, it was easy enough when Bates gave the Latin names, as Latin was international, used even on the 'Amazoons'. Finally, he handed the book back, and said: 'That is the best book I ever read. Everything Mr. Bates says is true. I know a lot of the things he writes, yet he explains them for the first time. For instance, that some insects mimic others. I know it well—for we have here a moth which looks everything like a wasp. Yet I never thought it was a law of nature.'

Jonah's son Rufus also often came along, for he was training to succeed his father. But not a single other Amerindian had been found who was interested. They nearly all worked in the forest—lumbering, charcoal burning, balata bleeding, hunting, fishing, collecting nuts and fruit—but they seemed to have no interest in its plants and animals, or in their own traditions. Indeed, it was hard to discover in what they *were* interested: their ancient domains had been invaded, their ways of life shattered, they were yielding all along the line. They had not yet acquired the purpose to hold their ground. They were polite, elusive, almost impossible to know, yet for some reason I particularly enjoyed working with them, and sensed that they might have more to teach me in the end than the more familiar-seeming, solidly flesh-and-blood Africans, East Indians, and Chinese of the Colony.

In the evenings, when we set off back towards Bartica from the Cuyuni or Mazaruni, it was sometimes necessary to avoid tide-races and other fluvial hazards by crossing the river and skirting the shore on which Aggie's uncle's house stood. I avoided this as much as possible, because if we passed we had to stop, and a stop meant so much drinking that the rest of the day—and sometimes the following day as well—was ruined for me. But Aggie knew our boat, and whenever we did pass close, she would wave determinedly on the steps until she saw us turn towards the landing. Once, when I disregarded her, she ran into the house for her uncle's rifle and fired a couple of warning shots into the water near the boat—whereupon we put about at once.

'Neek, you're a cool hound, trying to pass like that. Why, I never see you these days, man! You always too busy.'

'Aggie, I've had to go away for several days on end, as you know, and I've got so much to do. Besides, you've also been away—I called here the other day and there was no sign of you.'

'That's true, man. Well, come up and have a drink.'

Then we would climb up the steep, rough path to the house. It was a wooden house, set high above the ground on stone pillars, with wide eaves of palm thatch that swept down low over a verandah that ran all round the outside. From the back rooms and kitchen there could be heard the chattering of various Indian girls who did odd jobs about the place, or were merely living there; while on the balcony in his rocking chair, unshaven and in his shirt sleeves, would be the massive figure of Aggie's uncle. He had once been a splendid specimen of a Scotsman. Even now, in his eighties, when he stood up, despite his stoop he was over six feet tall. With shaking hands he would fetch a chipped decanter and two glasses off the sideboard (Aggie, being a woman, was excluded from this masculine exchange, though from past experience I knew that she could drink the entire bottleful given the chance). Then Jock, ignoring my protests, would pour out a tumblerful of rum for me and one for himself, and we would sit, saying nothing, for perhaps half an hour. There was nothing that I *could* say to him, for he seemed devoid of any ability to communicate, except through the almost holy act of drinking. After a while he would get up again heavily, tell me to drink up, and refill the glasses.

Aggie, meanwhile, would be sitting, squirming and wriggling, on a stool a few feet away, gazing at me with eyes full of devotion. She was evidently desperately earnest in her feelings for me, which was the last thing I wanted. As far as I was concerned communication had never begun, except on a very simple plane. I would have loved to have her just as a friend, for I was very lonely, but she wanted much more. She was already thinking in terms of living together, of having babies, perhaps even of marriage.

After sitting it out for an hour or so, I would say that we had to get back, refuse offers of dinner and spending the night, and we would walk down to the boat together, I half-paralysed by the strong liquor, while the men exchanged knowing winks at their boss's entanglement. Aggie was dying all the time for me to suggest that we go for a walk, or go hunting together, or just even to be given a kiss before the boat pushed off, but the wild look in her eyes was sufficient warning, and even when I was most desperate I managed to resist.

Then the boat would be on its way again, running along the dark, uninhabited forest shore, with miles to go before we reached the one tiny town in this wilderness. I would sit up in the bow away from the men and gaze out over the immensities of water and sky, and wonder what I was doing there. On one level I was a botanist with a fascinating job. On another I was seeking to find again something buried and forgotten deep inside myself.

When I was ten my father had died, and two years later my mother had taken me from the West Indies to grey England— and except for her, I had lost everything: all my most loved relatives—warm, intimate, intelligent, loving people who could never be found again; and beaches and islands, forests and blue seas, sunshine and singing of calypsos. Since then I had never found anyone, anything, anywhere, with whom or which I could identify myself totally. They say that happiness is reliving childhood's best times, and that is what I suppose I wanted to do. But even in its tropical nature Guyana gave me nothing like my soft islands—only brown water and titanic jungles, sea-like rivers and electric eels. Its countrysides were as harsh in their way as the burning deserts of Africa, its people anything but languorous, extroverted and gay. There were no cultivated eccentrics here like those of my naturalist family; no calypsos—except imported ones. Everyone seemed frightened, tormented, repressed—and to be watching everyone else. When passions broke through they were mis-shapen, lacking in beauty or even naturalness. I had experienced something of the same grossness underlying hypocritical rigidity in

a Scottish village where I had lived during the war—but there
the control had been nearly perfect. Here it disintegrated in
bursts of savagery—and even this release was not possible for
the better educated Negroes, East Indians, Europeans. Their
problems were fascinating to observe and analyse, but I could
do this only because I did not feel involved in them. They were
outside of me—and they gave me no solace.

Some sort of anguish had driven me here to live alone, to
leave my friends and fellows, and England—where after ten
years I had finally taken root, even though it could not give me
all I missed. I wrote one day to someone that I was seeking to
be a salaried hermit, but the truth was not frivolous, and far
from simple. I had a feeling that only by being completely alone
and quiet would something very shy and valuable in me—
my deepest treasure—be able to develop. It was as if I were a
cocoon inside of which, in darkness, something was waiting to
emerge and expand and encompass the whole of me. What it
was I could not guess. That it was there was all I knew—and
that it needed time and peace in which to grow.

Back in Bartica I would sometimes have dinner with Dennys,
his wife Margaret, and their beautiful tiny daughter Wendy.
We would plan expeditions and talk with excitement of
mysteries unsolved, discoveries to be made, in the jungles even
close around—and on leaving I would feel happy, resolved that
my problems were nothing. I should get married, said
Margaret, whenever she saw me looking pensive. Not yet, I
would reply—and indeed, even if I had wanted to, my salary
was still at a pre-war level (it had even then been considered far
from generous), and I could scarcely afford to buy myself a cup of
tea after paying for rent and basic food. My dignified-sounding
post of Assistant Conservator of Forests carried no housing or
overseas allowance—such as even a clerk from abroad in any
business firm was given, and had I not had the foresight to
bring my bicycle with me I could not have got around in
Georgetown at all, or even afforded a new one. (A car, of
course, was an impossible dream.) The Colonial Service before
the war had been considered a career for gentlemen of private
means: but it was not getting them, and it was doing nothing
about it.

Now, with my lame leg, it was impossible to continue my studies in the forests, where every walk was like a skipping, hopping and jumping exercise. And already immense rain-clouds had begun to hang in the sky every afternoon and the river level to rise, as the rainy season approached—during which all accessible forests would be flooded. It was decided, there-fore, that I should return to Georgetown until it was over, to meet the new head of the Department, Christopher Swabey, on his arrival from England, and the Assistant Deputy Con-servator, Maurice Taylor, who would be returning from leave at the same time. To see other sides of the Department's work and other forests, I would accompany Taylor to Surinam for a conference with the Dutch authorities on the control of timber-smuggling along the Courantyne River, which formed the boundary between the two countries. Meanwhile, prepara-tions for the expedition to the middle Essequebo region, to start at the beginning of the next dry season, could go ahead.

On the day before I left Bartica, perhaps incautiously, I accepted one of Aggie's invitations to go hunting with her. Early the following morning, at about 3 a.m., I left the hotel and hobbled down to the beach, where she had tied up her canoe and was awaiting me. She embraced me rapturously.

'Got your gun? OK, Neek, push off.'

Her boat was a narrow and extremely unstable corial (a kind of dugout canoe), very low in the water. We paddled noiselessly along, skirting the swamps of weirdly stilt-rooted fresh-water mangroves as we headed up the Mazaruni shore. It was sooty dark, with only a few stars to see by, and a light mist over the still water.

'What are we going after first?' I asked in a low voice.

'Labba,' she said: paca, a small rodent-like mammal, excel-lent to eat. We nosed into a small mud-shored 'creek', or tributary stream, utterly quiet—then she flashed her torch on. 'Hold your gun, Neek,' she whispered.

In the rays of the torch a pair of red spots showed low on the ground, on a muddy bank. It was an anaconda, a giant con-strictor snake about 12 feet long, slithering into the under-growth. Then two more red spots—a paca—but too far away to shoot. While she held it mesmerised in the beam, I paddled gently forward. Suddenly Aggie twisted round, almost overbalancing the corial, picked up her cutlass, and slashed wildly into the shallow water. There was a tremendous flurry and grunting, and a horrible whiskered face with a wide open mouth rose gleaming beside the boat. Another swipe, we grabbed and heaved—and a large, wet catfish, streaming with blood, flopped on to my knees.

This was one kill—but the labba meanwhile had disappeared. We lay quiet for a moment, then flashed on the torch again. Not an eye or movement showed.

Then out on to the grey river once more, in the pitchy night. Far away a dog barked over the water. Manatees, crocodiles, anacondas, fresh-water porpoises, giant lau-lau catfish up to 12 feet long—what dreadful beasts might not rise out of the blackness to engulf us? What about the much feared Water Mamma, a mermaid who carried men to their doom? I had my Water Mamma ahead of me, in the canoe, and a very wet and determined one at that.

The next creek, half an hour away over the water, had no signs of life in it either, but a few disturbed leaves showed where a frequented animal track came down to the water's edge. Stealing ashore, we tied up the boat and edged our way through the forest for a few yards. Weird sounds came from high in the tree tops. The first faint flush of dawn was far away in the east. Birds were waking up.

Soon we were under a hog-plum tree: scattered fragments showed that accouries and adouries had been feasting not long before. A dark silhouette among the leaves overhead! Aggie shot, and a big maroudi, or guan, a pheasant-like bird, came crashing down with Aggie on it like a wolf, crunching its neck with her teeth to finish it off. A moment later, I brought down its partner in a flurry of black feathers.

As I bent to pick it up a velvety black tarantula 6 inches across the legs ran crazily over my hand and away over the leaves.

We returned to the boat carrying the two heavy birds, and began paddling back to Bartica under a now coppery sky. I was due to leave in a few hours by the morning plane.

'You'll come back soon?' asked Aggie.

'Yes, as soon as I can.'

'This is real good, ain't it, Neek?'

'What?'

'Us two going so strong.'

'It's wonderful, Aggie. But remember, don't get serious. I am still in love with a girl.'

'But she's in England, Neek.'

'Yes, I know——'

'But this is B.G., Neek. Wouldn't you like to settle out here?'

'Maybe. But I don't know yet. Anyway, Aggie, please don't get so violent about things. You don't know me at all. I am just passing through, I told you I was in love.'

'Don't know you——! You certainly are just passing through. Anyway, don't behave bad to me.'

'Of course not, Aggie. We can be friends, can't we?'

'I'll get you if you treat me bad. I mean it, Neek. Nobody can do that to me.'

3

High Society (I)

From the seaplane base at Ruimveldt, a short way up the
Demerara River from Georgetown, the taxi took me between
dewy meadows intersected by canals, and clusters of crazily
leaning corrugated-iron shacks (with views to the far, tall
chimneys of Plantation Diamond's sugar factory), then past a
spindly wooden mosque, its finial crescents cut from an old
tin can, into crowded streets of stilt-perched wooden houses,
all painted white or gamboge, and all decorated with eaves,
windows, roof-lines, doorways of frenzied, frilly fretwork. I
glimpsed Stabroek market, a majestic late Victorian hulk
whose writhings were in red-painted cast iron—it might have
been in Brussels—soaring above piles of pineapples, mangoes,
bananas, jostling vivid-coloured throngs of Negroes and
Indians. Then the rich smells of molasses, squashed limes,
chickens, sugar and sweat gave way to those of newly-hosed
pavements as we swung along the yellow and brown collonaded
front of the 1832 Greek revival government buildings, and out
on to suddenly spacious streets. Two neatly-spired early-
nineteenth-century wooden gothic churches pointed primly
among breadfruits and hibiscus—and we swept into what I
always thought of as the 'zone of eccentricity'—where the Rev.
Ignatius Scoles, S.J.'s, town hall, in the form of a weatherboard
and cast-iron Rhenish castle, towered beside Baron Siccama's
masterly law courts—an enormous rambling concrete and half-
timbered Swiss chalet (1887), fronted by a dumpy statue of
Queen Victoria, and Blomfield's Anglican Cathedral—the
world's tallest, biggest, and perhaps ugliest wooden building—
in Puginesque Gothic, painted gloomy turd-Chartreuse-brown
(critics all describe it as 'magnificent').
 Further still, double-laned streets broad as the Nevsky
Prospekt crossed at right angles on the grid plan laid out by the

Dutch and French in the eighteenth century. Sometimes these streets still had Dutch-built canals running down their middles, but mostly these had been filled in, forming broad grassy or gravelled central avenues shady with saman trees (drifts of sticky pink stamens on the ground beneath) or flamboyants, cassias or jacarandas. Great barn-like wooden white-painted houses, like confections of snow, stood here amid enormous overflowing gardens. Mostly Georgian, Regency, or early Victorian in date, their classical details had been attenuated into needy elegance in the translation of stone or stucco into wood. 'Demerara Windows', vertically hung louvres pushed out from lacy fretwork sills by a pole, gave glimpses of cavernous interiors; while their 'wind-towers', enclosed spiral staircases with glassed-in-summit rooms, designed for hot evenings or to watch ships go by on the river, rose above the tossing foliage.

A juke-box blaring out 'Buttons and Bows' indicated our approach to Main Street's only hideous structure—my hotel, the Bristolburg, in badly-done wooden Plantation-Romanesque style. There were pleasanter hotels, if one could afford them, but this was where the men from the interior usually stayed.

'Hi, Nick,' came a relaxed greeting from a bloated, stetson-hatted figure rocking on the porch—Bill Leslie, the proprietor: 'A woman's been trying' to phone all mornin'. Sounded kinda desperate.'

Christ! I thought—Aggie. What *can* she want? 'Nice to see you, Bill,' I replied. 'Tell her I'm not here, at least for a few days. What's new in the zoo?'

The hulk rocked a few more times in the rocker, stirred, then rose, jerked an enormous pudgy thumb to indicate that I should follow, then shambled off towards the back of the yard. 'Only a new kibihi,' he called over his shoulder, 'Oh, and a tree porcupine.'

A series of hutches housed raccoons, parrots, mongooses, a little anteater, a kibihi (coatimundi), 2 macaws, a trogon, a collection of sugar-birds. The kibihi ran up to my shoulder, then hopped on to Leslie, while I inspected the porcupine: a ball of spines bearing a large soft nose and sorrowful eyes. It looked in need of sympathy. Responding rather too easily, I inserted a finger—and nearly lost it to a savage snap. How like a human, I thought.

It was a pretty yard, with its vermilion hibiscuses, sprawling flame and magenta bougainvillea, and sticky-flowered pale blue plumbago. But beyond its back fence lay a sea of black mud criss-crossed by planks, running from stilt-supported shanties made of old boards and sides of packing cases nailed together, papered inside with newspapers and sheets from magazines. Some of these houses were little bigger than kennels, but they were bursting with inhabitants. In the centre of the area a little naked brown boy was splashing under the single stand pipe that served perhaps sixty people.

It had struck me forcibly, when I first walked around George-town, how people of all classes were so mixed together, as the original plantation lots, each with its big house, had been sub-divided (even Government House had its adjacent shanty patch). But then this had seemed to me psychologically healthy—the rich could never forget the poor—by comparison with the newer, one-income-level suburbs that were being built on the outskirts. It added greatly to the human richness of a city that still looked much as it had a hundred years before, whose main street was still Main Street, and which was nearly everywhere not only beautiful, but was sometimes highly original and picturesque.

'I'm putting you in number six, upstairs at the back,' said Leslie, bringing me back to earth. His eyes were tiny and shrewd. They were scrutinising me minutely.

'Only room I've got. Leave your stuff and I'll get it taken up. Doreen! Take this guy's stuff up to number six!' I thought he spoke slightly grudgingly, but perhaps not. He really rather liked me, I felt, though I spent so little at the bar.

I returned to the taxi. A few hundred yards further and Main Street climbed steeply some ten feet or so on to a broad stone rampart that stretched to the right as far as the eye could see, diminishing to a distant hair line on which ant-cars crawled beneath microscopic palm trees. Georgetown is built on drained marshland four feet below high-tide level, and this rampart was the sea wall that protected the man-inhabited skin of terra firma. On the other side of it lay an expanse of fine brown mud, tufted with grasses and tangles of sea Convol-vulus (Ipomoea pes-caprae), stretching a quarter of a mile to where the chocolate sea slapped morosely in a line of foamy, beaker-at-bedtime breakers. It was a sight that always lowered my morale. Three hundred miles north, in Trinidad, the beach would have been shining yellow sand, the sea ultramarine. But from the Amazon to the Orinoco the coast of South America is mud. And for miles out to sea the water also is mud, bound to and merged with the land by unimaginable tons of suspended sediment, thick as chowder, horrible to bathe in, rich in fish and molluscs. Vast banks of shells along the shores bespeak its proliferating life; for the Guyanese it is but the first of many liabilities that weigh down the soul.

At the ultimate point where the sea wall met the Demerara River's mouth, a stone groin continued the river brink for a quarter of a mile further out to sea, to prevent silting up of the shipping channel. At the beginning of this groin, on the former site of eighteenth-century Fort William Frederick, stood the small wooden building that contained my office. When I looked out of its window there was no land between me and Africa, and the steady trade winds that buffeted us continuously were so insistent that every sheet of paper had to be held down with a weight—usually a specimen block of the local timber. It was the coolest, pleasantest working place in the whole city.

Among the other documents upon my desk was a long memorandum, from which I quote:

Notes for recruits from overseas

Professional Opportunity:

You are coming out to British Guiana as a qualified forester and you will have full opportunities to exercise your professional knowledge. Scientific forest management is in its infancy and we are only skirting the fringe of our problems, both in their fundamental biological aspects and in applied forest management. Thus you have every chance of making a name for yourself no matter in what field of forestry your particular interests may lie.

Responsibility to the Community:

With this background I would like to stress that your

technical aptitude is useless unless it is accompanied by the right attitude of mind. In the first place you must remember that your salary is paid by the people of this colony and that your primary loyalty is to the people you serve. Any decision you make, any work you perform must be judged by the yardstick of its value to the community.

Politics:

You must remember that the ultimate goal of colonial administration is self-government and that it is the duty of every officer of government to work steadily towards this end. Your knowledge and experience must be imparted to your subordinates, and every opportunity must be given to Guianese to qualify themselves for increasing responsibility. While you must take no part in political controversy, you should be in sympathy with the legitimate political aspirations of the country.

Tolerance:

You will perhaps find many things strange to you, conditions of life, points of view and attitudes of mind and at first you may find them difficult to understand. Do not be dogmatic and condemn these things. Remember that it is for you to adjust yourself to the country, not the reverse. The people of British Guiana are warm-hearted and generous and if they feel that you are attempting to identify your interests with theirs, you will receive unstinted cooperation and support. If, on the other hand, you are unsympathetic and over-critical, your path will not be strewn with roses.

This leads on to the problem of racial prejudice. You will appreciate how heterogeneous is the racial, religious and cultural background of our people. But while we make our home in the country we are all Guianese. The colour of a man's skin is completely immaterial and in any assessment of your fellow man you should be guided solely by character and not by pigmentation. You will be working largely with people of a different racial background from yours, and any attempt at racial discrimination is not only highly improper and logically indefensible, but will be your loss. You may come across racial prejudice from time to time and you have a duty to discourage it by your own example.

D

Relationships in the Department:

The maintenance of high morale within the Department, should be your constant care. Again, this is largely a question of your own example, the zeal and devotion to duty which you show and which you have a right to expect from your subordinates.

Treat your staff and colleagues with courtesy and consideration. Do not give orders which you would not be prepared to carry out yourself, but once orders are given, enforce them with firmness. You should constantly endeavour to imbue your subordinates with a sense of service and the fact that they (and you) are, in its true sense, servants of the public.

Relationships with other Government Departments:

You must remember that other branches of the service may view problems from a different angle from yours. If you have a good case, it should be possible to state it in simple terms and convince them by persuasion.

It is particularly important that you should be on good terms with the District Commissioner of your division. He is the senior administrative officer of Government in the district and you should seek his opinion and advice on all matters affecting his district. Never say 'This has got to be done'—say 'I suggest we do this, etc.'

Relationships with the Public:

(a) treat them with invariable courtesy and consideration.
(b) be accessible to everybody, however humble and however petty you may consider their requirements.
(c) deal with them with scrupulous fairness and avoidance of all prejudice.
(d) never gossip about matters which come to your official attention and never betray any confidential information which you may receive.
(e) never indulge in criticism of Government's policy (nor of individual government departments or officers) with members of the public.

Personal Life:

While your personal life is of course your own affair, it is obvious that any actions of yours which lower your status in the eyes of the public is bound to destroy confidence in you and in your official capacity and will bring the Department and the Service into disrepute. I will not labour the point.

For your own happiness it is of the greatest importance that you should adjust yourself to the ways of life of the country and join fully in the life of the community. It is very valuable to cultivate hobbies and interests outside your professional duties. Try and avoid any narrowness of outlook.

Try to cultivate critical and original thought and initiative. Never hesitate to put forward suggestions or ideas to the Head of your Department for the better operation of the Department—as it is still very far from perfect.

Christopher Swabey
Conservator of Forests.

I was puzzled by this document. Was it directed at me personally—I was the only newcomer to the Department? Or had it merely been sent ahead by my new chief to indicate that henceforth all our activities were to be conducted from the loftiest standpoint? In either case its recipients were seemingly viewed as hardly to be trusted among the unfortunates of the public and in other departments whom they would likely be roughing up.

That evening the Fanshawes took me to my first official party, so that I could meet some of my colleagues and one or two of the chief people of the colony. Our host was one of its great tycoons, a thickset, genial Yorkshire man with tiny, shrewd eyes. I recalled a mutual friend—for I had many introductions —and to my delight, on the strength of this, he invited me to dinner the next day. Then his cheerful-looking daughter came up, evidently a highly sociable and inquisitive creature, to find out more about me. But as we talked a look of dismay began to appear on her enthusiastic face. I did not play bridge; I did not drink; I felt no great fervour for the colony's sports of horse and goat racing—not enough to want to spend an entire day watching them. I liked reading, talking and listening to music. I might be a new male, but I was incomprehensible. I attempted to change the subject by complementing her on her necklace. This threw her off balance:

'You're trying to flirt with me!'

'Of course!'

'But we've only just met!' She frowned, strongly disapproving.

I announced that for the rainy season I might be sharing a house with someone I had met at the Bristolburg.

'But how *can* you?' she said. 'After all—his wife is *Chinese!*'

I felt helpless. But perhaps I had an ally: a powerful, flabby man standing near us had burst into laughter at my predicament. He had a soft, inane face, but I warmed to him. Then as he smiled again, our eyes met—and I noticed a curious conniving look. He had summed me up as a fellow homosexual.

The word 'Watkins' then came to my ears, and I looked around with interest, for I had heard that Major Watkins, head of an agency for developing the interior, was by profession an entomologist, and therefore presumably an educated man. Behind me stood yet another of the moustached and monocled, pigskin-complexioned men with whom the room was peopled: men who, with the dissolution of Empire, were evidently concentrating in Guyana—though I gathered from what I overheard that they had all known better places, like India or Burma. I had numerous questions to put to him about the marvellous insect life I had glimpsed at Bartica, but Watkins, for some reason, did not wish to talk shop. His obsession was road-aggregates, about which I knew little. Tactlessly I continued to question him. Suddenly he brightened:

'You're interested in insects, eh? Well watch out for those blasted jigger fleas! In the interior you pick 'em up everywhere. It's a great big flea, see? And it lays its eggs under your skin—they like going between your toes. The eggs swell up till they're as big as peas—I dug one out only the other day.'

This puzzled me: I had done a little entomology at Cambridge: perhaps Watkins had forgotten a tiny aspect of his subject? Deferentially I suggested:

'Isn't it the entire female that burrows under the skin—and the big, pea-sized object you get is not an egg capsule, but the female's egg-distended abdomen?'

'Eh? Yes! Now I think of it—I believe you're right!'

'It's rather like the big swollen abdomen of a queen termite, or better still, like Demodex folliculorum?'

He looked at me suspiciously, screwed his monocle into his eye and barked: 'What the devil is Demodex folliculorum?'

'The blackhead.' I explained—and my eyes strayed to his jowls. I had said the wrong thing. I dared not speak, but managed to avoid his eyes.

Could these really be descendants of the people who had built this elegant town? It was impossible to believe—and indeed they were not. For in Guyana there were no settlers as in the West Indies: only one British family remained that had lived in the country for more than two generations. All the rest of those who had so lovingly built these graceful houses and whose descendants might have lent some style, or at least love of the country to these gatherings, had gone, driven out by the decline of sugar, the gobbling up of the independent plantations by large companies. The Europeans around me were officials, business men, managers, here for a limited number of years like myself, but few seemed to have the slightest interest in the country beyond how to exploit it, make the most possible money in it while the chance offered, and get out in the least number of years.

There was only one attractive person in the room—a graceful, slow-moving, long-legged girl with large brown eyes, and a very shy expression. She had given me a sympathetic smile when I recoiled from the Major, so now I moved across to her and we began talking. She was a Guyanese—of largely Portuguese or Dutch blood I guessed, with some Negro—and lived in Berbice with her father, who was an official there. She had a detached view of the people around, and a strong sense of humour. She was sensitive, warm, voluptuous, and rather beautiful. I was very much drawn to her. When she left, the wife of one of the bank managers came up to me. 'I did not know you knew Sheila Van Battenberg? Was it the first time you'd met? Well, you must be careful, of course, Nicholas, who you make friends with—one can so easily get into the wrong crowd. You realise that the Van Battenbergs are local?'

Mostly these despised 'locals', as I began to discover, were of mixed blood, sometimes like Sheila with names that echoed the early Dutch or English colonists. Some were Portuguese, descended from indentured Madeiran labourers brought over in the mid-nineteenth century, and a few were East Indians (lawyers, merchants), or Chinese (doctors, dentists). At this date none were Negro or Amerindian. They might be incapable of ruling themselves in a manner of which my snobbish bank manager's wife would have approved, but they lived in the place and were concerned about it, and one day they would shape it to their own image. I was indignant and upset at her remark. Dimly it made me understand that, for Guyanese, independence would mean among other things freedom from people like those at this party to whom life in the colony had meant an enormous rise in social position, yet who only grudgingly 'accepted' the richest and most powerful people there. It was horrifying to think that large parts of the world were still ruled by their like. But perhaps the most dismaying thought was that if I stayed another twenty years in the Colonial Service and reached the top, I should be expected to become one of them!

When I got back to the hotel I wrote in my diary: 'I must be guarded in all I say and do, and above all avoid being witty. I am not going to be accepted by these men as a companion whatever I do. But I must try not to think of them as a bunch of loathsome human hippopotami.'

In the weeks that followed I went to many more such gatherings and with each one my sense of isolation increased. Friendships, conversation, warmth, discovery—even good living—were not the purposes of this society. Intimacy did not exist. It was purely a working group of ill-assorted, mutually-suspicious strangers, juggling for advantage in a complex artificial hierarchy based on concepts like 'seniority', but with real power over real people in its hands.

In the eyes of these people my real crime, it soon emerged, was that I drank only moderately, and evidently felt no need to get drunk—while they did. Powerful though they might be in their jobs, they were so lacking in social ease, so frigid with status consciousness that they did not dare make mistakes. What inner tortures these people are suffering, I kept thinking (not that this helped me). Drink was the smoke screen with which they covered their mistakes, their anaesthetic for frayed feelings. Without it no communication would have been possible, because mistakes would have been accountable for. Delicious and powerful, the ice-cold rum-swizzles, the whiskies, rum-and-gingers, gin-and-its, were knocked back, burying responsibility as they descended the gullet. Then, if someone made an error, saw a little bit of himself getting out of control, he could kick it away, reject it, stamp on it and claim he had been drunk. I had heard of drink-resolved societies of incompatibles under communist regimes, but I had never expected one as the establishment of an ostensibly free country.

My openness and ease were disconcerting to these people. I was like the voyeur at an orgy, just watching, not joining in with the rest. But until I realised this I went blundering on—showing my cards all the time, trying to make friends and understand those around me—while they just watched and smiled, thinking that I would eventually learn and become a spiritual trogolodyte like themselves.

Often in the evenings, when I had finished work, I would walk along the shore from my office, past the wizened shrimp fishermen casting their nets in the Cadbury-coloured foam, then out along the groin away from the sounds of shore. There I would watch the amazing colours of the sunsets—a braying of golden trumpets over the water; the lights going on at Vreed-on-hoop, three miles away across the Demerara; the waves glittering like dancing gold as they carried past me out to sea their islands of grass, bobbing coconuts, water hyacinths, floating branches. The long grey line of coast led far away to the west to the mouth of the Essequebo River, and on to Dauntless Point on Leguan Island, a scrub-covered bank built up in a few years by just such debris, drifting mud and sand, around the wrecked ship *Dauntless*. With such a volume of sediment, one would have expected the whole coast to have been a maze of deltas. But the continent was tilting, sinking in time to its growth eastwards, so that its river mouths were neither true estuaries nor quite deltas either.

The steady trades that buffeted in from out in the Atlantic would almost blow the clothes off my body, rocking the fleet of schooners, lighters, rafts and river boats in the shipping pool up river beyond a pretty pink and white liquorice-striped light-house, a collection of semi-derelict wooden wharves and warehouses—the port of Georgetown. One or two green-painted bauxite steamers would be swinging at anchor, on their way to or from Mackenzie, the bauxite mine a hundred miles upstream; or a Booker Brother's steamer might hoot, waiting to catch the tide on its way to England.

Nearer at hand, along the top of the broad sea wall, there would promenade each evening the wealth and beauty of the capital, out for an evening whiff of sea air: respectable white-clad family parties, ball-bouncing children, straw-hatted Negro blades, clumps of brown- or golden-skinned girls with vivid lips and gazelle eyes, dressed in dazzling orchid colours; sometimes a paler Portuguese or English face: jostling bodies, unfathomable eyes.

None of these eyes seemed to hold anything for me. In the West Indies on my way out I had felt at home. Here each time I opened my mouth I seemed to dig a trench between myself and the other person. I tried to reason with myself: at home I saw only friends, and was aware only of a tiny segment of people like myself. Here I was facing an entire community. Given time those who were like me would emerge. Meanwhile I felt intensely isolated. Was it that cocoa-sea that weighed these people down? Or was it my fault? With the simplest folk, like those at Bartica, I had no problem: it only arose when I turned to those among whom I might have expected to find friends. Yet if the world of the ruling expatriates seemed hostile and coarse, that of the local Georgetown people seemed divided into categories with none of which I could identify. As soon as I began talking my questions made people uneasy. They seemed like marionettes jerked to and fro by various dogmas—religion, class, colour, occupation—and insulated from self-knowledge. Habitually I questioned and sought causes for what I saw; but anyway I had no right to question, in the view of Swabey's recent memorandum: it was up to me to adapt.

'Be realistic, boy,' said a Guyanese at the Bristolburg one day. 'You British are on the way out in the Caribbean. It's the American who's making the grade since the war.'

'I suppose that must be so if *you* say it,' I responded acidly—my companion was dressed entirely in clothing bought from the U.S. Air Force base at Atkinson Field outside of Georgetown, and spoke with a strong Yankee accent.

'Sure it's so. People want what the Americans have got—money, and good times, and a big car—not a Baby Austin! They're the world's heroes. Europeans are just full of problems, and the British are plain hard up. Look man—if Britain

is so powerful why can't it pay a guy like you a living wage?—
here, let me do it, I work at the base and I'm *loaded*.'

This last was a particularly telling point. And my frustrations were exacerbated by claustrophobia. Unable to afford
taxis or a car, there was literally no means whereby I could
escape from Georgetown into the country beyond. The city
was ringed by swamps or the sea. Only two roads led out of
it—one to Atkinson Field 25 miles up river, and one along the
coast—both through densely populated areas. Beside each road
was a deep drainage ditch, while the very fields beyond were
of slush, the houses in them on tall stilts. Like the rest of
the population of Georgetown I was trapped on a crowded
raft.

I longed increasingly for the rainy season to end so that I
could return to Bartica, where at least I could go for walks,
and where my work was more interesting—or for any break
away from the thronged coastal mudlands.

One day the telephone rang as I was having lunch at the
Bristolburg, and the waitress answered that I was in. It was a
call from Bartica on the radio-telephone—from Aggie!

'Gee, Nick!' came a throaty voice. 'Why didn't you write,
man? Here I am waiting and waiting. Whassa matter? *Over*.'
Something boomed and echoed in my ears. . . . 'Whassa matter,
over? . . . matter, over.' The radio in the hotel dining room, as
well as those in nearby houses, across the street and thousands
more all over the city, were tuned in to pick up such conversations, which occupied part of the local broadcasting time on
the same wavelength. (Indeed, radio-telephone conversations
were regarded as one of the most enjoyable features of the day's
programmes.)

'Aggie, it's good to hear you—how has life been? Over.'
The crackle on the telephone was bad—I could hear much
better by listening to the hotel radio, to which the other diners,
faint smiles on their faces, were all intently turned.

'Oh, man, come back. It's lonesome here. Why don't you
come? How about next weekend? Over!'

'I simply can't. I've got so much work on here. Over.' (Nor
could I afford the $14.00 fare, I might have added.)

'Oh God, man, you driving me crazy!' my table companions
were smirking and smiling, 'I coming up myself to town. Over.'

'For heavens sake!—I may not be here! You don't realise I have to go off on inspections and things. Over.'

'Look, man, I go come up if you like it or not. You just fin' me place to stay. I postin' a letter to you tonight. Over.'

'Tim'es up now, I'm sorry, folks,' came the operator—for three minutes was the maximum allowed.

Blushing slightly, and with averted eyes, I made my way back to my table. In the far corner of the room a fat Portuguese woman was whispering to the cook. 'Das' one of de nicest conversations I hear for a long time.'

4

High Society (II)

Apart from conducting somewhat elementary research and giving advice to wood-cutters, timber dealers, etc., the Forest Department collected revenue—that was all. It had no legal control over forest lands, which were administered by the Department of Lands and Mines, which also issued all wood-cutting licences. This was an anomalous situation, dating back from before the war. It could have been fairly satisfactory if working plans for exploiting and replanting the forests in rotation had existed, giving the Lands and Mines Department a clear policy to follow. But nothing of the sort had ever been attempted. Instead, piecemeal licences to cut were issued to anyone who applied for them. Only large concerns, asking for exclusive rights over big blocks of land, were made to agree to any sort of conditions. But such conditions mostly concerned financial arrangements—they never mentioned the replanting or regenerating of the forests that were to be felled, and as a result the forests of the country, one of its greatest assets, were being mined out and replaced by valueless secondary growth or scrub at an incredible rate. World demand for timber was accelerating, and only the wildness of the country and the difficulties of extraction had saved Guyana's forests from total despoliation.

It was no secret that once the new conservator, Swabey, arrived, his prime task would be to alter this system. To do so would require tact, but he had a brilliant record. Returning with him on the same ship would be another forest officer who had been on leave, Taylor, so by the time Swabey arrived he would doubtless have a detailed picture of all that had to be done.

My botanical training at Cambridge and at the Imperial Forestry Institute at Oxford would be useful in any programme of scientific management. As an ecologist I would be able to suggest classifications for land use, ways of sampling the various forest types so as to discover their composition, and their content of valuable species, and ways of exploitation which would not permanently ruin them. Indeed, there might even be ways in which the proportion of valuable species could be increased. Meanwhile, the most basic statistics were lacking—few of the areas surveyed in the past could even be located precisely on a map!

I felt sure that I would like Swabey. Because he was said to have a tremendous sense of fun, he sounded a great relief from the dreariness of the colony's usual officials. So I felt a pleasant anticipation when the day came for him and Taylor to arrive. With the Fanshawes and Smeed, the Deputy Conservator (who was mostly concerned with administration), I went to the docks to greet the ship. In my hand I held a copy of one of the Colony's newspapers, in which 'Tweedledum and Tweedledee' by the Grampus, one of Guyana's two social columns, carried a photograph of a youth with a great mass of black hair culminating in a coif, above the headline, 'Swabey is new Forest Chief'. Fanshawe chuckled when I showed it to him. 'The photo is of Christopher I'm sure, but he's now over fifty—look, there he is.' And on the deck, as the ship drew alongside, stood a tall, stooping man, totally bald, with big pebble-lensed glasses and a jutting chin.

The gangway was lowered and Swabey descended, followed by a thin blonde with pale eyes, who never stopped talking in a high, authoritative voice—his wife (he had been married but a month). After them came a heavy fellow of about forty-five, with a hooked nose, moustache and monocle, followed by a swarthy, slanted-eyed lady (perhaps a Malay I thought?)— Maurice and Evelyn Taylor. Shaking with merriment as if at some secret joke, Evelyn introduced Swabey and his wife to the Fanshawes and Smeed—effusive handshakes, and then to me—a quick glance, a nod, and then he turned his back.

'Let's get ourselves out of here,' said Swabey—and Taylor went dashing off, barking orders right and left, organising the luggage and a convoy of taxis. During the drive, first to the Park Hotel, then to the Forest Office, I thought that Smeed was eyeing me somewhat oddly. I had had almost nothing to do with him because our work was so different. Could he have taken a dislike to me, I wondered? Fortunately my new chief, Swabey, and his wife were comparatively easy to get on with. I showed them the newspaper paragraph—she laughed, then stopped, seeing her husband's expression, for evidently he was far from amused. 'What useful work have you done?' he asked when we arrived at the office.

'For the moment, getting the departmental herbarium into order.' I explained that it was the most extensive collection of the colony's plants, and the Department's only means of identifying many trees. But its specimens, many of which were the 'types' from which new species had been described, had become badly jumbled over the years. Apart from that, I went on, I had been learning to identify trees in the forests, so that I could begin my ecological work. He muttered something about that being fairly worthwhile, and turned away.

It was obvious from the start that the new Conservator, Swabey, was the right man for getting what he wanted passed by the legislature. He had enormous enthusiasm and he needed it, for he met with much opposition, mostly because instead of working with the Lands and Mines Department as might have been possible, he proposed the more radical step of removing forest lands entirely from their control—which would mean that his Department would have to grow much larger—so his opponents were able to say that his policy was one of self-aggrandisement.

For me all of this should have been cause for optimism. Had I been in direct contact with him my life and work might have been very pleasant, but unfortunately he was almost inaccessible, so occupied were he and Taylor with the re-organisation of the Department. So, Fanshawe being in Bartica most of the time, I was placed directly under Smeed. To my dismay, I found myself being pushed more and more by him into the routine work of an ordinary forest officer which was all he knew about—licensing, timber and grant inspection, visiting saw-mills, and general administration—the excuse being that such knowledge would form a useful background for me. In truth the Department was short-staffed—it was hard to recruit anyone at the pay offered.* Had Smeed been pleasanter,

* My salary during most of my time in Guyana was £600 a year, on which I had to live as I had no other means.

I might have succumbed to his pressures. But he was not. Indeed, it seemed almost as if he were trying to break my spirit. But I was resolved not to waste the knowledge that I had spent years in acquiring—and I made it plain to him that I had joined the service purely as a means of studying tropical jungles, on the understanding that as soon as the proposed Colonial Research Service was formed I would be transferred to it. So every spare moment I continued my reordering of the herbarium, and began an examination of all the studies that had been made of the forests, and an appraisal of new methods of survey using aerial photography.

My apprehensions deepened when Smeed began to question the need for the expedition to the middle Essequebo region that Fanshawe and I had planned together. One evening by chance I lingered working late in the herbarium, and they began discussing me. The building had no internal walls, so it was impossible not to overhear.

'I just can't stand him kicking around the place, totally useless. Why the devil did they wish him on to us?'

'Well he *is* interested in the forests,' said Fanshawe mildly. 'A few months in the forests would probably do him a lot of good.'

'I see what you mean—throw him in at the deep end? Anything to get him out of our hair. OK, then. Go ahead with it.'

I blessed Fanshawe, and thought somewhat grimly, that the expedition would get Smeed out of my hair, also.

That night, after yet another appalling official party, I strolled back to the Bristolburg Hotel feeling desperate. I could hear the hotel from a block away as I approached: the juke-box was bawling out 'I'm looking over a four-leafed clover, that I overlooked before'. The bar was crowded with black-jowled miners and prospectors, mostly Americans and Canadians, but with a few British. Bill Lesley, rocking as ever in his rocking chair on the porch, rearranged his muscular limbs as I approached, and called out from under his stetson.

'Have a drink, Nick,' he beckoned, 'and meet Jimmy Smith and his bag of diamonds.' Jimmy Smith, bald and Jewish, with a lively face and gay, airy manner undulated towards us and sat down.

'No diamonds tonight, boy,' he said, 'got them locked up in the bank.'

'Amazing job!' said Lesley. 'What do you think? Jimmy took a party of investors up to Orindvik last week and just as they step out of the plane Jimmy sees a diamond on the ground.'

Lesley gave an enormous wink, visible to everybody. 'So Jimmy picks it up and hands it to Mr. Schmook from New York. Amazing stroke of luck, shows how rich that country is. Anyway, he's set up for about two years now, eh, Jim?'

Jimmy was shaking with laughter. 'For Christ's sake,' he said, 'don't spread it around.'

A roar from another table indicated that a big diamond had disappeared in a cloud of dust upon being given the steel pincer test. Now another stone was in the pincers, and the owner looked on tensely while the prospective purchaser strained his muscles to find a flaw. A hiss of relief and everyone relaxed.

I got up, determined to try to escape the confused mixture of emotions inside me, alienated from everything around. Upstairs the hotel was like an enormous barn—with decayed boarding dividing it into rooms, above which an open communal air space extended up to the rafters of the steeply pitched roof. Supposedly this arrangement made for coolness—but in fact it meant that there was no insulation, and little possibility of sleep until all the other occupants had composed themselves, for one could hear every noise coming from every other room. Tornado-like snorings, oaths and crashes from the drunken, sounded above the whine of mosquitoes. A few yards along the corridor my friend Dr. Edwards was evidently with his ten-year-old Negro girl, to judge from the sweaty smackings.

Unable to sleep, unenticed by the five feet six inches long iron bedstead (I was six feet two inches tall), under its conical mosquito net, I sat up trying to write at the substantial kitchen table that stood in one corner of the room. After a while there came a demonic yell from some animal—probably eating another, I thought—outside the window; then an extraordinary grating and banging sound. Getting up and looking out, I saw a creature the shape of a rat but the size of a dog walking

along the top of the galvanised iron fence that divided the
hotel from next door. It was a very large common Opossum—
a horrible looking mangy animal with sparse hair on its long
naked tail—and it seemed utterly oblivious of the tremendous
noise it was creating. I was curious to see it more closely,
so hastily I began to put on my shoes. As I tied the laces and
sprang towards the door, so as to get downstairs before it
reached the end of the fence, a gunshot shattered the night.

'Got him!' shouted Lesley from below.

'Oh Jesus!' screamed Dr. Edwards' girl, and leapt out into
the corridor. I bumped into her, standing naked and frightened
—eyes wide, mouth open and bright pink, pigtails in disarray.
All along the passage doors were being flung open, heads
thrust out, asking what had happened. 'Lesley's shot a yawarri!'
I called back as I ran down the stairs. But it had been blown
to bits, for he had leant out of the window and shot it at a range
of about six feet.

Now wide awake and thoroughly restless, I walked out
into the darkness. Heavy rain clouds rolled low over the towered
buildings. The streets, and the foliage of the dark trees which
lined them, were sopping wet, the air reeked of rain and
leaves and flowers. A curious mood was in the air. In the distance I could hear faint shouts and the sound of a steel band
(steel bands had only recently been introduced from Trinidad).
I walked towards it until, near the river and the docks, suddenly
turning a corner, I came upon it. It was playing in the street,
surrounded by a dancing crowd, everyone swaying and wriggling and jiggling. The thundering of the deep iron drums
obliterated every thought but the desire to dance, to follow the
dark crowd down the street. I saw a familiar face—Nora, a
maid from the hotel. Her mouth was open, she jerked her head
and shrugged her shoulders as she shuffled along. She was
about sixty, but full of life. Then above the din I could hear
another steel band, prowling in the distance. Each had its
own territory, someone said, and if the two met there would
be a fight—but the police would try to guide them down
separate streets.

'Now dere's going to be a real big fight!' said a friendly
Negro whom I began talking to at the side of the road. 'Ghengis
Khan only just get out of prison!' This was his band that we

were following, and his release had provided the excuse for
such unseasonable street music.

It was a relief to find oneself among people brimming with
exuberance. These huge Negro men and women who danced
or lolled in doorways, or swaggered about in lurid garments
yelling ribald remarks across the street, lived and enjoyed
all the superficial (or fundamental) aspects of life to a degree
unheard of in the intensely self-conscious middle-class circles
of the colony. They had never heard of inhibitions—they were
ultra extroverts, living a life which was a chain of wonderful,
unconnected events: dancing, singing, love-making, quarrels,
conversation, drinking, picnics, parties, between bouts of
necessary work. Trinidad was their Mecca, calypso their
religion, and the rhythm of calypso the intoxicant which
liberated their muscular, convulsive, shaking, semi-possessive
dances; while the words—compressed epics, generalisations
about mankind, commentaries on the affairs of the day—
at their best were poetry of greater significance than the
imitations of Eliot and Auden poured out by 'serious' West
Indian writers. D. H. Lawrence might have found in them the
Etruscans of the modern world, bearing the seeds of a dionysiac
civilisation which could be powerful medicine for Western
neuroses. Yet in Guyana this street dance was quite excep-
tional, there was no equivalent here to the saturnalian carnival
which precedes Lent each year in Port-of-Spain. Usually there
was no outlet for collective feelings, and one could sense
frustration twisting like a knife in the entrails, the desperation
that only violence could release. On a grassy verge in the
shadow of a wooden hut a mammoth Negro man and a woman
struggled and puffed together—evidently even love had to be
like rape, or it was not satisfactory: the mood of the country
was too savage for a lyrical approach.

Now I was in a slum quarter, a sea of tiny wooden or galvanised iron shanties. Everywhere music bellowed from radios
and gramophones, even after I had left the steel band behind.
There was no privacy, no intimacy possible in this spawning
ground for humans. The houses were paper thin, and every
door and window was wide open, to catch the breeze. Between
the pools of light from rooms of dancing people was darkness
alive with peeping frogs, marshy grass where the pavement

E

ended. Not 10 miles away the forests began, and stretched on a thousand miles to the Andes. The streets were crowded, full of shadowy, uncertain presences in the gloom. The warmth, the restless insecure world of darkness, called man, woman, and child out from the lighted circles to wander, adventure and return—looking the same, but perhaps altered by the things they had experienced.

I came to a small cafe full of Negroes. This was where by day I bought calypso records, for the best in town were sold here. The clientele had brought their bicycles in and leant them against the walls and counters. I went in and ordered a rum and ginger. Nobody took any notice of me, while I drank first one, then another. They sat around listening to the pounding of the radiogram and talking about boxing and politics. Their talk soothed me. I was frustrated in every meaning of the word—in the work I wanted to do, as well as philosophically, spiritually and sexually. I was lonely and my life in Georgetown seemed meaningless—a mere time of transition. Only the expedition that lay ahead gave me something to which to look forward, around which the hopes with which I had arrived a few months earlier could still cluster.

A block further the first floor was occupied by a somewhat notorious hotel, the Casablanca. A few months before, my friend Harrison, the doctor from the leprosarium, had been horrified when, on looking up at the dance floor, he had seen that all the men were dancing with their hats on. Later, standing in the shadow of the arcaded sidewalk, I glanced up at it's crowded windows. Suddenly I felt a nudge. It was Jimmy Smith, the diamond prospector. He was laughing into my face.

'Going up?' he asked.

I hadn't thought of it. 'No, just strolling,' I replied.

'Come on, old man,' he said, 'nothing like a bit of black velvet—nobody knows who the hell you are anyway.'

He gave a gusty laugh, seized me by the arm and before I could protest I found myself hustled through a doorway and climbing a narrow, creaking flight of stairs to the big dance floor.

As we entered there were shouts of welcome.

'Eh-eh!—it's Jimmy,' said one shapely little black minx,

rushing forward and seizing him by the hand. 'Come on, man, let's dance.'

A much larger, heavily voluptuous, white-powdered, coffee-coloured girl attached herself to me, and soon we were wiggling and shuffling round the floor to the thunderously pounding music. I could see Jimmy laughing merrily as he looked at me, and at the same time, I was surprised to find that I was enjoying myself, despite my initial reluctance.

'Healthiest place in the whole colony!' snorted Jimmy, 'for race relations!'

The ultimate act of courtesy and good manners, I suddenly thought: love-making, to produce a child. Perhaps in miscegenation lay the new White Man's Burden—everyone's burden, the future of the whole world?

Soon we were at a table, and Jimmy sat with one arm across my shoulder, and his other round his little black girl. My own, who smelt atrociously of sweat, was being very lady-like and reserved—perhaps I had not been quick enough in coming to an arrangement? Anyhow, she was clearly put out by me.

Jimmy leant across towards me. 'Get your hand up her skirt,' he said, 'that'll cheer her up. I know how to handle these.'

Setting an example to show me what he meant, he pushed his hand up his own companion's crutch. She obligingly opened her legs, and he twirled it around for a minute, while she gazed adoringly into his eyes: then he reached his two pungent fingers across to under my nose, and said, 'Meet the wife, old man!' At this the whole table burst into laughter —and an immense man carrying a glass of rum in his hand got up from another table, walked heavily over and introduced himself to me.

'Jimmy's a regular here,' he said. 'We've got everything he wants—ain't we Jimmy?'

'That's right, Captain,' said Jimmy. 'The only civilized place in town.' Meanwhile, another calypso had started, and a deafening uproar of stamping feet and shaking bottoms was going on all round. But I was feeling unforthcoming, despite Jimmy's efforts, because this evening I had already drunk too much and perhaps also because I was increasingly apprehensive about where this was leading me. I looked at these people around me, their fathomless eyes, and felt a

terrible despair. I could never get through. I was too idealistic,
or, perhaps, a terrible prig. I was terribly sex-starved, but
I could never have gone through with it here. Why is there
all this junketing around with sex, I thought? Why can't
everyone everywhere just be simple, instead of building
elaborate rituals around it? Why have I got to come to a
whore-house to get what is a natural part of life?

'I must have a pee,' I said, getting up.

'It's down the stairs,' said Jimmy. 'The way we came up.
Open the first door on the ground floor.'

Doing as instructed, to my surprise I found myself inside a
small shop. Overhead the ceiling was shaking, but in this
tiny shop all was curiously peaceful, with only a little illumi-
nation coming in though the slats of the shutters from the
street lamp outside. I recognised the shop now; it was the Chinese Gift Shop—filled with little porcelain dragons and horses,
hand-painted cups and saucers, joss sticks and various cheap
toys and things made out of bamboo and paper. The large
table in the centre of the room was covered with bottles of
jams and preserves.

I was confused and very unsteady, so clearing a little space,
I sat on the edge of the table for a minute. 'If I go upstairs
again,' I said to myself, 'I know I am going to end up with
Jimmy and those two whores. I'll get V.D. or something.
Also I just don't want to make love like that.' I felt as if I
were looking down a vast empty corridor, at the end of which
there was just blackness. I tried to collect myself, got up,
walked through the door and found the lavatory. A minute
later I stepped outside into the cool air of the street.

There, in front of me, magically, was a familiar face in
the lamp light, which softened into a smile of welcome when
it saw me. It was Sheila van Battenberg.

'What are you doing here?' I said.

'I was just walking home to my aunt's,' she replied.

'Come inside,' I lurched forward, and seized her by the hand.

'Oh no, I couldn't,' she said.

'No, I don't mean in there,' I said, somewhat incoherently,
dragging her through the doorway and into the Chinese Gift
Shop, so opportunely open. I bolted the door behind me
and for a moment we stood there. Uncertainly, she looked

into my eyes and then smiled, I put my arms round her, and kissed her. For a long time we stood there, then gently I reached under her skirt. She stood paralysed, then her tongue came into my mouth again and with a decisive movement she slid off her panties. Hastily we began to clear a space on the table. I slipped the straps off her shoulders, undid her bra. In the dimness she was unbelievably beautiful, with her black hair falling on to perfect shoulders and arms, and her breasts two soft targets for kisses. With utter rapture we embraced each other. It was the first moment of release that I had experienced in the many months that I had lived in the colony. Neither of us spoke; no words were needed. We were just totally, instinctively happy to be together. We lay looking at each other, while overhead the reverberatings of the band and of the dancing drowned every sound we made.

Suddenly, in the middle of renewed caresses an awkward movement brought an avalanche of jam-jars, stuffed alligators, and other curiosities crashing to the ground. Twisting sideways to see what had happened, Sheila fell off on to the floor with a thump which crushed half a dozen little balata-gum-coconut-palms-with-groups-of-monkeys-underneath, made for tourists.

Alarmed by the noise, she suddenly panicked. 'Let's go. Someone is bound to come and find us!' she said reaching out for her clothes—and hastily we both dressed. Rapidly I replaced all the fallen objects on their shelves.

'I'm going back to Berbice tomorrow,' she said. 'I have to.'

'That's terrible,' I said. I would love to see you again. We must meet.'

'We will,' she said, 'I'll 'phone you whenever I get into town.'

Opening the door cautiously, I crept out into the street to see if all was clear, then rapped on the window for her to come out. As if we had never seen each other we walked apart in the darkness, she to whatever her life concealed, I back to my hotel and my loneliness. Yet in the days following I thought of her, and felt more serene because of her—*someone* had accepted me just as I was.

Then came an alarming note, though initially it amused me. For in the morning paper I read: '$2,000 raid on Chinese

Gift Shop'. The paragraph ran roughly as follows: 'Mr. Cheon-Hu reports that on Wednesday night thieves broke into his Chinese Gift Shop under the Hotel Casablanca, in Main Street. They stole $2,000 worth of valuable speciality goods, mostly imported from Hong Kong, besides doing damage estimated at $500 to the contents of the shop in an act of pure vandalism, before escaping with the goods. Mr. Cheon-Hu has requested that the Hotel Casablanca, from which he suspects that the thieves made their entrance, be relieved of its licence. The police are understood to be on the trail of the criminals.'

What if someone should mention my name, or call me as a witness? Fortunately, Jimmy had meanwhile returned to the bush. There was nothing for me to do but stay quiet and hope that the police investigations would lead nowhere. And indeed after a week nothing had apparently been discovered and there were no further mentions of the raid. Meanwhile, I had been thinking about the likely maximum cost of the damage I had done—so putting two $5 bills into an envelope I mailed them to Mr. Cheon-Hu.

Relief from Georgetown came with the trip to Surinam. At 9. a.m. one morning a rusty taxi collected me, and I sat in front with the Indian driver, while the Taylors sat in the rear.

All day long we drove eastwards along the coast on the colony's only main road, traversing an utterly level watery landscape, punctuated occasionally by the vertical note of a sugar-factory chimney. The details of this tropical fenland repeated themselves over and over again, as I noted whenever fully alert, for heat, dust, and the rocking of the car soon lulled me into a torpor. Half a dozen miles outside of Georgetown the road became of red 'burnt earth', with two narrow metalled strips for car wheels to drive along. Whenever we passed another car it meant getting off the strips, and throwing up clouds of dust as we slithered over the earth, perilously close to the deep drainage canals that ran beside the road. These canals, or 'trenches', were full of scarlet flowering Nymphaeas, water hyacinths with pyramids of flickering mauve flowers, Salvinias, Azollas, Marsilias, a delicate white flower like a water buttercup which I did not identify, and—most wonderful of all—great banks of lotus, naturalised from Egypt: at each moment of growth perhaps the most beautiful plant in existence, with its tall velvety dark green peltate leaves, buds fat and gracefully pointed, flowers like enormous translucent pink or yellow single paeonies, and wine-glass shaped fruit like giant poppy capsules.

Beyond the trenches lay meadows of incredible lushness, dotted with cattle and buffaloes wading knee-deep in the richly-flowering mud. Everywhere there were flowers and birds—white egrets, white herons, blue herons, storks, gallinules, grebes, big black orioles with long yellow feathers in their tails, hovering rusty-and-grey coloured hawks. Soaring overhead were ghoulish vultures—occasionally they would be in clusters beside the road feeding upon some dead animal, and scuttling and flapping away with indecorous haste as the car approached. To our left there was always the low line of the concrete sea wall that protected this wonderful polder landscape from flooding with salt water at high tide.

At first all the villages were pleasant looking, full of pretty white houses with fretwork gables and balconies, perched high on stilts among embowering mangoes, hibiscus, coconut palms, and vegetable gardens. Idyllic—yet only two years previously almost all their inhabitants had had chronic malaria, and the hospitals throughout the country had been filled with malaria cases. Now they were healthy, for malaria-carrying mosquitoes had been almost entirely eliminated by a colony-wide campaign of spraying with DDT. The hospitals were now empty, but the birth rate, formerly stagnant, had shot up to become one of the highest known—3·7 per cent per annum—which meant that the population would double every twelve years. The implications of this were not pleasant to contemplate—for already 96 per cent of the 600,000 population of the entire country was concentrated in a strip 5 miles deep and 150 miles in length along this very road, between the sea and the swamps that barred the way to the vast, empty jungle and savannah country inland. Already most of this population had no work—so frustration was added to claustrophobia: a simple society, a crowded society with its options apparently exhausted. Now came the first great sugar estate: an avenue of stately palms

leading to an enormous grey-shingled house of Georgian style;
clustering factory buildings; an intersection of canals, with
iron barges tied up near a sluice; and beyond, row after row of
what looked like rather ramshackle dog-kennels. These were
'barracks' built for the estate workers. Each row was perhaps
300 feet long, and divided into thirty sections, each of which
was a 'house', consisting of a single room about ten feet square,
and a section of the balcony in front, on which cooking was
done. One stand-pipe for water, and one lavatory hut over
a ditch, often overflowing, served each of several dozens of such
rows, all set like soldiers on parade on a huge acreage of bare
earth crisscrossed with drains. All the sugar estates had similar
acreages. I shuddered each time we passed one. What was
worse, all the new housing I saw was merely an amplification
of the old—still as appallingly regimented, still set in those vast
bare areas with never a tree, a bush, a flower, under the
furnace sun. Taylor and his wife were asleep in the back.
I turned to the driver:

'Why don't they grow a few vegetables, or a banana tree,
just to make the place more like home?'

'I say so myself, sir—plenty time. Yet they always has a rule
to clear de bush. That way nowhere for mosquito to breed.
There is almost no maleria left, yet they continues with this
rule because they is too stupid to change it.'

Originally each unit had housed a single family. Now they
were frequently occupied by several: relatives, descendants, or
simply squatters who had moved in, and who had nowhere
to go.

It was unbearable to contemplate what life must be like in
them. They reminded the ecologist in me of boxes of seedlings.
But in a seed box the individuals are thinned out as they
develop—or they simply choke each other. In these barracks
there was no provision for spacing out, and even if there had
been, their uniformity gave little scope for individuality. But
then, individual development was doubtless not desired in sugar
workers.

I began to think about egalitarian societies occurring in
nature: I thought of bees and ants, of fields of corn or cabbages.
In all instances their apparent equality was a product of
pressures equivalent to totalitarianism among men, except where

societies of the same species of plant or animal existed as a brief juvenile stage in development towards 'higher', more mature and stable societies. But such juvenile stages, like a cabbage field left alone, are rapidly invaded by other species that can utilise the spaces in their ranks—i.e. their unexploited raw materials and wastes. As a result we get the development of a series of societies (called a sere), which might run something like this, among plants:

Bare rock→colonised by mosses and lichens (egalitarian phase)→then ferns and bushes come in as the rock breaks down into soil→these grow into a scrub woodland→and finally, when a deep soil has been produced from decomposed rock mixed with vegetable humus, a mature society—the forest— appears, where there are trees of many kinds, as well as shrubs, ferns, mosses, climbing plants and others. Or, to take another instance, a pond or lake which gradually gets filled in by reeds, shrubs, and finally forest. Both these processes result in the same end product, forest, which we thus call the 'climax' vegetation of the area. Could this concept of societies as developing through various stages to a climax be applied to human societies? I pondered:

$$\left.\begin{array}{l}\text{bare rock}\\ \text{unoccupied land}\end{array}\right\} \to \left\{\begin{array}{l}\text{mosses and lichens}\\ \text{pioneer settlers}\end{array}\right\} \to \left\{\begin{array}{l}\text{ferns and herbs}\\ \text{hamlets}\end{array}\right\}$$

$$\to \left\{\begin{array}{l}\text{woodland}\\ \text{villages}\end{array}\right\} \to \left\{\begin{array}{l}\text{forest}\\ \text{towns}\end{array}\right\} \to \text{climax} \left\{\begin{array}{l}\text{maximum forest}\\ \text{metropolis.}\end{array}\right.$$

At once I saw an extraordinary analogy: in nature the earlier, more 'egalitarian' societies produce relatively abundant debris, which accumulates and provides a foothold on which the species of the later stages nourish themselves. Similarly egalitarian human societies of, say factory workers, produce goods which are overabundant for their own consumption, and which are sold outside of the production area. This then, I thought, is the true meaning of exploitation of the masses: instead of enjoying the surpluses produced by their own labour and using them to develop a mature society for themselves, their products are exported for the benefit of others, while they are kept in the strait-jacket of juvenile social conditions where production is the only goal. To substantiate the analogy one would have to measure inputs and outputs. But it was obvious that all egalitarian human societies above the primitive level produce materials and energy which should enable them to develop into something more complex. And yet this does not happen—incredibly because egalitarianism has become a social goal! Marxists, egalitarians, even builders of uniform housing estates, beware! The societies you are so eagerly producing are blueprints for revolution! How desirable this is, is another question; but planners should at least be aware of what they are doing, and of its place in a more general view of the evolution of human relationships and communities.

We crossed the Mahaica, then the Mahaicony rivers, driving cautiously on rickety bridges, with glimpses of olive water, stilt-rooted mangroves, and the sea beyond. Then the country changed, the villages grew poorer looking, and a desolate note came in. Even the metal road strips were left behind, and the road—monotonous, full of potholes—stretched straight ahead, blazing red under a burning blue sky. Between snatches of sleep I looked up. Gradually the pastures gave place to acres of stinking grey sea mud, slimy ooze on which ghastly clusters of rickety pile-dwellings stood on top of their middens. When the tide was up these villages actually stood in water, or on tiny squares of mud surrounded by water. In the filthy channels between the houses women were washing clothes, or fishing neck-deep with tattered brown nets. Sullen, hostile groups stood by the roadside. The rags, filth, and squalor were indescribable.

I turned to the driver again, and asked: 'Why wasn't the sea wall continued along here? Or is it broken? How can the Government allow this?'

He smiled. 'Don't feel sorry for dese people, Sa. Dese is rich—and always been healthy. Dere is never no malaria at all in dese part, 'cause of de sea-water. Sometimes dey does break down de sea wall to let it come in! They'se dirty is true. But they is freeholders—dey *owns* de land. Just a short way in there is big rice fields. I tell you dese is proud people—dey refuse Government aid. Dey don't want no obligations.'

'How is it that you see so few men in some villages?'

'In the Indian villages they out working rice and coconut. In the black villages the men gone to Georgetown for work.

They leaves the women and baby behind—that is family life
in B.G.! And that why women so powerful—they is the head
of the family. Each man send money for he child. But sometimes
a woman have child by different men. I tell you there is every
type of marriage here—man with ten wife, and woman with
ten husband!'

We crossed the Abary River, and about noon arrived at
Rossignol, on the bank of the Berbice River. Here we waited in
a procession of motor cars, lorries, vans, cyclists, and donkey-
carts, for the ferry to take us across to New Amsterdam, the
colony's second city, spread out along the opposite bank.
Evelyn Taylor, now awake, began unpacking the lunch, while
I strolled to the waterside. Great patches of water hyacinths
and grasses were floating past on the murky flood. The crowd
awaiting the boat consisted mostly of women, taking baskets of
chickens or provisions into town, together with a few men,
probably plantation workers on their day off.

Haranguing the crowd were a number of speakers, and I
drifted over to the nearest to see what he was saying: 'Is a most
holy condition, I telling you, I have many witness. But is not
a simple t'ing. Dere is four sort of you-knocks, and four sort of
you-knocky. . . .'

I could not think what the man was talking about.

'. . . First there is those who are *born* you-knocks' (eunuchs!).
'Then there is those who bee-come you-knocks by a natural
development, like for old age or illness. Third, there is those
who make theyselves you-knocks, as it were by divine calling.
And last there is those who have you-knocky thrust upon
them. . . .'

'Which is de bes', man?'

'De bes' is de t'ird. De wus' is de fort! . . . yes, man?' (He
was addressing a woman.)

'Is it possible for a woman to be a you-knock?'

'Yes—is possible in de spiritual sense, both *and* in de physical. . . .'

'Wha' you saying deh, man!' came a shout from a heckler.

'You big mout'! Shut up!' yelled the incensed woman,
turning at him. 'I got moh' balls dan de lot ob you!'

'Quiet, *quiet*, please, ladies and gemmun. Dis is *holy* meeting.'

An even larger crowd was assembled a few yards further on—

a crowd that seemed unusually quiet. I moved towards it, and
found myself beside our chauffeur. In his hand was clutched a
$5 note—and to my surprise I saw that many others of those
around me in the silent throng also held up $5 notes. The
speaker, who stood in the back of a small Ford pickup, was
dressed entirely in white, and wore a tall white-and-yellow
mitre on his head—evidently a bishop of some sort. He spoke
so softly that I could not hear his words, every now and then
stretching out a be-ringed hand to rest it on the shoulder of
one of those nearest him, while with his other be-ringed hand
he took the proffered $5 notes and stuffed them into a school
satchel at his side.

'Oh, Gawd, I mus' get close before de boat come!' muttered
our chauffeur.

I clasped his arm. He spun round, eyes fearful, then softened
as he recognised me.

'Is de wish-come-true man, Sa. He only come once in a
while—an' I t'ought you was a policeman.'

'What does he do?'

'He makes everybody wish come true, *if* he take de money
an' he say de words.'

'What if they don't come true?'

'Dat never happen without a reason—else you break
somet'ing he says.'

His face was so intent that I questioned no further as we
passed forward. Indeed, I searched in my own pocket for a
$5 note, wondering desperately what to wish for. The chauffeur
reached the inner circle, and held up his money, his face shining
with hope. Deftly the wish-come-true man took it from him,
and bent low, muttering, his right hand reassuring on the man's
shoulder.

'Nicholas—lunch! Hurry! the ferry's coming.' It was
Maurice Taylor, on the edge of the crowd. The spell was
broken. I was irritated, but I no longer wanted to spend money
on magic. I turned, pushed my way out and walked back to
the car, thinking somewhat cynically that the wish-come-true
man had evolved the purest, simplest way of making a living
that I had ever heard of, the very archetype of confidence tricks.

When the chauffeur returned, excited and pleased, I could
not help asking, 'Why do the police want him?'

'Dey say he t'ief our money, I 'spect—or something like dat. Anywise, dat is why you have to catch he when you see he. Sometimes it is three—four years and you don' get no other chance. Nobody know where he from—maybe he come from Suddie way, dat is what I hear.'

We drove on to the ferry. I got out of the car and leaned over the rail alone until we disembarked. To my surprise, when I rejoined them the Taylors were talking about 'Sheila', saying what a pity that her brother made her live here. My heart leaped at the name although it was evidently a different girl they were referring to, and I wondered whether we might glimpse my Sheila as the car crawled through the dusty streets of this hot, bedraggled little town.

On the outskirts we passed a beautiful old house, its front supported by a range of decorated Doric columns, a style suggesting 1780, though it was probably later—a relic, anyway, of the affluent days of slavery. Then we crossed the Canje River, and entered a mudland with villages even more derelict than before. The road was thronged with pedestrians and animals: sheep; weird pigs with woolly coats; tiger-striped curs; lumbering oxen and buffaloes; donkeys—patiently plodding or obstinate with twitching ears; crazily-running cows pursued by shouting men, and avoiding thrown nooses with practised ease. Few of these villages had names, but all had numbers. It seemed significant of the anonymity of life in this human spawning ground.

Heavy clouds began to fill the sky, lurid and foreboding. Then as dusk fell we turned off at Village 63, at the mouth of the Courantyne River, and bounced along a rough road to the main Government rest-house of the region—a large house with roofed verandahs all round. I got out and stretched. A frog-filled lagoon and a line of mangrove trees screened us from the sea, loud-roaring, foaming turbulently on to a beach of shells. Then a couple of thunderclaps brought rain rumbling out of the clouds in drops the size of coffee-cups. Dinner was ready as we ran into the house. Starving, I fell on a delicious dish of fried chicken with rice, plantains, potatoes and yams, pleasantly served by a gentle old Negress. Hours later, after I had gone to bed, I could hear Evelyn telling the awe-stricken old woman about how things were done in the East; then tiredness and the buffeting of wind and rain on the roof and walls carried me off to sleep.

A rendezvous had been arranged with our Dutch opposite numbers, so next morning we drove to Springlands, on our shore of the Courantyne River, where Wilson, the Assistant District Commissioner, awaited us—a tall, affable, slightly stooping coloured man with glasses. As we cast off in his launch the clouds began to liquify and rain poured down, lashing the river's surface into spray a yard high.

When it lifted we were swinging round a point on the Dutch side into the Nickerie River. About half a mile away the shore showed low and jungly, above a beach dotted with curious black blodges. Could they be rocks? A rock would be a real event—for there are no rocks in coastal Guyana, only mud. The river was narrow and winding, with sloping mudbanks fringed by stilt-rooted mangroves. We passed a rickety looking group of timbers in mid-water: 'Old Nickerie,' said Wilson. 'That's all that remains of the old town. The whole coast has sunk into the sea.' Then a few houses spread before us, a saw-mill, a discharging sluice gate—and the town of Nieuw Nickerie.

At a well-made jetty stood our opposite numbers—the Dutch Commissaris in an immaculate white uniform with gold buttons and epaulettes, and a Forest Officer in smart khaki drill. With the most perfect courtesy they helped us ashore—I in a blue Aertex shirt and brown shorts, Taylor in scruffy khaki trousers and a once-white shirt. Only Wilson looked at all presentable.

'Professionals *v.* amateurs,' I thought. 'These people must believe in themselves!'

The downpour renewed as we shook hands. Were we English perhaps cleverer, seeing through uniforms and other such disguises? Or were we merely shifty, unwilling to proclaim our statuses and intentions, in case we changed our minds? Reluctantly, I concluded the latter. An American limousine of immaculate glossiness awaited us, and we drove slowly towards the Government rest-house, where we were greeted by an enormous Negress dressed in magnificent traditional 'Kota Missie' costume (*she* certainly had no doubts about herself). With a kindly smile she led us to our rooms, walking

ahead, brilliant as a triumphal bouquet of flowers in her layers
of rustling starched cretonne skirts, her bustles fore and aft,
her capacious flounced bodice, her elaborately folded and
peaked bandana head-kerchief.

The Commissaris saw my interest and smiled. 'These cos-
tumes are getting rare!' he said. 'They are too expensive compared with modern clothes. Yet what a pity!'

'They are so attractive!'

'Yes—yet they were designed to be *unattractive*, by the
eighteenth-century missionaries! To disguise the female form.'

Changed into dry clothes, we went to the Commissaris' home,
the upper half of a graceful columned-and-verandahed early
nineteenth-century building. The bookshelves were full of
works in Dutch, English, French, and German, there were
beautiful and interesting objects—works of native art, rich
rugs, attractive pictures, tasteful furniture. It was obvious that
the Dutch valued education more than we, and were prepared
to pay to have educated men in their colonial service. I could
think of no equivalent room in British Guiana.

Coffee in giant cups piled high with whipped cream was
brought to us on an open terrace. Then we descended to the
Commissaris' office and discussed the smuggling. The entire
Courantyne River was Dutch, as far as low-tide mark on the
British shore, so the onus of inspecting timber rafts fell largely
upon them; but the problem affected both sides, for it was easy
for any timber-cutter floating his logs down the river to claim
they had been cut on either bank and so evade duties on which-
ever side he sold them. A large number of mills on both sides
were delighted to saw up this cheaper smuggled wood as fast
as it reached them. After a short discussion we agreed upon
the joint enforcement of a system of marking logs, and the
establishment of four customs-posts.

Business over, I pointed to a series of maps of timber grants
on the wall, and asked the Commissaris and Forest Officer
Snijders whether they were of areas in Surinam. I had often
prepared similar maps during my training at Oxford, to show
different types of forest, different densities of timber, dates for
felling and for replanting or regeneration by seed. They formed
a complete set of forest-management maps for a particular area.
But I had seen nothing like these in British Guiana.

Taylor was evidently embarrassed: 'Come, come, Guppy. Don't let's waste time.' But I insisted: 'This won't take a minute.'

'Yes,' said Snijders. 'These are in Surinam. We conduct exploitation on very strict lines. We survey each block of forest, then ask for tenders for it from the different timber companies. Then after exploitation is complete we go in and replant or resow—at the timber company's expense!'

'We could never do that in B.G.,' said Taylor.

'Why not?' asked Snijders. 'You have greenheart, which is much more valuable than any timber we have here! That would pay for it!'

I thought with dismay of the immense ruined areas of forest in British Guiana, logged out and left to regrow haphazard, if at all. And especially of the 'Bartica triangle', the country's most magnificent timbered area, and one of its prime capital assets, in which despoliation was just beginning.

'No, we just couldn't afford it,' insisted Taylor. 'We just don't get enough in royalties to be able to afford to do things on that scale. We haven't the personnel—it would take years to build up a department capable of that sort of treatment.'

'Oh no!' interjected Snijders. 'We've done it in two years— since the war. It pays for itself, I assure you.'

'Of course it pays for itself,' I asserted. 'In the long run it is the only possible way. We just allow the forests to be devastated in B.G.'

Taylor glared. I said no more. Then an unworthy thought entered my brain: were we British really so incompetent? Or was this a plot—taking everything and putting nothing back; spending not a penny, leaving the colony sucked dry, and then abandoning it? But surely not—surely there was no intention on the part of the British Government to leave Guyana, except at some vague time in the future, when it had been built up economically and was ready for self-government? How could I be sure? We—meaning our bosses in London—were either being wicked or crassly stupid, if well-intentioned. I concluded the latter—it was more comfortable.

After lunch we had a siesta, and I lay on my bed thinking dark thoughts about my chosen career. Why should the Colonial Service *have* such depressing people in positions of

power? I could not feel that they represented England—from
the people she sent abroad it was impossible to believe that
England was a civilised land with a history of which she could
be proud. To the Guyanese that civilisation meant a great
deal—it was the only thing they really wanted from England.
They wanted intelligent, cultivated men; but England sent
them scout-masters and centre-forwards. They wanted help
in creating a worth-while society; she sent them failures in the
competitive world at home, who sought vengeance on their
frustrations by recreating the atmosphere of a third-rate public
school. They wanted friends; she sent them racial snobs, to
whom a job abroad meant servants and a big step up socially.
No wonder the Englishman abroad was as disliked as when he
returned home! A common bond of incompetence seemed to
hold the Colonial Service together: it was a pyramid of mutually-
propping buck-passers, increasingly fearful, as they reached
retirement age, of intelligence or innovation. From the summit
down the last thing any of them wanted was to tackle a problem
(let it burst on the next fellow). What they wanted was
Budleigh Salterton and a pension (the interest, steadily
diminishing in real value through inflation) on a capital sum
they had earned, but would never realise, poor imbeciles!
Fewer, better-paid men on a series of short contracts would
have been preferable—especially if some outside firm could
have calculated their efficiency, including their use of capital
tied up in buildings and equipment. For the effective, 'seniority'
(if that was really of value) could be acquired through each
new contract, while continuity would be assured when a newly-
independent country requested a man to stay on. If I was right,
why then—'unless the fruit rots, the seed will not grow'. If I
was being hasty, time would correct me.

After lunch, we were driven to inspect an irrigation scheme.
Where in British Guiana there would have been Indians from
India, here there were Javanese, inhabiting picturesque
villages of houses with high, delicately pointed eaves.

Taylor, at his most bristling and authoritative, was haranguing Snijders about the relative working abilities of different
brands of 'coolie' in the parts of India where he had served,
and I listened, wondering what compulsion could drive him
so to caricature the Indian army officer.

F

Rice was the chief crop of these irrigated fields, and beautiful it looked in the gently moving afternoon air. The rain had stopped, but the sky was still cloud-hung, with spreading blue patches and shafting sunlight. Beyond the rice stood a wall of forest, and from this twelve large hawks came flapping slowly side by side: flapping then gliding, flapping then gliding, through the moist air, turning their heads as they scrutinised the sopping rice-lands below. Then one by one they closed their wings and descended upon some mouse, lizard or snail, forced out into the open by the flooding of its place of concealment. Then up they got again, flapping heavily back to the trees, there to alight, eat—and return. For half an hour, as we stood there, they kept up a sort of continuous avian shuttle without once ceasing; and so abundant was their prey that none was ever aloft for more than three or four minutes before swooping.

That evening we strolled through the streets of Nieuw Nickerie. The shops were small, and full of the things that village general-stores sell everywhere—coils of rope, cheap cloth, tinny wristwatches, hurricane lanterns, kerosene, bars of chocolate—but they smelt of molasses, rum, spices, tar, salt-fish, in a wonderful rich compound that could be found only in the tropics.

The bubble, gurgle, rattle, buzz and boom of innumerable and varied frogs came from the marshy ditches beside every street, while the air was a soup of singing, stinging, malaria-carrying mosquitoes. Even in bed, safe inside my mosquito net, the wild humming of frustrated mosquitoes was enough to keep me awake for a while. In British Guiana, at least, this was a thing of the past. Here the hospital beds were still full.

5

Over the Falls

'Dat is one big problem you got, Mr. Walker,' said Stanislaus de Courcy, my barber, pausing for a moment to consider and test the reactions of his audience. I had come in to have my hair cut very short, to last three months, before going to Bartica for the start of the expedition. Half a dozen clients awaited their turn, or had remained to read the papers and magazines and to continue the talk. For a Georgetown haircut sometimes took half the morning, and was a major social event, a time for acting out roles and for philosophical and sporting discussion. We had dealt with racing and boxing. Now Walker, a well-known 'sweet man', had come up with his problem—a married woman.

'She jus' drivin' me crazy, I tell you. But dat bloody old man of hers, he nebber go out! Even if she go to market, he go wid she!'

'You got to make him weak an' lazy.'

'You tellin' me! Oh, Chris' man, she got bubbies like watermelon! Wherever he fin' dat woman? Somewhere in de country? An' he's a real randy sod, you know—he work she well. She don' need for nuttin!'

'Dats what I'm sayin', Mr. Walker. De pawpaw treatment is yo' only hope.'

'Wha' you mean, man, eh? Paw-paw treatment?'

'Well dat is de one way you get she for certain. I use it myself. Dat is how I get my present ol' lady. You mus' get a young *male* Paw-paw tree, an' plant it upwind from where dey lives. Now when dat tree get big, in a few months' time, de pollen go fly—an' den you will see.'

'Wha' happen den?'

'Well, you know dey use de leaf to wrap up chicken and tenderise meat? Its de same thing wid de pollen, only mo' strong. I tell you dat man will not be able to operate within one week of de tree flowerin'. Den you mus' speak to she. But remember—it mus' be male tree, because dat is de one dat shed pollen.'

'Man, I go get paw-paw right now in de market,' and Walker bolted from the saloon. De Courcy winked, and summoned me to the barber's chair. Had they been serious, or had this all been an elaborate leg-pull for my benefit? I could not guess.

Since returning from the Courantyne life had been easier. I had received £100 in compensation for a suitcase lost on my way out, and my mother had also sent me a gift of £100—so I was less pinched than before. Feeling readier to take risks I accepted an invitation to share a house with a pair of young men, a geologist and an accountant at Bookers. With them I went out more often, even sometimes on Saturdays to dance at the local night club, the Carib, situated on the breezy sea wall a short way out of town, or to the Palm Court with its curious decor of tropical plants, on picnics into the bush near the airport, or along the coast to swim in the brown sea. Life was brighter. I had more friends, including some interesting new arrivals in the colony, and there were enough of us to form an oasis insulated from the depressing, intrigue-ridden tensions of the local and official scenes. Perhaps it was that we were merely younger? Though noticeably one or two older people began to prefer us to their peers, including a delightful Dutch business man and his wife, a retired Harley Street doctor who had come to the colony to continue his life-time hobby of butterfly hunting, and the head of the local airline. Some were expatriates, but many were Guyanese.

Not that I had changed my views about Georgetown, but continuing my ecological analysis I had begun to see its social structure not as something to which I should conform, but as something diseased which inevitably must be overthrown. It was an overmature society, like a woodland in which all the dominant trees are old, and suppressing the young saplings that should be growing up to replace them. The conditions which had called this world into being had changed: its old trees were for the chopper—and as they had produced so few young, those who would take over would be very different indeed.

The pressures at my office, however, remained as strong as ever. Nothing is more demoralising than the feeling that one is disapproved of, regardless of one's efforts. I completed my work on the herbarium, was congratulated on the catalogue that I produced, and was paid the compliment of having it duplicated and bound in hard covers. But I felt I could make no contact with my bosses. One day I blew up over some trifle and was horribly rude to one of the office staff. I blush today when I think of it; and even more at the fact that he apologised for *his* behaviour.

But the rainy season was now nearly over, and increasingly I was occupied with preparations for the expedition. It puzzled me that I could find only fleeting references to the region I was to survey. Was something wrong with it? No one ever seemed to have stopped there, only passed through as quickly as possible, and there was no record of any inhabitants.

However, I found a number of maps at the Lands and Mines Department, and obtained copies. The whole area seemed to be untouched jungle—and there were virtually no names on the map except along the river itself: the guttural Arawak 'Urumaru Creek' and 'Mocca-Mocca', the soft, mysterious 'Arisaro Mountain'; the gentle Creole 'Plantain Island'; the romantically evocative 'Gold-Workings' and 'Balata Bleeder's trail'. But I could form no picture of the region from there.

The most detailed map, dated 1917, had been prepared by the Government surveyor, Hohenkerk. On this I began to plot my future survey lines, to be cut at roughly right angles to the bank, 1 mile apart, on alternate sides of the river. Each was to be $3\frac{1}{2}$ miles long—considered the maximum economic limit for the extraction of logs. Under normal conditions surveying a $3\frac{1}{2}$-mile-long strip of forest 100 feet wide was considered a reasonable day's work, giving a total journey on foot of 7 miles.

A pre-planned random scatter of lines over the area would theoretically have produced a better sample but under the likely working conditions of the survey such lines would be nearly impossible to locate accurately. If aerial photographs had been available I would have suggested making a rough map of the different vegetational types in the region, and then sampling each—but they were not. So my figures would have a margin of error that would be both wide and hard to estimate.

What then were my objectives?

1. To sample the forests on both banks of the Essequebo River from Gluck Island to the mouth of the Potaro River, and to find the volumes per acre of all the different types of trees present which were over 12 inches in diameter 'at breast height' (an arbitrary point chosen to eliminate the basal swelling of the tree trunks; or above buttresses, stilt roots, etc.).

2. To discover, describe, and photograph the vegetation types in the area, their ecology, developmental relationships with one another, and the effect of wind, fire, pests and diseases upon them.

3. To collect botanical specimens, particularly of new species, or of species previously unknown in the area. In particular I was charged with collecting ferns and the curious plants of the family Podostemonacae for Dr. Phillipson of the British Museum, and mosses for Dr. Catcheside of Cambridge.

4. To examine the topography and soils.

As assistants I was to have with me my old friends Jonah and his son Rufus from Bartica, Jothann Fredericks, an Amerindian ranger of the Forest Department, Kenneth Lord, a young Negro ranger undergoing training, and Basil Tracey, half-Amerindian, half-Negro, to run the boat and engine.

Besides these the Bartica office engaged some fifteen other men, mostly Amerindians or of largely Amerindian blood, some of whom had been on previous surveys and understood the work. Nearly all had beautiful or unlikely names—among which I noticed Julian James. For our boat an old river craft had been rehabilitated, which was said to be very easy to handle in rapids. And to pilot us up through the mighty rapids and falls above Bartica an old river captain named Skeet had been brought out of retirement.

To cook for me, to wash my clothes, and generally look after me, I needed a camp attendant. Several villainous-looking men presented themselves, and I was beginning to despair when a thin, sooty-black Indian called Boodhoo, with eyes so red that they glowed like rubies—I have never seen their like before or since—presented himself. He sounded conscientious and described himself as a good cook—but

above all I liked his mild and timorous countenance. I gave him
a few dollars to buy things for the trip—and he ran out of the
room so rapidly that I had doubts about whether I would ever
see him again. 'Don't worry, Sir,' said one of the office clerks.
'He go fast in case you change your mind.'

Food for the men—salt pork, biscuits, butter, condensed
milk, rice, tins of salmon, etc.—had been purchased for the
first part of the journey and awaited me in Bartica, and further
supplies would be despatched from Georgetown by Taylor.
My own food, including a few luxuries—tinned asparagus,
capers, olives, Worcester sauce, herbs and condiments—had
been crated and shipped to Bartica; and I had selected a few
books that might be good reading on a long trip—Proust, and
The Magic Mountain in particular; and assembled all my old
clothes, including several pairs of very light rubber-soled
canvas 'miner's boots', a camp bed and mosquito net, a torch, a
shaving mirror. Finally I obtained supplies and instructions
from my doctor friends for treating the likeliest bush ailments,
and bought a tin trunk, or 'canister', and a duffle bag to fit all
this into.

I was looking forward to seeing Bartica again, even if only
for a few days. And also Aggie. Despite her wildness I liked
her and felt that she was really a friend—for we had had
several more conversations over the radio-telephone, and
exchanged several letters. Again and again she had suggested
coming to Georgetown to live with me, but that would have
been difficult in a hotel where I could hardly afford to live
myself; and even after I had moved into the house, I had
hesitated to ask her because I felt she would regard it as a
total committal. Perhaps in my few days in Bartica I could
persuade her that I did not want to get married—only to be
friends.

The very day before I was due to go there a parcel from
Bartica awaited me when I arrived home in the evening. Inside
it was a sponge-cake with thick icing, and the word 'Nick'
entwined on the top: it looked rather loving—but with it was
a letter:

'You Heel. I guess this is the end. Johnny S. [the young man
studying for the ministry] saw you in G.T. and I suppose *she*

is why you playing so hard to get. You double-crosser, I never
thort you was so low. Next Wednesday I coming to town and
if you can explain make it good.

                                                    Aggie.'

It was Tuesday! Could this mean that Aggie was arriving
the following day—just when I was leaving? I had so re-
peatedly *not* returned to Bartica that evidently she did not
believe I was actually coming. But how could I stop her? She
had no telephone of her own—she used the radio-telephone at
Bartica. There was no telegram service over the telephone, and
the Post Office was closed. Even if I could send a telegram it
was unlikely to reach her before she caught the plane. Just in
case, I wrote one out: 'Arriving Bartica Wednesday, see you,
Nick', and gave it to one of my house-mates, to be despatched
early the following morning. Then having done so, I nearly
took it back again, for my heart sank: it would undoubtedly
be misconstrued by Aggie, and cause her hopes to soar. At
dinner time I cut the cake: there was something hard inside.
Delicately prising the layers apart, I saw that in the central
creamy area was an object carved out of wood. Before my
chuckling friends I drew it out: a dagger! The cake meant
love—undoubtedly—but the knife was a warning!
    When the amphibian plane reached Bartica next morning,
and I disembarked into the tender that rowed us ashore, I
gazed intently at the line of passengers waiting on the jetty
for the return flight to the capital. It was only as I mounted
the steps that I saw Aggie. For one second our eyes met and
I started to speak, to explain about my telegram. But she just
glared at me with an incredible hatred. Then she turned aside,
brushed past me roughly, and ran down the steps into the
boat.

Roar, crash, rumble, bang! Amethystine rain clouds came
tumbling their torrents over the Essequebo, drumming on the
tin roofs, battering on the thatch, lashing water, muddying
ground, making the palms toss and hurl their football nuts. A
quarter to six in the morning, and my room was a tangle of
cards and paper, scraps and ends. But I was packed. I had
written a long letter to Aggie. I was wide awake and nervous.

Breakfast: Miss Correia, the hotel owner, was full of sympathetic words. 'I was out in de bush myself, you know. Yes—six months wid my brudder Eugene. . . .' Up and down her voice lilted, her hands making gentle benedictions. 'We came down from Issano in *one* day. Over fourteen rapids, and I was never so glad to get back. . . .' (What had I forgotten to pack? Would it all ever get in the boat, together with the mass of provisions and equipment we were taking—and twenty men?) '. . . Dey lost a lot of lives in dose falls—dey *very* dangerous you know—be careful, Mr. Guppy . . . will you settle for that last coke you had, Mr. Guppy . . . ?' Her face was gentle as a cherub's.

Despite the rain the river level had dropped several feet in the last few days, the rainy season was over, the dry season setting in, and our departure date had evidently been well calculated.

Our boat was called the *Tacouba Express*—a lucky name, said everybody. A tacouba is a log or dead tree, and she would be encountering plenty of them, floating or submerged. Thirty feet long with a spoon-shaped bow and a wooden tent amidships (whose tarpaulin flaps could be let down when it rained), she had never been beautiful, but her hull was still sound, and her draught was fairly shallow. She had a screw for raising the propeller when travelling amongst rocks or floating snags, but her engine, though no worse than those of many of the other river boats, had developed an irregular paralysing cough and stopped unexpectedly at times. Perhaps it would stop when we were in the grip of a whirlpool? But Basil was confident—and in any case we had paddles.

While we were loading he drew me aside: the trouble was fixed. He had made two new valves from old tin cans, improving the performance enormously, while the insertion of a rubber shoe heel was responsible for the new silence of her running.

Painted along the boat's side was a white stripe, the Insurance Mark, a sort of river Plimsoll Line which must show above water for a boat to be licensed to travel through the falls. I looked at the twenty men, the boxes of rations, the piles of equipment weighing at least 6,000 lb. Much of it was still on the quayside, and the Insurance Mark was already threatened. Hastily I commandeered a second smaller boat, the *Moroballi*, which we could tow behind, and an outboard motor, so that she could be independent in the rapids. Into her went part of our stores, and seven men. From our first camp above the rapids she would be sent back with the river captain and his bowman.

Loaded, the two boats looked as unstable as teaspoons tottering full of sugar. The baggage was covered with tarpaulins, and on top of everything numerous fishtail-handled paddles, baskets, warishis (Amerindian basketwork rucksacks), axes, bows and arrows, gumboots and other oddments were lying loose. It seemed hardly possible that men could be added to all this without overturning. Last to arrive was Captain Skeet, greatest and indeed almost sole survivor of the old river captains, in a solar topee and a pair of ragged khaki trousers. With tremendous dignity, planting each naked widespread foot in front of the other with the deliberation of a wading bird, he pushed his way through the small crowd of loafers and lookers-on, and handed me a letter, which looked like a bill or circular. Now all together we went along to the Police Station, and solemnly registered that with a certified River Captain we were about to proceed through the falls. Then we embarked. Amazingly, with everything aboard we had two inches to spare below the Insurance Mark. Two large paddles, the bow paddle and the 'awkward paddle' (for use in rapids), were laid on the roof. The engine started, Skeet waved his topee to the crowd with a claw-like hand, and the boat staggered out into the stream, towing the *Moroballi* behind. It was 9.30 in the morning.

Among the crowd stood four or five gentle fawn-eyed Amerindian girls with babies on their backs, looking longingly at the husbands they would not see again for three months. No kisses or emotional last embraces—just a quiet word, a nod, a wave. Tears began to trickle silently down their faces as they stood there. Then they turned away, got into their dugouts and began to paddle off across the river, to their huts beside some hidden creek.

With the Negroes of the party matters were different—a barrage of abuse, endearments and obscenities volleyed between the two partners even after we had cast off, and a knot of wives followed us along the shore in order to prolong the parting till the last possible moment.

Soon we were coasting past the crumbling stone river wall, the puffing electricity station, the saw-mill: washerwomen waved, the Negro wives yelled their last. Then jungle closed in, edged by half-moon bays with palm trees and thatched houses. Dark water curled past the prow, breaking into creamy foam and vanishing, bubbling, in our wake. Above it a clump of giant cabbage palms waved dark green beside the Police Station. The town began to look very low on the water, a mere line of glittering tin roofs.

Under the tent a small space had been kept clear for me amid piles of suitcases, hampers, baskets of fruit and vegetables rising to the ceiling. At first I tried to settle down in here—but at last I crawled out on to the top of the tent and sat on a rubber tyre which was lying there, a pleasant nest amid the litter.

In front and at the back, the men were sprawled on piles of luggage, chatting or attempting to sleep. Looking at them, it was hard to believe the common reputation the Amerindians had for deserting their masters in the bush, even for murder. Julian James, snoring with the mildest of faces, I had last seen attempting to cutlass a harmless kite-flier. Gouveia, my trader friend, had warned me strongly about several others who were still just unidentified names: bodies whose faces were hidden by the weirdest, most picturesque assortment of hats I had ever seen—not lifeless and impersonal, but as indelibly moulded to their owner's characters as once the hats of cart-horses or of coalmen used to be. Reassured by these, I glanced at the captain—very straight, steering with the huge steering paddle —remembered, and opened my letter.

FOREST DEPARTMENT
BRITISH GUIANA

0.025/50

Courtesy and Manners

1. I have been distressed to observe a few cases of discourtesy by certain members of the Department and I must insist that all should pay particular attention to this.
2. Senior officers should treat subordinates with invariable patience and courtesy: discipline can be maintained far more easily by quietness and firmness than by swearing and shouting. At the same time they must see that their instructions are

carried out and are entitled to expect loyalty, obedience and respect.

3. Junior officers must always show courtesy and respect not only to officers of this Department but to officers of all other Departments. There are many little ways in which this can be done, by saluting if in uniform, by raising the hat if not in uniform, by rising if seated, and so on. Senior officers of any Department should be addressed as 'Sir'. These are traditional marks of respect which all of us should observe.

4. Finally, officers of the Department must show invariable patience and politeness with the public and do all in our power to be helpful: the use of abusive provocative language is never necessary. At the same time our duties must be carried out without fear or favour, with firmness and patience. The ability of an officer to 'get on' with the public and with his colleagues is an essential pre-requisite to promotion.

5. I look to all members of the Department to build up a tradition of courtesy and service and I will take a very serious view of those who are not prepared to do this.

Christopher Swabey,
Conservator of Forests.

By mid-morning all softness had gone from the landscape. The air danced with a thousand pin-points of light, and a luminous haze veiled the shore. The glare was terrific. I baked on the roof, barely able to move, but enjoying the breeze produced by our motion. In my inner ear the drum-beat theme from Sibelius' *Tapiola* kept time with the throb of the engine. Long boat journeys in the middle of the day made one inert, hypnotised.

By two o'clock heat and glare combined to make an inferno. We were too far from the shore to take any interest in it. Only occasionally did we skirt a point or pass a little grove of thatched dwellings from which people waved. Moraballi Creek, Monkey Jump and Winiperu were left astern.

By three, piles of foam were coming past in the current, some standing a foot high, like monstrous meringues. The river was running faster, its surface strained. Soon we were passing islands and drawing closer to the banks. Each low bush we passed was a nest of insects: the shrilling and chirping came clear to us above the noise of the engine. Here and there mangrove trees showed that the river was still tidal; while from the tall trees which lay behind the riverside vegetation hung curtains of lianes spilling over and floating in masses on the water. Some were in flower, and I noticed one with panicles of magenta-coloured trumpet flowers, and a dark red convolvulus with heart-shaped leaves. Sometimes we disturbed a wisp of little river bats—and away they went flitting through the air, suddenly to vanish clinging like tiny bits of bark to some lichenous branch.

An hour later as the sun declined, its rays again began to pick out details of foliage and clouds, waves, and headlands. A new softness like that of an old aquatint came in to the air; colours intensified. Now it was a magical experience to travel by boat through this wonderland of colour—whose existence depended on the time of day.

Everywhere huge prussian-blue kingfishers with russet breasts, enormous bills, and white bars on their wings, swooped low over the river. We drove one ahead of us for about a mile, before with shrill alarmed cries it had courage enough to double back past the boat. A few yellow butterflies were bobbing about in the air ahead, points of colour against the sombre green of the trees.

The current grew faster and the channels between the islands narrower as we advanced. There were glimpses of rocks ahead or to one side, but our own route was free from them. The foam was in great piles; the few yellow butterflies had changed into an endless cloud crossing the stream from east to west, as thick as flakes in a snowstorm.

Mixed with them were a few day-flying Urania moths, emerald-green and black, with long silver tails. Where did they all come from? Where were they going? Were they part of a similar horde I had seen on the Courantyne a few weeks before?

To give our boat extra power, we now transferred the out-board motor from the *Moroballi* and fixed it astern. Then the captain and bowman began to fit the 'awkward paddle' to the starboard side, tying it with ropes in such a manner that it could be swung in any direction. One of the men was stationed at this paddle, while the captain himself took up position by the main steering paddle on the port side, and stood on the narrow seat at the extreme bow, tensed, his eyes scanning the water ahead for signs of submerged rocks.

The water was now running swiftly, amber coloured and translucent, full of bubbles. Ahead lay a flickering line of white, with occasional dark rocks showing: the first rapids! A few yards away a little wave broke—the bowman threw his weight on his paddle, heaved—his shoulder muscles contorted, relaxed—Skeet shouted, the water foamed and boiled beside us, then ran smooth.

In front there were vistas of towering red and grey boulders, pink-rimmed at the water's edge by masses of ice-cream-pink flowers, and crowned with gnarled, water-twisted trees and shrubs, bearing sprays of delicate pale green leaves. There was a dark smooth rush of water between the rocks—and beyond, a mile-wide stretch of white tossing foam.

Now there was hardly time to think, for I was nearly flung off the roof by the shuddering and rolling of the boat as we struck this surging, tumbling cataract. Inch by inch we began to climb, both engines racing madly. All hands seized paddles, and desperately we dug into the water, for we were hardly moving forwards at all. The water formed an inclined plane, sliding dizzily past—one could see the angle from the horizontal. All around us it boiled in huge rolling blisters. Whirlpools foamed, cauldrons of spray leaped into the air, dashed into our faces. The captain flung his arms out, pointing the course with dramatic gestures, or heaved the reluctant steering paddle. The bowman crouched in front thrusting into the water, shouldering us round invisible rocks. The boat trembled and jumped, the terrible roaring and rushing of the water struck the ear in hammer blows—yet the beauty of the scene was such that one forgot all danger. We were in the midst of a grove of wild guava trees growing on submerged rocks: sunlight danced on water and leaves against a placid blue sky. The air was champagne.

Now a crumbling wall of water four or five feet high stretched ahead right across the river. How on earth could we go through? Shouts from the captain, ropes were flung out, and the men leaped overboard like a shoal of mackerel, dragging the boat through shallow water on to a shelving bank of rock.

The bow cut crisply through thick seaweed-like vegetation and came to rest. I leaped ashore on to a carpet of pink star-flowers, in a little Eden of dark-foliaged trees.

This was Karuabu portage, and here we would camp for the night. Whether we were on an island or the shore I did not know. No sooner was the boat securely fastened than a great bustle of activity began: boxes were unloaded, and the ring of axes and cutlasses sounded above the rush of water, as clearings were made and tarpaulins put up for our night's rest. Everywhere the air, deliciously cool and fragrant, vibrated with the thunder of the falls. A smell of water mixed with that of the riverside flowers—wonderful hothouse shrubs whose families I recognised: Rutaceae, Myrtaceae, Malpighiaceae; Melastomes with pale mauve and white flowers, and velvety leaves with prominent purple veins on the underside; Rubiaceae, glossy-leaved with waxy-looking inflorescences of a brilliant vermilion; and on top of all this the whiff of acrid wood-smoke drifting from the many camp fires now beginning to glow in the depths of the groves.

At the waterside, little beaches of coarse sand and gravel had collected in sheltered places among the rocks. Where broad shelves, dark grey with occasional splashes of red, emerged from the lapping flood, thick tufts of the pink star-shaped flowers were growing from what looked like masses of decayed seaweed. To the men these were 'pakuweed', because upon them the delicious paku fish is supposed to feed. To me they were one of the things I had come in search of—plants of the extraordinary family Podostemonaceae, adapted for living in tropical waterfalls and rapids, where the water is highly aerated. Their roots, stems and branches have been transformed into rhizone-like structures which creep, closely attached to the rocks, clinging by special sucker-like organs. Their leaves (in this species anyway) are leathery and divided, like seaweed-fronds, and offer little resistance to the force of the water. For most of the year these plants live completely submerged. Then during the dry season, when the water level drops, they are exposed to the air, and immediately, as the stalks and leaves decay, from the horrible rotting mass of plant flesh the buds burst forth, flower, and set seed with amazing rapidity.

Some six inches above the present water-line the rocks and

weed were still damp, showing how rapidly the river was falling; and along this narrow transitory zone between air and liquid—and only there—the flowers were in full bloom. Below water not even traces of buds showed. They appeared an inch above water, brown at first, then pinkish, developing green stripes before they burst into flower. And a mere inch above, the weed had already dried, and the ripe seed capsules stuck up into the air like apple seeds on thin stalks. Evidently the whole process from bud to setting of fruit took place in a few hours.

In this particular species flower and stalks were all a delicate pale pink, and the petals were reduced to scales, so that it was the ring of stamens which gave the star-like appearance, reminiscent of a beautiful saxifrage, their nearest relatives. This species was relatively primitive with large flowers, but in specialised members of this strange family the leaves are reduced to moss-like proportions, and the green creeping rhizome becomes the dominant organ; the flowers become so reduced that they may consist of only one stamen; and from being insect pollinated they may become wind- or even self-pollinated. Looking at one of these most advanced, specialised forms, it is hard to believe that the plant is not a liverwort or moss, instead of a member of the highest group in the vegetable kingdom.

The low sun was tingeing the tossing water and sending crimson sparks off the frail leaves of the guava trees whose aerial pastures fluttered so delicately above. Silhouetted in the stern of the *Moroballi* sat Basil, the engineer, fishing with rod and line for the green-scaled paku-fish.

'This is a famous place, you know, Mr. Guppy,' he shouted out to me.

I jumped aboard and sat beside him.

—'Yes, Sir! This is where the Sultan nearly get drowned.'

'Who was he?' I asked.

'He was a famous pork-knocker who strike rich many times. Well, one time he hear of a big shout up Potaro way, so he catch the firs' boat going up. When dey reach here de water higher, so dey decide to steam through, instead of portaging [unloading and carrying round]. So dey strike a rock further up and de boat overturn. Well, de Sultan get on a rock out deh, an' an old friend came floating past and reach up and say "Sultan, help me man, gi' me a han'!" But de Sultan jus' shove he off, an' say, "Had de Lord intend you to live you would have reached here fus! Pass on friend to eternal life!"' Basil chuckled.

'Who told the story?'

'He friend! He wash up jus' below! Another time de Sultan strike rich an' land at Bartica, and his mother run forward to greet he. But he jus' wave her away, an' say "Touch me not woman, for poverty is an infectious thing—an' I'm on me way to the Bank of Canada."'

'With his biblical turn of language he should have been called the Bishop!'

'Oh, dey have another one call' de Bishop! An' den there was Ocean Shark, an' many more with names like dat. Ocean Shark was a really bad man, he kill many people, but dey could not catch him because he was always shelter by Indian women. Finally it was an Indian man what kill he.'

'What about bad women—were there any of those?'

'Plenty! Dey is a really terrible lot! One of de mos' famous was Gertie Inner-Tube. She was 'bout 6 foot tall, a black woman, an' strong as a heffalum. She specialise in "lunch tongue", but she sometimes a little rough an' one or two men no good after a session wi' she! One night when she was up Mazaruni she hear dat dere is a strike, and de men comin' in along a certain trail with dey diamonds. All de other whores is waiting for them, but Gertie decide to get there firs', so she start walkin'. Dat night she take fifty-two men and mos' of dey diamonds, and walk 11 mile! Den dey was Maudie Wood-Horse, an' Deep-Strippin', and Bush-Fire, and Pensive Two-Mouth—an' plenty mo' like dey. Dey get plenty money, jus' like de men, an' spend it jus' as fas'.'

Basil had English and Negro blood as well as Amerindian, and his enthusiasm and romantic disposition made me warm to him. How well I could understand his excitement as a boy watching the seething boatloads of prospectors, prostitutes, traders, adventurers setting forth from Bartica for the gold and diamond fields! Even now the sight of those huge open craft laden with bundles and batelles, hammocks and cut-lasses, salt pork and fish, sugar, tea, matches, cartridges and

G

guns, and other needs of the bush, was infinitely thrilling.

The sky overhead had faded to a dusky blue, the leaves had turned from green to black, and the sun had slipped below the distant wall of forest on the far side of the river. I walked back to my tent over a carpet of rustling leaves. It was already dark under the shelter of the trees. I lighted the vivid, white flaring Coleman lamp; the red-eyed Boodhoo was grilling sausages over a low fire, and coffee was on the boil. I was hungry and tired, but enormously elated, with a wonderful feeling of loneliness and freedom: to have escaped from Georgetown, into a cleaner, purer world.

As I ate, frogs uttered typani-like strokes in the bushes all around ('Huge frogs', said Jonah). Suddenly one leapt on to my tent with a tremendous thud. Startled, I went outside and shone my torch on the canvas roof. Big brown eyes looked unblinkingly at me and long, flat toes curled round my fingers as I picked him up. He was olive brown and exceedingly sticky, and offered no resistance. Then, like a spring uncoiled, he leaped a clear eight feet on to the ground and away into the bushes. No sooner had he gone than my hands felt quite clean, without the least trace of gumminess or smell: evidently these frogs exude an adhesive from their feet, which they reabsorb at the moment of leaping.

To the sounds of rushing water, the drum-beats of the frogs in the bushes, the sifting and drifting and falling of leaves and twigs and flowers from the forest roof on to the ground and my tarpaulin, I undressed and lay down, and within seconds was asleep.

Next day we were up in the bitter cold of early morning, with the stars still in the sky. Shadowy figures were cooking or warming themselves at fires on the rocks as I went down to the river to bathe. I found a safe spot away from strong currents and slipped in. The water was surprisingly warm, glimmering in a deep basin. A sweet smell came from the decaying paku weed. The river had fallen a few more inches and another strip of pink flowers had appeared. Flying around them and clinging to them were many small stingless bees which probably effected cross-pollination.

Whilst I had my hot coffee and bacon and eggs, with Jonah in charge the boat was completely unloaded so that it could be hauled through the rapids, and everything in it was 'drogued' to the other side of the portage, a distance of about three-quarters of a mile along a cavernous tunnel in the trees, a scramble over rocks and boulders slippery with filmy ferns and mosses. I was amazed at the enormous burdens the men shouldered—some must have weighed 120 lb. Charles Sandy laughed when I mentioned this, and said he had known men who carried 180 lb. for 37 miles in one day. At the far end the baggage was piled on banks of rock which sloped steeply down into deep water in which were growing half-submerged palms, guavas, and many other trees.

Next ropes were tied to the boat and all clothes were shed— except for hats, it being considered dangerous for the head to become too hot or too cold—and into the water everyone went, pulling, pushing at the huge craft, straining, clinging with prehensile toes to the slippery river bottom, hanging on to the small bushes and rocks which projected above the water. The engine was started, and roared away, giving what help it could. Inch by inch the boat moved forward against the battering force of the water, over the long arching waves, behind and among the trees. Through fully a quarter-mile of rapids it was pulled forwards, until just below the head of the portage it stuck, entangled in prickly palms, its prow raised high in the air, its belly swaying on a ridge of rock over which the water surged in waves that bumped it up and down. The engine raced, the ropes stretched, everyone cursed—the river bed was full of unexpected potholes in which we floundered. Then suddenly she was clear, in the shade of overhanging trees which rose out of the water all around.

Bringing the *Moroballi* up was easier, after which we re-loaded both boats. There were still 5 miles of rapids to negotiate, but the going was easier. Sometimes whirlpools would appear, and suddenly sweep past and vanish. Some-times foaming rushes of water carried us backwards; then everyone would seize a paddle and dig furiously into the water to assist the engines, until the danger was past.

Except when paddling I sat on the roof taking photographs and making notes. It was like being in the middle of a fantastic ballet, or the world of the Red Queen in *Alice in Wonderland*, for we had to run fast just to stay in the same place—but at different speeds in different places. Eye and brain could hardly adjust to the sudden shifts in time and rhythm—the unexpected calmnesses after the splendour of gold and silver water tearing past; the shocking stillness of rocks and islands, the lazy swirl of backwaters—one's senses were thrown out of gear yet also delighted by the sparkling, sunny beauty of the scene.

On some of the rocks long-necked darters stood, gazing into the flood. I saw one plunge into a racing current—it was impossible to believe that it could survive, yet it appeared again, swimming nonchalantly some 50 yards downstream. Everywhere wiry guavas and ice-pink paku weed flowers waved, all of the same kind except once when I saw a single showy pyramid of about a dozen pink flowers, like an English ground orchid. Although so delicate in appearance, these were the only plants tough enough to survive in this savage environment of bare rock alternately dry and torrentially drowned. In human terms, they were pioneers. In other places, where rock had been pulverised into rubble and sand, and where the water was less violent, other species also grew—the beginnings of later, more mature and 'civilised' societies, I reflected.

Then came danger: Skeet attempted a water slope, and half-way up the engines and paddles did not have the power to get through. We began to turn, to drift back over a liquid precipice towards the black serrated rocks below. At the last moment we managed to seize some guava bushes and clung breathless, saved by their rock-entwined roots.

There was only one thing to do: lighten the boat. We put two extra men in the *Moraballi*, giving her a crew of nine paddlers, for with her shallow draught she could negotiate a channel closed to us. Her crew were taking a considerable risk, but there was no alternative. Then we fastened her outboard motor to our side. Our load lightened, with both engines racing and everyone paddling we charged again. The boat reverberated as we struck the frenzied water-slope, spun round as if seized from below, and for a minute we were on one side, with the water seeming to stand above the gunwhale, and I thought we were lost. Then we were through into comparatively calm water which stretched in an 'S' bend between the cataracts. Ahead we saw the *Moroballi* and with deep relief tied her on again.

All through the morning we negotiated falls with lovely names—Aharow (Big Fall), Epiru Malali (the worst when the river was in half-flood), Mapihi (the worst when it was highest), Tamanado. Then I was aware of an unstrained smoothness and darkness about the water, a silence as it lapped the shores. Rocks gave way to clay banks; and clay banks to a sheer wall of vegetation rising straight from the river. We had passed the last of the falls—but so much had they possessed me that it was like entering a strange country. By mid-morning we were skirting the 7 miles of Gluck Island, largest island in the Essequebo. The riverside was tangled, with trees lying horizontally over the water, down to which lianes swept in confused cordage. Behind, on the banks, rose a forest of majestic Mora and Kakaralli trees. From the river the Moras (Mora excelsa) were easy to identify, for they looked like gigantic elms, with the same characteristic curling-over of the boughs, and similar dark-green foliage. But their trunks stood a hundred feet without branches, and each of the main branches was the size of a full-grown oak. One of them was in young leaf, a blaze of purply brown. Young leaves in the jungle were often as colourful as flowers—their reds, purples, yellows, and browns being supposed to screen harmful sun rays while their delicate tissues grew.

Jonah, who sat with me, told me that chips of fresh Mora wood and bark were sometimes thrown into the water by the Indians. Any fish which snapped them up would die after a while and float to the surface, where it could be picked up, cooked and eaten, for the poison is weak. Sometimes also the bark was made into a tea and drunk as a treatment for diarrhoea and dysentery. It was hard to believe that these vast trees belonged to the family Leguminosae, which in Europe we associate with creeping herbs—peas, clovers, and vetches. Similarly the enormous Licanias which were sometimes visible were of the rose family! But the other commonest big trees, the Kakarallis (Eschweilera spp.) belonged to a family largely peculiar to South America, the Lecythidaceae. The trees of this family have extraordinary fruits—shaped like enormous flower-pots in the Brazil-nut tree and the Monkey-pots, like huge fetid spheres in the Cannonball tree, or slender graceful pipes in the Kakarallis (sometimes called Monkey Pipes) and Wadaras (Couratari). Their flowers also, which are fertilised by crawling insects and humming-birds, are often weirdly shaped, hooded by a pendant central lip fringed with stamens, and of strange waxy textures and tints—coral pink, yellow or white—grossly fleshy, discolouring at once when bruised, and strong smelling. Some kinds stink like rotten meat, others exude an unearthly fragrance. The Kakarallis along this stretch of river were of the latter kind and just beginning to come into blossom. Each tree that we passed gave forth a piercing scent sweet as jasmine, dropping occasional flowers, pale cream and daffodil yellow, into the water. In my comparisons between men and trees I had mentally labelled the Kakarallis (because of their abundance yet tendency to occupy good positions) as 'white-collar workers'. Now that I saw their beautiful flowers I upgraded them to 'executives'! By twisting their bark, which comes off in vertical strips as long as you like, the Indians make ropes and string—or else they pull it apart into delicate papery layers and use it for wrapping parcels or rolling cigarettes.

The lower stretches of forest along the riverside consisted mostly of other kinds of trees—Wallabas (Eperua spp.: the commonest 'workers' in my classification), with frilly leaves, white flowers like Rhododendron blossoms, and enormous scimitar-pods hanging on 18-inch long bootlace-thin stalks; acacia-foliaged Sarabebes, laburnum-like Warakosas (both Inga spp.); and perhaps most beautiful of all, Trysils (Penta-clethra macroloba), against whose dark feathery leaves the long white plumes of their flowers stood out like so many crests of the Prince of Wales, while their long, curling, velvety seed pods were the richest golden brown. Boiled in water, the inner bark of this tree produces a cherry-red infusion used by the Indians in treating fever, bronchitis and colds, as an antidote for scorpion stings, as an emetic and purgative, and as a blood coagulant. But most curious of all is the way in which the Indians scrape a foam from the fresh inner bark and apply it to a cut, where it dries to an antiseptic healing plaster through which the wound can breathe—an idea which perhaps some pharmacist will copy.

As lunch time approached we began searching for a place
to land. The forested banks looked solid and impressive enough,
but whenever we drew close we found that water stretched
away between the trees, with not a sign of dry land. At last
a melancholy narrow strip of mud appeared, with gloomy
flooded forest behind it. Fires were lighted here and meals
cooked, while I lunched on sandwiches and a bottle of Coca-
Cola, sitting on a damp rotting log under which was the
recently sloughed skin of a sizeable boa constrictor.

Two hours later we reached Rockstone—a nasty scar of red
broken earth, a rusty single-track railway line of minute gauge,
and three decrepit wooden shacks, rotting in rain and sun. One
of them was a balata company's store, while the others contained stores and a wireless transmitter and receiver belonging
to Hamilton's Transport Company, which operated a supply
boat for the goldfields far up river.

Searching the scrub I found the six nondescript brick pillars
which once, in the days of the township's glory thirty years
before, had supported an hotel. The railway from here to the
Demerara River had circumvented the Essequebo falls we had
just ascended, and had then carried a considerable traffic.
Along the railway line, as it curved in to the riverside, stood
a stately avenue of Eucalyptus trees, planted when the future
of the little place had seemed assured.

I spoke to one of the half-dozen inhabitants, a grizzled Negro
in a leather jockstrap who had an indefinable air of authority.
Sure enough, he was Hamilton's captain, and he told me that
the line to Wismar had just been reopened and a crane set up,
in order to transport the two picturesquely rusty pontoons
which lay half-sunk in a nearby backwater of the river, and
which were destined ultimately for a gold dredge being built
by B.G. Consolidated Goldfields some 80 miles further south.
He promised to bring us our mail and supplies on his fort-
nightly run.

I then showed him my map and told him of our plans, all
of which puzzled him considerably. But he promised to do his
best. Then we continued, anxious to reach a good camp site
in the survey region before night fell.

Except for a mining camp marked at a place called Omai,
the country above Rockstone was apparently uninhabited for

150 miles—as far as Apoteri at the mouth of the Rupununi River. Nor were there any records to show that it had ever been inhabited in the past. None of the old travellers— Schomburgk, or Waterton for example—or the records of the Dutch colonists, mentioned settlements. People had passed along this stretch of the river on their way further inland to places where they hoped to find gold and diamonds, but for some reason that I could not fathom they had never settled here.

The river curved like a muscular arm between patches of dry land bearing tall forest and areas of lower growth. Where reeds would have grown in the temperate zone the shores were fringed with dense swaying banks of gigantic arums called 'Mocca-Mocca' (Montrichardia aculeata). Their graceful stems stood 10, even 20 feet out of the water, were up to 8 inches in diameter, and were clothed in blunt thorns: monstrous herbs, relying for strength not on wood, but on their circular cross-section of tough skin kept in shape by crisp, turgid white pith within. At the top of the stems were bunches of the large heart-shaped leaves typical of arums and, at certain times of the year, yellow-spathed flowers or oval fleshy fruit knobbled like hand-grenades.

On slightly firmer ground stood clumps of a tall grey-green palm, every inch of whose trunks and leaves was clothed with long sharp spines, so that from a distance they looked as if rimed by hoar frost. Both these plants formed part of a 'succession', occupying mud and silt banks as they were built up, until in turn when the ground grew yet firmer they were replaced by the trees of the riverside. The palm, known only from this part of the Essequebo River, had never been scientifically described—largely, no doubt, because of its horrific prickliness—and it was one of my objects to bring back the first specimens. It was apparently a new species of Astrocaryum (star-nut palms), and for it Jonah and I invented the name 'Awaraballi', Arawak Indian for 'like the Awara Palm' (the common edible star nut, A. tucumoides). Now that I had actually seen it I was not so sanguine about getting specimens. Jonah, however, was reassuring: 'Not so bad, Chief. Dere was one man I know climb right to de top when a cayman chase he!'

As the afternoon drew on we left Gluck Island behind and the river expanded into a gently shimmering lake of level azure infinities, with delicately blue-green softly sculptured promontories and islands. Perfect white clouds sailed above, like yachts in a sky regatta. The sunlight slanted in straw-coloured beams, and a dream-like calm fell over us, despite the dire warnings implicit in the scene. For the entire countryside was overflowing, like a pasture after heavy rain. The puzzlement of the old Negro at Rockstone began to take a new meaning. This was my survey area, but all but the tallest trees were inundated—where could I even set foot or make camp? It was getting late, and within the next hour we would have to find a camp site of some sort, for sleep in the overladen boats would be impossible.

I leaned on my elbow on the roof beside Captain Skeet, trying to locate our position on the map and scrutinising the miles of riverside for a place that might be above water. The captain was a garrulous fellow but unfortunately difficult to understand.

'Dat,' he said, pointing to a light patch on the distant shore, 'is de mout' of a big lake.'

'That's interesting,' I replied, poring over the map and failing to find it, then pointing into the distance. 'And over there, is that an island or the main?'

'Dat is a small, small bird.'

'I mean that piece of land sticking out there.'

'No good for eatin', Boss.'

'No! I don't mean that kingfisher.'

'Dat what, Suh?'—he craned his spidery neck forward, and directed towards me a leathery, trumpet-like ear, delicately fringed with white hairs, his lips writhing affably round his three teeth.

'You see there?'

'Yes, Suh—dat itabu?'

'That what?'

'Eet ees an eetabu, a water path'—he pronounced each syllable with great distinctness. 'A water path go round so— and it have a *very* little current.'

'You mean that over there is an island, with water all round it?'

'Ho, ho, ho, ho, ho!' He uttered a surprisingly powerful laugh for such an emaciated man, then took off his sun helmet and sponged brow and neck with a pink palm. We were at cross purposes. He was a little deaf, and, anyway, our words did not mean the same things. It seemed that an itabu or water path was something like an ox-bow, an almost cut-off meander of the river through which water still flowed at times. Evidently the piece of land it separated did not count as an island—indeed, probably it was *not* an island except when the river was in flood.

I could locate the point of Gluck Island both on the ground and on the map, and also the wide expansion of the river. But where were all the other features so clearly shown? Inlets, capes, peninsulas, islands? Skeet knew only the main channel some mile and a half wide, and he pointed to another marked name, a green patch of forest far ahead which he said was Plantain Island. But he knew none of the other names on the map and indeed nothing else seemed to match. In a nightmare one's distress is increased by the inexplicable behaviour of people whom one knows in real life; similarly my confusion was made worse by the distorted resemblances which I occasionally found between the map and the reality. Here was marked a group of islands—but none showed on the river: had they been submerged or swept away—or joined into that peninsula? Or were they merely the invention of a map-maker who had never visited the area? It was hard to decide.

The river, Skeet said, was usually very shallow: we were now sailing over sandbanks which in a few months time would be exposed: already—and he pointed to a line of debris in the trees—the water level was falling fast.

By guessing the height of some of the palms and other trees whose crowns we were skirting, I estimated that the level might fall by as much as another 30 feet. Rain might be still falling inland, and this vast mass of water was held up by the rocky barrier of the rapids. Hohenkerk had probably drawn his map at the height of the dry season when things would look very different. Yet even this could not account for everything. Since 1917 erosion and deposition had also evidently altered the whole superficial structure of the countryside, sweeping away islands, building up sandbanks, uniting archipelagos and joining them to the mainland by isthmuses. In my innocence I had trusted this straightforward-looking piece of paper, and laid my survey plans according to it. The possibility of any landscape changing so much so rapidly had never crossed my mind. It was bewildering, but fascinating.

Meanwhile, even examination of the scene presented problems. Continually, as we cruised along, I had to correct what my eyes told me. On the Courantyne I had met with optical illusions—but here everything had an unreal, hallucinatory feel. My eyes had to acquire a new sensitivity merely to see what the men around me saw—to separate a green island from the green mainland behind, to tell the far bank of a river mouth from the near, or the paleness and blueness of distance from those caused by variations in colour—even height as a guide to distance was misleading, for often far off trees were taller because they grew on different soil.

Plantain Island was now my one point of reference, and when we had been unsuccessful in finding anything but deep water among the trees along the left bank of the river, I directed the steersman to cross towards it and explore the opposite shore. As we approached two small colour variations in the riverside foliage began to show, one of which looked like the mouth of a small river, the other like a clearing of some sort. Nearer, it proved indeed to be an abandoned camp—probably that of some surveyors who had been in the region a year before, said Skeet—for in front of it was a survey-mark, a diamond-shaped wooden hoarding with six foot sides, painted white and faced by its pair, a mere speck a mile away on the opposite shore. Along the 50-foot frontage of the clearing the river bank was above water level—the only 'land' we had seen since leaving Gluck Island.

The boat drew up beside the hoarding, and I jumped out on to a fallen tree trunk. The ground was soft wet clay, sticky and unpleasant, and obviously only recently exposed by the falling river. Here we would have to camp, and in the morning, if it seemed worth while to stay, we could clean the place up.

While tarpaulins were being put up I bathed, standing on a log and throwing bucketfuls of water over myself, and Boodhoo prepared some tea. I felt content—but then there is no easier contentment than that which comes of being dry, warm, fed, and with a place to sleep, after being wet, cold, hungry, and uncertain, if only for a few hours.

Before the sun set I decided to make a rapid trip round Plantain Island, which was just upstream, and to explore the river mouth or lake entrance which I had seen from across the river. As we untied the *Moroballi* from the upright post which carried the surveyor's mark, I saw that written small upon its white paint in pencil, but still easily legible, was the word 'Hopeful'.

The water in the lake was inky black, broken here and there by a ring cast by a rising fish or dipping fly. Spiny palms and gnarled tree trunks emerged from it like dripping bearded monsters, wreathed in epiphytes, mosses and orchids. We passed over submerged woodlands whose upper branches alone showed above or below the surface. The lake was quite short, parallel to the river and cut off at the far end by a screen of feathery acacia-like trees. There was no life to be seen: no cayman, duck, or manatee; and no sound to be heard, save the murmur of the water in the leaves.

Then we went up the channel which separated Plantain Island from the bank. Again mirror-blackness—until a four-foot fish jumped, making a silver fountain; nothing more. As we came round the far side of the island, with its prostrate trees lying along the water, its tremendous liane-hung Mora trees darkening overhead and dissolving from view, night fell and wrapped the whole mysterious landscape in a blacker obscurity.

In the morning Skeet, his bowman, and his engineer left in the *Moroballi*. Unladen, they would be able to shoot the rapids, and should reach Bartica by evening. We still had some lesser rapids to negotiate, but we would have to manage on our own.

'Well, Sir, you treat me nice,' said the old fellow as we shook hands. I was touched. As the *Moroballi* pushed off I felt momentarily isolated—in this strange new world, among these twenty or so men of whom I was now in charge and most of whom I had never set eyes on before the previous day—except for the one who had tried to kill or maim a fellow man when drunk a few months before; Jonah, whom I knew and trusted; and his son, Big Rufus. But a few words and smiles had been exchanged and I had been summing up those impassive faces,

as they no doubt had been me—and there was the interest of
my first real exploration to take my mind off personal feelings.

While most of the men set to work improving the camp
Rosoleno Gonzales ('Kunyow'), our half-Arawak half-Spanish
huntsman, picked up his shot-gun and went off to see what he
could kill. As he reached the edge of the clearing, he turned,
smiled, and waved. It was extraordinary what that trace of
Spanish blood could do—his face, body and gesture were those
of an El Greco saint, charged with ancient nobility. For a
moment he was a figure in some baroque painting—the forest
vanished, and there were the plains of Brabant, the porticoes
of Jerusalem. Like Ruth Draper he created his own scenery,
peopled his own stage. But he was a poor illiterate forest
dweller, quite unconscious of the existence of the backcloths
that he summoned up.

I wrote a few letters, sorted my notebooks, while all around
trees groaned and crashed to the ground in sheaves, so closely
were they bound together by 'bush ropes' (lianes). It was
useless to attempt to fell a single tree, for it would be held up
by the tangle. Instead, after careful scrutiny, five or six trees
were selected and cut through, only the key tree being left.
Then this would be attacked, and with great splintering a
whole slice of forest would thunder down.

A dense growth full of spiny palms covered with mantles of
bush ropes grew out of the water in front of my tent. Though
difficult to clear, I insisted, and eventually the men produced
an opening through which I could view the constantly changing face of the river.

Smaller trees were now cut into lengths, and laid down to
form a corduroy floor in the mud under the tarpaulins. With
the felling of so many trees sunlight and fresh air began to
reach the ground, which rapidly became less sticky, while
numerous sun-loving butterflies of the tree-tops were pleasantly
deceived. Instead of the slow-fluttering black and red Heliconias typical of the forest gloom, sprightly vivid butterflies
came whizzing in to explore the new sunlit area we had
created. Yellow Pierids bobbed around, or settled in clusters
to drink moisture from the ground; skippers skipped, and
Crackers ('Musical butterflies', Ageronia feronia) spread their
barred and spotted wings on leaves or bark, and produced

loud 'Crack, crack' sounds as they circled the tree trunks. Individual butterflies appeared to develop preferences for certain places: a skipper insisted upon its particular leaf, upon which it rotated slowly in the sunshine, occasionally dashing off and returning; a brown leaf-shaped butterfly with two cream-coloured bars on its wings liked sitting on the edge of my tea cup. Each time I drank, it whisked away and settled on my tent pole. Then back it would come as soon as I put down the cup. Cautiously it would manœuvre, then unroll a long tongue with which to sip delicately at the cool edge of the liquid. Eventually it became so bold that when I put the cup to my lips it merely moved an inch or two to allow me to drink.

By late evening Kunyow had not returned to camp, and we became worried. There were all too many tales of even experienced bushmen being lost in the jungle, even near settlements, and being found only weeks later, dead or imbecile. At night the cold and damp in the forest was intense and wild animals roamed; by day there was little or nothing to be found to eat, and there were no paths—only bewildering animal trails leading in circles. Hoping that Kunyow would hear, Philbert Thomas and Albert Smith, our two strongest men, began beating the buttress of a giant Mora with axes. The tree was hollow and each stroke sent a dull reverberating sound booming out over the forest: a sinister sound, a warning and guide to the lost man.

After more than an hour, just as the sun was setting Kunyow emerged from the edge of the forest, his gun over his shoulder. Behind the camp lay a swamp with deep water, he said. He had gone through that and had reached dry land beyond— but there was no game. All the animals had moved away to higher ground yet further inland, beyond still other swamps. Trying to come back he had been cut off by deep water and had lost his way. Only the sound of the beaten buttress had guided him back.

6

To Mocca-Mocca Point

At 7 the following morning Jonah called out 'Everybod . . . y!
Everybod . . . y!' his long-drawn cry like plain chant among the
trees. The men assembled and got into the boat, and we pushed
off—then minutes later the engine stopped. While Basil
tinkered with it ('It would take some time,' he said), we drifted
and paddled slowly towards the faraway almond-green wall of
Gluck Island, then turned into the bank at a point where a
patch of trees was hung with a net of yellow-green flowers. I
decided to cut one of my lines from here, which approximated to
the beginning of line 2 of the survey as fixed by me on the map.

Theoretically our lines had been placed 1 mile apart alternately on each bank, but without accurate maps, aerial photographs, or any means of locating our position precisely, and
with limited time at our disposal, I had to cut wherever was
actually possible, and try later to adjust the figures produced.

With cutlasses and axes we slashed into the vivid, tangled
riverside foliage, forcing the boat between fearsome prickly
Awaraballi and Bactris palms for a distance of about 30 yards.
Then in the gloom we saw a bank of mud about a foot high. I
turned to give Jonah some instructions before jumping into the
shallow water—and there beside our stern a vast black salami
4 feet long and as thick as my leg nosed the surface, gave a
muscular undulation, and sank again. An electric eel. Though
their shock might not kill a grown man, it could stun him, and
in deep water cause a swimmer to drown. There was no turning
back: with the maximum of splashing we jumped over the side
and began clambering through roots and bushes or along
paddles placed between prickly palm branches.

Once ashore the men sharpened their cutlasses, placed a
stake to mark the beginning of the survey-line, and prepared for
the various jobs I had assigned to them.

Our plan was to measure all the trees of exploitable size along a strip 100 feet wide and 3½ miles long—each mile constituting a sample-plot of 12 acres. Ordinarily a traveller follows paths along the easiest route, or walks along the ridges of hills, or goes by boat along a river. But our compass lines would take us straight through every sort of country—through swamps and over precipices—until we had finished or it was impossible to go further.

At a signal from Jonah, Everard Thomas went forward in the lead with the compass, cutting due east; then followed three cutters—Philbert Thomas, Justin Joseph, and Elias Joseph—clearing a path through the dense undergrowth along which the rest of us could follow.

Behind the cutters two men, Charles Sandy and Edward Wong, marked off distances with a measuring chain (and at every quarter-mile would insert a numbered peg); while on the right, 99 feet away from the first line, a second 'offset' line was cut parallel with the main line, by Kunyow, Leno Thomas, and Julian James, while between the two lines two boys, Levi and Little Rufus, ran with a measuring cord to keep the separation accurate. Next came the experts, three men with callipers who measured the trunks of all trees between the two lines over 12 inches in diameter. These men were expected to know the names of the 400 or so commoner trees of these forests. Jonah, Jothan Fredericks, and Big Rufus were the calliper men today, but in emergency Philbert and Leno could have stood in for them. 'Mora 24 inches, Kakarall 12 inches, Konoribi 12 inches . . .' they called—and I, walking along behind, took down these measurements, plotted the position of the trees on a diagram, kept rough notes of changes in soil and topography, and described and photographed the different forest-types we came upon. Behind me came the axe-man with axe and warishi (a large wicker-work rucksack), whose task it was to cut down any tree of whose flowers, fruit, or wood we needed samples, and to carry these and any other specimens of herbs, rocks, soil, etc., that we collected, and to act as a general odd-job man. Finally, Lord, the ranger in training, worked with the calliper men, learning the tree names. Later he would study other aspects of the work.

Once started, the line moved forward rapidly and precisely,

Hauling through the rapids

The Tamandua monkey

Wading through swamp forest

with some of the beauty of all well co-ordinated manœuvres.
But it did not get far. The bank of mud on which we had landed
sloped up for a little way, and then very gently undulated
downwards. Within five minutes we were walking in slush,
then there were cries of 'Water! Watoooo!' from in front, and
soon we were ankle deep, then wading to our knees in the dense
gloom, tripping over submerged logs, thrusting our feet into
underwater morasses of decomposing leaves and twigs. There is
nothing more unpleasant than getting wet gradually, but we
were in excellent humour. Many jokes were bandied around,
all of the most elementary banana-skin variety, but received
with roars of laughter. There was keen competition as we waded
along to keep the 'Insurance Mark' above water, by finding
shallow places to one side or another, or *tacoubas*—fallen trees or
branches—to walk along. A good tacouba might carry one
forward as much as 60 feet, if lying in the right direction. I was
following Jothan (regarded by all as the best 'tacouba hunter')
along a particularly thin and slippery specimen, balancing by
placing my feet crosswise, when loud shouts of 'Ai, Little
Rufus' insurance mark gone!' announced that those stratagems
had failed in deeper water ahead (Little Rufus, the shortest of
us, had been carefully watched as a sort of human depth
gauge). Then came the cry: 'Little Rufus swimming!'—and
soon the rest of us were, too. The water was chill and murky,
and stretched as far as we could see into the forest, apparently
getting deeper and deeper. It was quite impossible to measure
trees or check distances under such conditions.

We turned aside and clambered on to a neck of dry land
which ran a short way to the left, and tried to go further inland
along that. Then that too shelved into the motionless brown
water. When Everard's hat and compass alone showed above
the water at the front of the line, we stopped. We had come 400
feet from the riverside, instead of the $3\frac{1}{2}$ miles which we had
confidently set out to achieve.

Wet, but not dispirited, we set off back towards the boat.
Near it the air was filled with a sweet scent—and on the ground
lay a single cream-coloured larkspur-like flower. Neither Jonah
nor I had seen this flower before, but we guessed it to be that of
some new or eccentric species of Bauhinia liane. We craned our
necks, and gazed upwards towards the gay, sunlit, wind-tossed

H

roof of the forest 120 feet above. At last Jonah pointed to a slender tree whose crown he said was carrying the liane. The axe-man set to work, and before long it lay in wreckage on the ground. A few shafts of sunlight struck down and illuminated its dull-foliaged crown—and there among them shone resplendent masses of yellow flowers in bunches at the ends of short twigs of sickle-shaped leaves, while all around long snake-like stems trailed from other trees—and far above, spilling over the edge of the gap we had made, were yet more clusters of creamy blossoms. We collected the few sprigs required by science, put them in the vasculum for pressing later, and left the rest distilling their rich scent into the gloom, soon to moulder away.

The engine was working again, so over a river that had become choppy in a strong easterly breeze we started downstream to see whether we could make headway with survey line 1, which was planned to start from the riverside at Tipuru Inlet, in the very area that had most puzzled me two days before.

I settled down on the launch roof to compare the map with the actuality. One largish island, half a mile or so in length, had evidently been swept away completely. Another—distinguished clearly by its higher, older forest—had become the tip of a peninsula past which we were now gliding. While, when we turned round the point of this, we found that between it and the mainland a completely new tongue of land had formed, which divided the former bight into two long winding channels. The outer channel, which I decided to call Tipuru Inlet, was about three-quarters of a mile long, and wound placidly between walls of tall swamp trees growing out of the water. The inner, which I dubbed Tipuru Lake, was similar, but larger. At its inner end it opened by means of a short sinuous waterpath through the trees into yet a third long channel—'Inner Tipuru Lake'. All three channels had gently flowing water of a Stygian blackness, made darker and more sinister by the blazing light of noon.

We went up Inner Tipuru Lake for about a mile without finding its end or any possible landing-place. The branches of the trees along its sides were profusely laden with orchids, Anthuriums, and giant Bromeliads with brilliant red flowering-spikes. But under them, water stood 6–10 feet deep. Silent, seemingly deserted by animal, bird, and fish, there was an air almost of daylight-haunting about these three inlets which made us want to get out of them as fast as we could. As we were leaving, behind us there was a most colossal splash, as though some monster had risen to the surface to throw a parting curse after us. We turned and stared, and saw only a wide-spreading ring of water:

'No fish or cayman or manatee make a splash like that,' said Jonah. 'I never hear that noise before. The only thing—perhaps a cayman when he calling fish, when he crack the water with he tail—only that is much sharper.'

We lingered, puzzled, but there was no repetition.

Back on the Essequebo, we searched for a large river, the Urumaru, marked on all the maps, at the mouth of which I had planned to start my third line. But it had completely disappeared.

Next day we cut behind our camp for a quarter of a mile before reaching impassable water. Then we crossed to the opposite bank and tackled line 5. I decided not to bother to start dry, so at the exact location we jumped in up to our waists. We waded until lunch time, when we reached a small dry knoll. I ate my sandwich lunch seated on a log, watching some brilliant blue and red macaws in the summit of a tree whose base was only a few yards away, and whose crown showed in a large gap in the canopy, down through which the sun poured its scorching rays on to me. It was marvellous, sitting there in the sudden heat, shoes off and sopping trousers steaming, while all around the brown jungle water stretched away under the trees.

In fact the floods had their compensations, for as a result of them the notorious insect pests of Guiana—mosquitoes, cow flies, kabaura flies, bush ticks, Bêtes Rouges (minute harvest-mite larvae that burrow under the skin and cause a terrible itching)—were pleasantly absent. Ground-dwelling snakes also would have been driven, along with other potentially dangerous animals such as jaguars, on to higher ground. And in the water we had little to fear except electric eels or breaking a leg. We hoped perai would stick to the main river; as also should caymans and anacondas—or near higher ground, so as to be near their prey.

Cheered by such thoughts I started to wander, looking for fallen flowers with Jothan. It was as well that he came, for my perceptions were then not as acute as later. There was a thick layer of dead leaves, some damp and rotten, others loose and dry, upon the ground. We bent low, searching with our fingers through the litter, exploring every inch of an area about 6 feet square. After about ten minutes of search I saw a slight movement beside one of my feet and stepped back rapidly, but not hastily. Like an image suddenly focussed on a screen a small snake became apparent, about 9 inches long, dark brown and mottled, coiled upon the leaves. I had stepped upon the tip of its tail—and it was rearing its head to strike when Jothan quickly killed it with a stick. He turned it over to show me the pale yellowish area under the tip of its tail—a yellow-tailed Labaria, one of the deadliest kinds in Guiana.

A hundred yards further, just after the half-mile point, the leading man began swimming. So we returned to the boat and cruised upstream looking for the beginnings of lines 6 and 7. But the water was too deep at either place for us even to disembark.

Disheartened, we returned to camp and began packing. There was nothing we could do but move upstream in hopes of finding drier ground. We had arrived a month too early, said the wise men of the party. We should go back to Bartica and return later. It was useless to keep starting and abandoning lines. Besides, even now heavy rain might fall far away in the Pakaraima mountains or along the Brazilian border, cause the river level to rise in a few hours by several feet, and sweep us from our camp site—our safety margin was only a few inches. Faint hearts, I thought. We must push on until we reached the Potaro Mouth, the upper limit of the expedition, surveying where we could: then turn back and tackle these earlier lines—if they were by then passable.

Yet there was something melancholy about leaving a newly-built camp in which we had hoped to live for many days; perhaps tonight we should have to string hammocks in trees over the water, like the Warrau Indians of the Orinoco delta?

We pushed off early, crossed to the far bank, and went upstream close inshore, almost brushing the trees. A 4-foot-long iguana plunged into the water from an over-hanging branch and swam away submerged, leaving a trail of bubbles. In the top of a tall tree, flaming red and gold in the sunlight, sat a big male howler monkey, hunched up, eating some large fruit. He did not even glance at us, as we went by with racing engine, so impervious was he at that moment to distractions. A tiny black-and-white dipper flew low above the water; a gigantic heron flapped hastily from a branch, all pretence of dignity gone. And every now and again one of the big blue and red kingfishers darted up the river like a projectile, or skimmed the surface with his beak.

The river was like a vast silk sheet, smooth between its jade forest walls. Not the faintest ripple disturbed it: air and liquid seemed spun of the same opalescent substance, lilac, green, and palest blue, shot through with straw-yellow sunshine fingers. Only an occasional floating pink trumpet flower defined the surface. Overhead regular processions of pyramidal clouds floated all at the same height, like a tray of meringues; below, a second perfect hemisphere, a crystalline inversion, and between the two worlds the boat, poised at the arrow tip of its own wake, that far back stretched from shore to shore.

The sound of the engine passed into limbo, and I was aware only of silence. I felt like crying out aloud to proclaim this perfection: there could be no worries in such a dream of wafting colours. Yet in an hour the angle of the sun would be higher, the water vapour that veiled the river would have blown away, the illusion would have changed. It was just as well. A few weeks or months in such a light and a man would lose his senses and forget the world. Georgetown—did it exist? My life there, my past few months had vanished. Nothing was important beside the silence of the forest, the solitude, *the light*.

The landscape was like the abstraction of some stupendous baroque design, a natural Versailles in green—monstrous as the real thing but a hundred times bigger: perspective after perspective, Grand Bassins followed by courtyards or wings, endlessly the same parts combining and recombining—yet at the same time as mysterious as a Tanguy painting, for sometimes I just could not *see* what was in it. The Indians could see features on the shores as invisible to me as the hidden numbers on a colour-blindness test card, or fish in the dim waters, beneath the play of surface reflections which they had trained themselves to ignore.

Sometimes even the solid banks and trees would lose their reality to me. A puff of wind ruffled the polished river ahead—

and an island suddenly appeared detached from the shore, floating high in the air. To one side a log hung suspended—and a few hundred yards in front the river surface ended in a sudden precipice. We were sailing straight for the edge of the earth! Then air liquefied, broke into wavelets, embraced the floating island again—and as suddenly smoothed into another sky-mirror. Sometimes a succession of magical horizons came and went, leading the eye to distances whose vanishing-points were at variance with those created by the shores. For the river-sides of course were neither parallel nor uniform in height; but to the eye they appeared either one or the other: at one moment a higher place drew nearer; at the next the illusion would be of a canal with exaggeratedly low or high forested shores. Overhead also tricks were being played: the dark-shadowed undersides of the clouds formed a level ceiling—until the eye met a group of clouds slightly higher or lower than those around, and one felt oneself tilting. When halted in a railway station and the train alongside moves, one may for a moment think that one's own has started. Similar illusions were being produced in this conjurer's landscape through optical effects that threatened reality at one moment, yet at others made me feel as secure as if I were in an infinitely vast monastery cell with walls of tones and colours, and its floor a luminous carpet on which I floated while marvellous lighting effects were switched on and off.

In this dream we passed Plantain Island and three small islands, unnamed on the map, which I called the Trinity Isles. Upsteam from them a grove of trees stood half submerged, the river murmuring through their branches.

Suddenly, excitement among the men in front—'Mountain! Mountain!' they shouted, pointing upstream. And there, emerging above the blue distant forests was a solitary shape of forlorn simplicity: a vast wedge resting on its broad side, a tremendous escarpment, its tail disappearing miles away in the tree tops, its beetling thousand-foot face hanging almost perpendicular over the river. A minute later, before we could quite grasp its existence, it disappeared, hidden by a slight bend in the river. It was the first mountain I had seen during my six months in Guiana, and it assumed a disproportionate significance. Perhaps from its solitary summit we might sight yet other mountains far away across the plain—the Pakaraimas, even the Kanukus a hundred miles further south? But it was still 10 or 15 miles away, and if we found dry lines to survey it might be a week or more before we reached it.

The entire left bank of the river was inundated, so near midday we crossed to a small promontory called Mocca-Mocca Point, where we found dry land, disembarked, and began to make camp.

While an opening was cut among the trees, and frames made from saplings bound with twisted lianes were put up for the tarpaulins, I took Jonah's nephew, Little Rufus, to look at the jungle around the camp. We walked along the crest of the riverside bank (here some 50 yards wide, between the river and the floods) and began to cut along it from the edge of the clearing. We had not penetrated a dozen paces before I realised that we were in the finest Mora forest I had ever seen. Looking obliquely upwards through the lower trees, at any one time five or six huge columnar trunks were in view (and about a dozen trunks of lesser trees), smooth and perfect cylinders soaring 80 feet and more to their first branches, and above that to the continuous dense leafage of the forest roof. Six or seven out of ten of these were Moras, the rest mostly Kakarallis. The base of each column was finned like a rocket by tall supporting buttresses, which formed neat triangles between trunk and ground, sometimes trailing out into a surface root.

The largest trees, I discovered, were frequently hollow, with much of the base of the trunk and the buttresses rotten and fallen away, looking as if they might collapse at any moment. For a few more years their dark curling broccoli crowns would rustle 130 feet up, then one by one they would crash to the earth or into the river below. The previous night there had been a long-drawn-out thundering near our camp. . . . Now the nearest giant groaned loudly, swayed by the wind, and we moved hastily away. In some places the colossi grew so thickly that they even touched each other at the base.

Was this an over-mature society dominated by elders—like that of Georgetown—I wondered? Probably not, because all around the ground was dotted with seedlings—the new generation, waiting as long as they could survive—perhaps several years—in the dark undergrowth, ready to shoot upwards the minute a canopy tree fell. Mostly of the Mora itself, they were spindly things 4–8 feet tall with few leaves, carrying at their base the two halves of the huge bean from which they had sprung. I picked up one bean—it must have weighed half a pound, a rich endowment of food for a socially dominant tree to hand on to each of its young. No wonder Moras only flowered and fruited on a large scale once in several years. The strain was equivalent to the launching of a débutante—and the failure rate for the young, even in such patrician circles, was very high by human standards. A socially 'mobile' tree, on the other hand, typically blanketed the jungle each year with small seeds with little reserves—no staying power if success was not immediate after germination.

Over-topping the seedlings were a few small understorey trees, about 20 feet tall, nearly all belonging to the Custard Apple family (Annonaceae). They had strongly aromatic bark, with a cinnamon or clove scent, prickly fruits, and branches arranged in whorls like those of a fir tree. And there were also a few small trees of the Myrtle family.

Little Rufus was quite invisible sometimes as we crawled along, cutting through the thick undergrowth. But I followed his line of cut twigs and bent branches. We came to a fallen Mora, a chest-high hulk of soft mush dotted with protruding fungi. But for the rapidity of decay, these forests would be impassable with monstrous wreckage. Instead, there was little humus, decomposition was so rapid and complete. We walked on a very thin layer of dry, rustling leaves, with dark-brown clay immediately beneath. Full utilisation of waste products indicated that this was indeed a mature vegetation—would this also signify maturity in a human society? If so, our advanced civilisations, over-productive of unused wastes, must (however complex) be juvenile phases in a potential sequence of development—and artificially kept so because our political and moral ideologies did not allow the maturer phases to follow.

From the ceiling above tumbled tangles of lianes of curious shape, mimicking cables, ladders, trellis-work. 'Monkey ladder' and 'Granny Backbone', which Little Rufus named, were Bauhinias, source of an ingredient of curare arrow poison; another was a Passiflora, and yet another, slashed by little Rufus so that the scarlet sap oozed, a Machaerium. They hung

idly, looped and twined about one another, or fell in coils on
the ground before rising again to the canopy. It was impossible
to tell where any liane began or ended. Many were thicker than
a human thigh, and in volume as big as trees, but pliable, not
rigid. Few showed leaves—those were out of sight, carried on
myriads of lesser twigs half smothering the tree-tops.

How do lianes get up there? Very few actually climb. Some
germinate from seeds left high up by birds or wind, and send
long probing roots to the ground in search of water and
nutriment, then thicken. Others have stems which grow
gradually up a trunk while the older parts die away behind, so
that in the end they are connected to the ground only by roots.
While yet others wait year after year in the crowns of saplings,
until the time comes—if it ever comes—when the sapling bursts
through, carrying them with it up to the canopy—like the
favourites of an opposition leader who gains power.

Clinging to these lianes and to the higher parts of the tree-
trunks, wherever the sun occasionally fell, were yet other plants
countless in number, epiphytes many of them, like the orchids
and bromeliads, just sitting there and living on air and sunlight, on debris collected by their roots and leaves, and rain
drops or mist. Some had traps in the form of leaves or tangles of
roots, which collected plant remains and moisture, forming
private soils high up in the branches (which might in turn
nourish other plants and animals), into which they sent their
absorbing roots. One orchid, with sinister maculate leaves and a
long spray of mauve flowers, had its knobbly tubers embedded
in a garden of small seedlings, all growing from earth brought
to it by the swarms of powerfully musty-smelling ants which
nested amid them. Its tubers were water reservoirs (many
epiphytes have water-conserving devices of the sort we expect
among ground plants only in a semi-desert). The finger-like
aerial roots of one orchid were sheathed in highly absorbent
phellogen tissue, and showed green where moist, silvery where
dry. Another plant, a pretty little aroid with green-and-white
striped and spotted leaves stored water in bulb-like petioles;
and a Nautilocalyx, upon which any northern greenhouse
owner would have leaped, had soft, velvety, mucilaginous,
water-storing leaves, purple beneath. Still other epiphytes, like
the bromeliads, whose pineapple-top leaf-rosettes clung to

twigs and branches by means of tight little clusters of roots, had thick leathery skins. Some of the bromeliads were as tiny as starfish; others had leaves as long as swords, and central flaming torches of vermilion flowers. In the hollows between their leaves decomposing humus and water collected, and were absorbed by the plant. Sometimes a rich flora and fauna of algae, bladder-worts, water-fleas and mosquito larvae also developed in them—so rapidly exploited was every opportunity in this fantastic world.

I pulled at one slender green life-line, stepping aside to avoid the showers of humus and water which fell from above, and tried to trace it to its source. Extremely elastic, it would spring back 6 feet after each pull, causing a momentary stir in the leaves above. 'Mibi', was Little Rufus' identification: 'Good for making basket.' It was an Anthurium with yard-long heart shaped leaves. Monsteras, Philodendrons, and a Carludovica (from which are made Panama hats), grew on the same tree. Then I saw an even more impressive cluster of hanging roots, each as thick as a stout rope. They descended in a straight line to the ground, were dark brownish-green in colour, and covered with little raised corky warts. When I slashed one it exuded a sticky saffron-yellow sap—and on the ground beside it lay several fruits like coconut-sized onions, and a single white flower, like a deliciously-scented magnolia blossom 9 inches across.

These could belong only to one plant: 'Kufa,' said Little Rufus in confirmation: Clusia grandiflora, the monarch of all epiphytes, and a member of the Mangosteen family (Guttiferae).

Excitedly I searched the tree-tops—and in doing so discovered that the 80-foot canopy at which my eyes had previously stopped was in fact only a middle stratum, composed of the crowns of Trysils, Waraias, Warakosas and other medium-sized trees, but that the great trunks of the Moras and Kakarallis passed clear through, to regions far above.

I walked until I could find a gap, and looking up saw, some 40 feet higher, the crown of a Kakaralli. Its branches were white against dark foliage gleaming in the sunshine, stirring gently in the breezes—on one a wild pigeon cooed—and sitting in its crown, grew another tree the size of a small oak—my

Kufa. Its leaves were dark glossy green and as big as table-tennis rackets, and from it hung those cable-like roots that I had first noticed. The branches of the Kakaralli and the neighbouring Moras were almost invisible, so densely were they incrusted with epiphytes, mostly bromeliads. Those summit epiphytes were quite different from the broad, delicate, dark-green-leaved epiphytes that grew in the saturated, cathedral-dark forest depths—not surprisingly, for only a quarter or half of 1 per cent of the light that falls on the rain-forest canopy reaches the ground, according to the few trustworthy measurements that have been made. Desiccating up there in the abundant sunshine and breeze, they had small, tough leaves, usually bright yellow in colour. When a tree falls, or a clearing is made, the more delicate plants dry up and die—and soon the tree-tops species begin to establish themselves lower down, and may even grow upon the ground.

Comparing forests objectively is hard—on a dark day a light forest may appear gloomier than a dark one when the sun is shining brightly. And when the same rain falls alike on adjacent wet and dry types of forest, who is to tell which has drier conditions throughout the year, or how much water penetrates through or evaporates from their different types of crown? But as a quick rule of thumb, if we can say that certain bromeliads, usually found only on the top branches of the tallest trees in rain forest, grow only 6 feet above the ground in another kind, this gives us a more useful idea of its lightness and dryness than a few irregular readings with thermometers and photo-electric meters.

By the time that Little Rufus and I turned back the sun was low, sending its rays into the jungle and illuminating the columns of the trees, the network of lianes and pendant roots. The structure of the forest stood out in amazing detail, intricate, luxuriant, utterly alien to someone accustomed to the friendly woods of Europe. Here (to continue my human analogies) was the Tokyo or Manhattan of the plant world—where vegetable growth had attained a maximum complexity—where the forest had itself become a major environment supporting lesser environments that had evolved only within it.

Yet why had this particularly rich development occurred only on a narrow strip of land between raging river currents and

placid swamp waters? I thought of the other forest types we had
cut and waded through, and of the unexpected variations in the
heights of forest along the river banks, and suddenly it made
sense—we were in the middle of a classical example of 'levee
topography'—levees being high banks that form on either side
of a river liable to flooding.

In civilised lands rivers are tamed. We think of rivers as
eroding valleys, but we have few images of how they build up
plains—which is what the Essequebo was doing in this area.
For such plains, being richly fertile, are usually intensively
cultivated or developed, and the only levees we know are usually
man-made—walls and embankments designed to prevent any
further flooding.

In the dry season the Essequebo would be eroding its bed, and
carrying the resulting silt, sand and mud downstream. But in
the rainy season the volume of water was too great to pass down
through the barrier of the rapids and their adjacent hills, so it
overflowed and formed an enormous lake on the upstream side.
This silt-laden water would drop its main load of heavier
particles close to the main channel, at the point where its speed
was checked as it spread over the landscape—thus building up
levees along the riversides with a soil relatively coarse and free-
draining, while away from them where the smaller particles
were dropped as the water speed slowed down further, it
became finer and finer, and eventually a heavy, sticky clay in
the deeper places where we usually had to start swimming. This
wide flood plain was being built up in the rainy season by
materials dropped in differing places according to water speed;
while when the dry season came it would doubtless reveal itself
as an undulating level of clay, traversed by high-banked rivers
scouring their way along meandering channels on their way to
the mighty mile-wide Essequebo in the middle.

How would such a continuously changing landscape affect
the forests and other vegetation that grew upon it? It represented something very different from the northern ecologists'
idea of a 'hydrosere'—a sequence of landscape development
from open water, with the debris from its various stages of
aquatic vegetation building the bottom level up until finally it
could carry land plants, and eventually high forest. In the first
place the bottom level that was being built up here was of sand

and silt only, because of the rapid decay of all vegetable debris when exposed to the air during the dry season.

There was thus no possibility, short of a major geological change, of the land level being raised above that of the highest floods, so that drier forest types could take over. Secondly there was no question of permanence even of the highest levees, for the river and its tributaries were liable to change their courses at any time and sweep away whatever was in their path, only to deposit it again somewhere else.

I had to accept therefore that the vegetation that grew on the different parts of this topographical system would evolve and reach 'climax' stages in ways very different from those found in the drier areas around—indeed, that there might be many different climax plant societies in Guiana. As a first step to describing them I decided to call these forests 'Flood Plain Rain Forests', or 'Swamp Rain Forest'.

7

Wading

The following day we sailed down river to a point opposite the Trinity Isles, and began a line at an attractive spot where a small Kakaralli tree emitted a thrilling sweetness from tresses of soft fleshy white and golden flowers, which swarmed with black ants come to feed at the nectaries. Nearby a Malpighiaceous bush bore panicles of scented pink flowers amid dark glossy leaves. The water here was olive-brown, almost black, slow running and very deep. We nosed in, tied up and jumped ashore, while Basil got out his fishing line. Having worked out what the submerged topography of the area was like, I was determined to push through to higher ground along this line. But fifteen minutes later we returned, having encountered water too deep to pass, despite my resolutions. In this short time Basil had caught six perai: powerful ugly monsters with a pugilist's thick lips, saw-sharp teeth, and red-gleaming eyes. They were all apparently dead, but when I cautiously probed an open mouth to test one's teeth with a pencil, its jaws came together like a pair of rose-clippers and snicked the end off clean. We stayed another half-hour, replenishing our food supply with these fish. Basil had started off using a bit of powis leg as bait; now he was simply tying bloody strips of the rag it had been wrapped in to his hook. There was no problem in getting the fish to bite—only in embedding the hook in their bony mouths and hauling them in before they cut the strong wire leader of the line with their scalpel teeth. The secret was to give the line a terrific jerk at the slightest bite and to haul in as fast as posible. As each new catch came thrashing out of the water we tried to kill it with cutlasses instantly. There was a positive panic when a 12-inch specimen (most were 7 to 9 inches long) slipped off the hook and leaped about cracking its teeth together in the boat bottom.

Silently Julian, who had killed it, held out his hand from
which two fingers had lost their end joints: 'Dat happen two
years ago. I have me hand in the water, scaling a fish by de
boat side. Jus' by Bartica stelling.'

But no one had actually heard of a human being killed by
perai. People were just too careful. 'This is a real bad-looking
perai hole,' mused Jonah. 'The water so deep an' black, and
trees hanging over, so plenty of animals bound to fall in, like
insects, and lizards and birds—it would be a very dangerous
place to swim.'

'Up the Courantyne the Indians scare them by clapping
their hands under water,' I said, remembering the surprisingly
loud muffled boom, very hard to imitate, that I had heard
them make by bringing their hands hard down, edge on, to
meet just under the surface.

'Even if dere was six here clapping I don't jump in for no
money!' said Basil, 'You watch—*every* animal we shoot here
going to have a mark from dese perai! I seen deer with it, and
bush cow (tapir), even camoudi (anaconda). Only otter
escape—because he feed on fish! If dey did live in fas' water,
nobody could go up through de falls.'

'That's right,' agreed Jonah. 'And this is the sort of place they
breed. Sometimes you see a mother with eggs—she lays them on
roots or on leaves in quiet water. And she fans them with her
tail.'

Leaving the perai hole we sailed between and through the
three islands—now mere banks of tree-crowns emerging from
the water under a tangle of lianes, some with bright flowers:
purple and white Bignoniaceae, a cerise-flowered convolvulus,
a golden legume. A few curious leathery straps hanging from a
tree, dark green or sometimes purple or brilliant red were
'Alligator Tails' (Epiphyllum sp.), the only cacti found in these
forests. At one point an Awaraballi crown in fruit projected
above the surface. Should I collect it, and make a useful contri-
bution to knowledge? But I decided not—not yet, anyway.
Every inch of it, leaves, spathes, nuts, was clothed in a terrible
array of spines. It would be a ghastly thing to have to carry
around for three months. Instead I contented myself with
photographing it.

As we drew away into the open river, we found ourselves

carrying a load of riverside dragon-flies, big fat fellows and slim demoiselles, which evidently regarded the boat as a convenient advanced base for operations in mid-stream, for whenever we left the bank we were usually accompanied by a screen of them hawking around, nipping out over the water on short flights, or settling with complete confidence on all parts of the boat and on us. Sometimes they accompanied us for miles . . . and, as Little Rufus said sentimentally: 'If they got homes they might never find them again.'

Four times more that morning we attempted lines; but at each the water was not shallow enough to jump overboard into, even when we had cut through into the forest. Then at our final attempt a bank appeared, drier than usual. We jumped ashore, took up positions, and moved forward up a gentle slope, then slowly down again, walking upon soft mud, then in slush; ankle deep, knee deep; then wading steadily, up to our waists.

Soon the front men were swimming, only their hats visible above the still, black water. I looked for ripples round leaves and twigs, but there was no sign of flow. In the mirror surface the gloomy columns of the trees hung reflected; above, their branches closed with not a chink of sky to be seen between. As we swam forward in the chilly depths, I resolved to go as far as possible. Loud cries of 'Cayman!' followed by an imitation of the splash of its tail and its angry roar; then 'Perai! Ow!' and, 'Jaguar' (snarl) from ahead were designed to terrify and amuse me. Lord, a natural butt because of his inexperience, had emerged shivering on a root: a yell, then a laugh indicated that he had been deceived by the movement of a twig made to wriggle like a snake near his foot by Big Rufus, Jonah's son— who caught my eye and burst into a fit of giggles.

A hundred yards further I reached shallower water and began to wade again; then came to a patch of dry land. Here I waited while a succession of hats followed by naked brown figures emerged from the water—somehow one expected suits. Kunyow removed his inflated blue egg-like dome with its frilly down-turned brim, and produced from it underpants and shirt, cigarettes and matches, then settled down for a smoke and to dry himself in a small patch of sun. Big Rufus swam up, tiny, like an elf without antennae. Inside his jaunty pale green Robin Hood hat he carried his carefully folded shirt and shorts, all

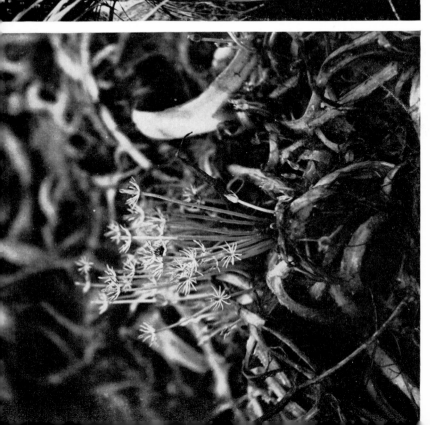

Paku-weed flowers

A half-submerged Awaraballi crown

The camp at Mocca-Mocca point

wrapped in a large banana-like Heliconia leaf. While the rest of us bent exhausted over the inky water and drank out of our hands, or by sucking at the surface, he sipped fastidiously from his leaf, now twisted into a cup. I plucked a large praying mantis with waving legs off a twig and offered it to him. To my surprise he—who had lived his whole life in the forest—shrank away, almost in terror.

We settled down for lunch on this dry spot, and I took off my trousers to dry them: light cricketing flannels dyed brown. The dye had run, beautifully mottling the lower part of my body so that I looked like a design for *L'Après-midi d'un faune*. I thought of wearing only the bathing trunks that I had underneath, but decided that wet or not, my trousers gave some protection against scratches. I wore my oldest clothes (avoiding anything of hard-surfaced cloth, which clung clammily when wet), and basket ball shoes, so that I could slip through the tangled under-growth, clamber over logs, or jump across creeks. They wore out after a month, but were cheap to replace. It amused me to think of the conventional explorer's khaki suit and leather knee-boots: anyone in such an outfit would have had to be carried.

After lunch we were soon all swimming again—and this time there was no sign of drier ground. Wearily we gave up. We had come three-quarters of a mile from the riverside—our best effort to date.

Big Rufus steered on the way home—he had asked to be allowed to do so—and there was tremendous chuckling as purple rain-clouds began to build up in the sky. He, who had been so pernickety about keeping his clothes clean, neat, and dry, while the rest of us were soaked and filthy, now began to look alarmed, and asked if anyone would like to take over. But no one volunteered. Instead we all crowded in under the awn-ing, leaving him alone in the open. A positive tornado of rain then dashed across the water, drenching him before steadying into a downpour. Five minutes of this, then the sky cleared and the sun shone, just as we reached camp.

Day after day for another week we began and abandoned lines after only a few yards. Our days were cold, wet and uncomfort-able, yet from each few yards measured I was beginning to construct a scheme of these Swamp Rain Forests, and of the series of successions they formed. Everything confirmed my

i

surmise that the over-riding factor defining these series was the landscape-forming process.

Then unexpectedly came drier land, upstream from our camp. From the river's bank we cut through low straggly forest; then for about a quarter of a mile waded through a swamp of waist-high sedges and razor grass with only a scatter of small trees a few years old. The sharp edges of the sedges cut our flesh and tore our clothes; our arms were a mass of blood. The sun was blistering hot. It was obvious from charred logs and stumps that the whole area had been burnt.

Suddenly a loud hum came from a small sphere hanging in a bush a few yards away. It had a hole in the bottom, like a Chinese paper lantern.

'Tiger-head marabunta!' whispered Jonah. 'Keep low and as *quiet* as you can.'

One by one we stole past—but with each man the hum grew louder. Then the wasps rushed out like a squadron of jet fighters and, lashing themselves into a fury, raced in widening circles. Although by now about fifty yards away, copying the Indians I dropped flat on to the mushy ground, but not quite in time: two wasps entangled themselves in my hair, and I was stung. (My head throbbed for two days afterwards.) We lay quietly until the wasps had returned, then continued in thoroughly bad humour. Two men beside myself had been stung, but none severely.

'That was Tiger-head,' said Jonah cheerfully (he had escaped). 'You lucky you only get stung through your hair, else you feeling really ill—maybe get fever and have to stay in bed! And there is even worse kinds! Like "Saucepan cover". These have a flat nest with all the holes underneath. They drops in a mass straight down, and if you is below they can kill you. Afterwards they rise up and fly round slowly, in circles, and finally they goes off and builds another nest. Then there is "Kwako", which is all black, and builds a clay nest on a stout branch. He is very bad, but don't attack unless you shake he nest hard. There is also another bad kind like a big black-and-white ball, near the top of a tree. And another that builds a clay nest always on a dying tree. You have to be careful, for the nest is scaly, just like a certain kind of termite nest.'

The trees grew thicker, the water deeper, colder, darker, the mud soupier; and soon we were wading waist-deep beneath a dense growth of Corkwood, Awasokule, and Manni trees. We hacked our way between fantastic buttresses and stilt roots, over rotting logs crawling with nauseous giant millipedes and squelchy worms; through thick black mud and chill water, tripping, slipping and falling, while spiders' webs wrapped themselves round our sweat-streaming faces and fierce stinging ants rushed out to attack from certain undergrowth trees.

Every now and then one of us would be flung face downwards as he stumbled into a submerged pothole, tripped over a snaking buttress of one of the Corkwoods or an underwater stilt root of an Awasokule, or hooked his foot into a root of the Manni trees. These covered the bottom like thousands of concealed croquet-hoops, rising above the ground in loops—for they are pneumatophores or aerating roots, found largely in trees growing on permanently waterlogged soil. Being tripped up once is bad enough, but being tripped up for a whole day is almost unendurable. To add to our joys the cut-off roots and twigs of both Manni and Awasokule exuded a thick, treacly, adhesive yellow latex which set firmly on our limbs and faces, so that soon we were coated as if in a mass of sticky chewing gum. Yet, even this was not the limit of our torments, for on top of all this there was the eye-strain of avoiding twigs and branches swinging in our path. Finally, cow flies abounded—great inch-long streamlined creatures, sleek as sports-cars, with glittering green-striped eyes—which flew up noiselessly, hovered, settled, and then stabbed with a sharp needle-jab, drawing blood. Almost as much of an irritation were their enemies—large yellow-and-black sand-wasps (so called because they nest in holes in sand) which in turn pursued and preyed on the cow flies. There were large numbers of these, and their intentions were of the highest order, but they would usually arrive when there were no cow flies about, and buzz a foot from one's face, twiddling their feet together and scrutinising one. Then they would pounce on a button or anything even faintly resembling a cow fly. Unfortunately upon my cheek I have a small dark mole, and throughout the day wasp after well-intentioned wasp violently tried to drag it away. I offered one a small piece of leaf and he picked it up, but dropped it at once and returned to my mole.

Slowly we plodded on cutting through this morass, always in near-darkness; for though there were few trees of any size, the canopy was dense and we seldom glimpsed the sky. I was numb with cold, tired and wretched, with an all-dissolving desire to escape, wash, lie down, and sleep. But always when we thought we were stuck we found a way on, for I was determined to go on to the limit—to form some picture of the countryside, and if possible to complete a line.

At 11 in the morning we stopped for lunch beside a creek. Ringing its muddy banks were beautiful Jotoro plants (Dieffenbachia), with 4-foot-tall leaves like giant green rabbits' ears sprouting from the ends of twisted rhizomes, which lay, like so many old hose pipes, on the surface of the ground. We took care not to handle these, for like many of the other large herbs around they had a blistering sap—they are the 'Dumb cane' of the West Indies, where their juice was used by the Spaniards for torturing slaves: a few drops in the mouth caused the tongue to swell and made speech impossible for several days. Or the slave would be beaten with the rhizome, and painful weals would rise on his back.

Sunlight streamed through the gap in the canopy left by a fallen tree, drying our clothes, warming our chilled flesh. Sitting on a prostrate trunk with feet dangling in the air, a little way from the chatting men, I ate my sandwiches and read *Manhattan Transfer*. For a while I escaped into the New York of the 1920s. It was a shock when I looked up and found myself in the jungle. I ate my last sandwich, put on my partly dried shoes, drank a gulp of brown swamp water, jumped into the creek up to my waist, swam to the other side—and away we went again through the flooded, vilely uncomfortable jungle, slowly feeling our way forward with our feet.

Now for long level stretches we had to cut through thick plants like giant irises, with man-high saw-edged leaves (Spathanthus and Rapatea), or dense thickets of horribly thorny Bactris palms. Yet I began to notice unexpected beauties, such as the delicate Rapatea flowers—heads of thin-stalked blossoms like miniature onion flowers, each with three white petals and long golden stamens; while out of the mud grew small plants of surprising daintiness and beauty: gentians, raising solitary trumpets into the air, or little inflorescences of tiny rusty orange, yellow or white bells, star-shaped and curiously anaemic, for they had no green leaves or chlorophyll, but were saprophytes living on the rich humus of the soil—a far cry from the resplendent blue gentians of Switzerland.

Occasionally there were the twin spiral cymes of Burmanniaceae, borne like the gentians on hair-thin stalks. Filmy ferns were abundant: their leaves' membranes only one cell thick and strangely luminescent—in certain lights glowing a grassy green like cats' eyes. They formed tiny clumps, but one, Trichomanes elegans, grew quite tall and differed from the rest in having a blue metallic lustre. Some grew up the sides of the trees so closely pressed to the trunk that they looked like frost-traceries on the bark. I pulled at one of these, and stripped off what turned out to be a single wiry-petioled leaf eight feet long, with many large lateral leaflets of dark translucent green. This fern had altogether three such huge leaves, which sprang from an inch-long rhizome buried in the soil at the base of the tree. Another filmy fern was in fruit and its fertile leaves extended out at right-angles from the tree with tiny horn-shaped receptacles along its edges, from the centre of each of which protruded the hair-like stalks of the sporangiophores.

Sometimes I found curious insect ghosts sitting on twigs—each a perfectly preserved insect, but quite hollow, anchored by a circle of threads and surrounded by a halo of tiny pink-and-black clubs.

'The Amerindians call these "moonstruck",' said Jonah. 'Instead of sleeping, they went out at night when the moon was full, and looked into her face. And this is what happens.'

In fact they were riddled with a parasitic fungus called Empusa. No one knows quite how these fungi are transmitted from one insect to another, or how, after they have grown to some extent within its body, they set the final paralysis in motion so that the poor creature is found gripping a twig. The fungus then throws out a web of filaments which attach the insect even more firmly, spreads its way through the whole body, bears its club shaped fruit, and dies.

Another object which interested me looked like a green grape attached at one end to a leaf. It was exactly the same size and shape, and had exactly the same lustrous surface as a grape—but it was hollow, a membranous-skinned balloon; and within, stretched from end to end, was a white thread containing a few white blobs. I scrutinised this with my pocket lens, and decided that it must be some sort of egg capsule (perhaps of a snail), which protected the eggs within from enemies, and perhaps provided a local climate which favoured their develop-ment—keeping out too much water or too much sunlight.

By three o'clock, after seven hours' work, we had cut 1½ miles inland: four hours and forty minutes per mile. There were still two miles left to be cut and charted. It took us two hours to walk back to the boat along the cleared path.

The following day we struggled out to the point where we had left off, again taking two hours: I was determined if possible to finish this line, for our friendly sand-wasps must be nesting on dry white sand, and somewhere ahead we should find it.

Sure enough, the forest began to change as we cut on, turning gradually into a low dense woodland of small-stemmed trees including many Barabara trees (Diospyros, with a charcoal-like bark the under layers of which are used as a fish poison), and full of palms, mainly Bactrises with long black prickles and a few tall Ités (Mauritia flexuosa). The soil too changed, first from a brown clay to a whitish clay; then I found that this was only an inch thick, passing below into white sand—and soon we were walking on dry, level white sand: my white sandhills! Thirty feet above I could occasionally see the sky.

Slowly the vegetation became more and more small-leaved as we passed into a different soil and micro-climate: Cyrilla antillana, a delicate, twisted shrub with myrtle-like leaves in tufts at the twig-ends, appeared in numbers; Ité palms became more numerous—then there was a shout ahead, and we stumbled out into the blinding light of day, into an open savannah of high Rapateas and tall, thin, straggling ferns (Lindsaya aquatica), thickly overgrown with high bushes of Cyrilla. All around against a brilliant blue sky rose majestic fan-leaved Ité palms, singly or in clumps, while amongst them I noticed two clumps of a similar but smaller and more graceful palm whose stems were covered with large thorns: Mauritia aculeata, a species I had not seen before, and which I never saw again on this expedition. Still wading to our waists we cut on, feeling happy as our backs dried in the sunlight. Occasionally we would pass through an island of taller trees, mostly Mannis (some bearing their exquisite waxy coral-red flowers), and Bactris palms; but with nothing of sufficient size to be included in the survey.

Finally, two and a quarter miles from the river's edge, Little Rufus and I climbed a Manni tree and scanned the horizon. As far as we could see there was an endless plain of Cyrilla bushes with Ité palms waving above, and no sign of higher forest. There was nothing for us to measure—everything was below exploitable size. So, having made notes on the vegetation, we abandoned the line and returned towards the boat, drenched by a passing shower as we entered the forest.

The journey back through the Manni swamps and the razor-edged sedges was almost as bad as the journey out—it was almost a pleasure to think back to our previous days of wading waist- or neck-deep in cold, brown water, stumbling through mud, clay, and rotten humus. But when at last we reached camp I found that Boodhoo had tea waiting and a bucket of warm water with which to bathe. Little James (Philbert Thomas' eight-year-old son—secretly brought along for the trip, then accepted by me as Boodhoo's aide), took off my soaked shoes. I washed and changed, covered my exposed skin with dimethylphthalate to drive away insects, and sat out in the open, blissfully happy from pure exhaustion.

Tea, a few cakes or scones which Boodhoo had baked in an oven made from an old petrol drum, and I began to revive. Every evening the sun set in a fanfare of scarlet and yellow, with grey or sooty clouds floating, glowing, and fading high up in the air over the blackening forest wall of the opposite shore. Perhaps a tree or two standing above the rest would catch its last rays and fling aloft green spangles of light.

It was usually quite silent—but tonight the howler monkeys were singing far away in the jungle roof, their voices like no other sound on earth: sometimes elusive, a mysterious whisper like the wind in the tree tops, dying away or rising to a murmur. Then bursting forth clear, triumphant, a vast swelling chorus that one felt could come from no living creature, but must be the voice of the forest incarnate.

Darkness fell, except for a lingering tawny glow over the far bank. The mile-wide river slid past smooth and powerful, with here and there a silver circle cast by a rising fish. Occasionally the baffling eerie sound of the howler monkeys rose again from the other shore, but otherwise a great stillness; then the drum-strokes of the tree frogs, and the sounds of the night began.

I did a little reading, had dinner (fried perai—dry, rather woolly-fleshed, and full of long, pointed bones), then grilled powis (Curassow), and some cabbage from the heart of a palm-tree, and went to bed, feeling content (for at least I knew that one line was finished), to the sleep of sheer exhaustion.

8

Mountain

Next morning we packed up camp and set out upstream, rolling heavily on the choppy inland sea of the huge river, our destination Arisaru. Rounding a bend, we saw the mountain not far ahead, then a long island obscured it before it came into sight again, looming across a broad expanse of water. The river became full of islands, and the foaming main channel straight ahead looked perilous. Although we could see no rocks, we thought it wiser not to ascend it, but to cross to the mountain shore and creep forward in the shelter of a long, shallow bay.

As we approached, Arisaru's seemingly vertical near face towered above, clothed in thick forest with here and there a projecting crag of bluish-brown rock. All sorts of estimates were made of its height and distance from the river—some men said 5 miles, others 7—it certainly *looked* a long way. But by comparing the trees on its sides with those near at hand (and with tree crowns I had seen from the air), I tried to make an accurate judgement, and concluded that it was only about a mile and a half inland. And by roughly estimating the diameters of the tree crowns, and counting them as they stood one above another on the slope, I calculated that the face was about a thousand feet high. Perhaps it would not count as a mountain in other parts of the world, but in the flat countryside of Guyana it was an astonishing thing, a sheer wall of verticality where all else was horizontal, rising above the river plain as dramatically as does the great cathedral of Ely above the level fens.

Moments later, the near wall of jungle hid the mountain from view. The current became fast and the water full of bubbles. Slowly we rounded the point at the end of the bay, and landed at the very toe of Arisaru, on a steeply sloping bank of hard earth facing across the narrowest part of the river, through which—constricted by the high ground on either side—

the water ran in a smoothly hissing sheet. A single jagged tear down the middle showed where rocks lay just below the surface.

We unloaded on to a shelf of rock. The ground was dry and well drained, the air was cool, the view up and down river fine: it was delightful to find such a perfect site. We felt gay, for the mountain meant higher land and hope that we might escape the flood waters and be able to finish a number of lines; so we decided to take more trouble to make ourselves comfortable.

Other people had camped here before, and the whole place was overrun with dense tangles of razor grass (Scleria), scrambling over bushes and festooning the lower branches of the trees. First we had to clear this, and our arms, legs and faces were soon criss-crossed with networks of thin lines of blood, while a curious and horrible smell, like a rotten tooth, began to seep out of the soggy undergrowth. This was caused by wood decay, and for a while it was almost unbearable. But as the ground dried it disappeared.

Next, saplings were cut in the surrounding forest to make the supports for our shelters. My own consisted of a square of upright posts supporting a central ridge-pole across which was stretched a heavy canvas tarpaulin, its sides and ends tensioned by springy rods stuck in the ground. The men's tents were similar, but much larger, to accommodate six persons each, and had stout horizontal beams along the sides of the roof from which to hang hammocks. The canvas roof swept down to about 4 feet above the ground along the sides, but sides and ends were otherwise completely open for coolness—although that meant that rain and spray could sweep right through. To minimise this I placed my camp bed in the exact centre and had brought an extra supply of towels, which I spread over my possessions each night against dew, and with which Boodhoo could cover things during the day if necessary. My mosquito net afforded a good deal of protection against spray—even so, at Mocca-Mocca Point rain had blown in and soaked me, so I now kept a bath-towel handy to cover my blankets with. It was extraordinary to lie in bed at night under four blankets shivering violently with cold due to the saturation of the air, and at the same time sweating from heat and humidity.

At one end of the tent I put my working table-top supported by a frame of fresh-cut sticks, at the other a peeled rod as a rudimentary clothes horse. Along one entire side a trestle of thick straight branches was built high enough to be sheltered by the overhang of the tarpaulin roof, and upon this I placed my luggage: two waterproof tin 'canisters' (trunks), a medicine chest, a duffle bag, two ration boxes and three plant presses; and beneath it a few logs for my shoes to stand on—for they would otherwise have gone mouldy overnight. Along the other side of the tent I placed a folding camp table, a 'barbricot' (a table made of sticks and slats of wood) which I used as a book-shelf, and two canvas chairs. Next, a small thatched shelter was built a few yards off for Boodhoo to cook under, and some way off in the bush, along a path, a deep pit was dug (giving a very interesting soil 'profile'), crossed by a horizontal stick held up by two forked branches: my lavatory. Finally all around each tent a deep drain was dug, to carry away surface water during heavy rains.

When all was complete and set out at the day's end I had a most comfortable dwelling—in fact, it was not much less comfortable than my Georgetown hotel, and with Boodhoo and Little James to look after me I had better service.

From my tent I could see upstream for several miles through a thin screen of trees (charcoal-barked Barabaras, hollow-trunked Cecropias with big palmate leaves, delicate guavas) growing out of the water. Downstream a tiny promontory similar to mine carried the men's camps; while between, cutlassed tunnels wound through the thickly razor-grass smothered bushes. It was like living in a sort of green rabbit-warren with saw-sharp walls.

It was curious to feel that just behind us the mountains towered up—as if a hole has been knocked in our ceiling. Night fell, moonless but with the stars so brilliant that they made the eerily swirling water look like milk, their reflections long pale lines on its surface. The men's camps were too far away for me to hear them. There were only the muffled drum beats of frogs, the splashes of fish or cayman. Leaves rustled and lifted without visible cause on the ground around my circle of light, as I sat reading—as if moved by tiny ghosts. I put the light out, and lay in bed listening. I could hear the gentle rain of debris falling from the tree tops, the sibilances of insects and other sounds without apparent place of origin, enwrapping me in their mystery. One was like the hiss of dry grass in the wind, or the crawling of the hair on one's scalp, and it came from all around, pervading the atmosphere as if the entire surface of the earth were moving.

I awoke to the sound of calling birds. The mountain! We were back in dry, animal-filled regions again. From a little way inland sounded the melancholy, piercingly sweet whistle of a tinamou, sometimes wavering, sometimes clear, repeated every now and again. Overhead, irresponsible gurglings and tinklings came from bunyahs (Oropendola), black mocking birds with long yellow tails, whose hanging nests were a-sway in a Kakaralli tree top at the edge of the clearing. Vocal virtuosi capable of singing straight, they have descended to comedy and hideously maltreat their voices; in the middle of a beautiful pure melody comes a sound like a child on a xylophone or a stone rattled in a tin can—'Tonka-tonka-ting!' A noise like a fountain bubbling came from a small spotted-backed wren working its way through the bushes along the edge of the river bank. Another unknown bird played a monotonous scale.

It was Sunday, and I could relax. I got up and shaved, then settled down to breakfast. As I sat eating my porridge something called confidingly low down in the trees nearby: 'Who-who? who-who?' in positively human tones. I sat very still and replied 'Who-who?' Presently it answered nearer, and I answered again and began tiptoeing in to the jungle towards it. I scrutinised the dark lower storeys of small trees and shrubs as I called, and at last saw an inconspicuous bird, the size of a blackbird, sitting gravely upright on a twig. Its two long, slender tail feathers ended in round discs, like a pair of badminton rackets. It was a motmot, a bird wondrously irridescent in the hand, sky-blue, purple, white and rufous—yet here perfectly camouflaged. They are said to be born with complete tail feathers, but to pluck all but the mid-ribs and tips as they get older. I looked down, and at my feet, in a tiny depression in the leaves of the forest floor, were five highly polished turquoise-blue eggs, like china darning eggs: a tinamou's nest, perhaps that of the bird that had been calling.

I returned to my seat and began to write up a report on my work, but not for long. Patrolling the riverside bushes were parties of hideous, hook-beaked black birds with rasping voices,

called 'old witches' (Crotophaga ani), a type of cuckoo which
builds large communal nests in which all the females lay. Now
a group assembled a few yards from where I sat and began
bowing and displaying to one another, flipping their long tails,
arching their wings, and screaming raucously, creating such an
uproar that I could hardly think. I watched them for half an
hour. Then the uproar was too disturbing and I got up and
chased them away. From a branch above them a big turkey-like
bird, a guan, rose and flapped off heavily, while below me on
the beach (the river bank was deeply excavated) several huge
Morpho butterflies, with metallic blue wings 7 inches across,
fluttered and hopped upon a decaying banana that Boodhoo
had flung out. An owl butterfly (Caligo), equally large, but
with sullen mauves, greys, and staring eye spots, came and
settled on a twig near them—a 'Mort bleu' as it would be
called, appropriately, in the French West Indies. Later, when
I was sorting some plant specimens, there came from the forest
an exquisite little fluting, with the lilt and emphasis of a musical-
box tune. At first I could not believe that it came from a bird—
but when I whistled in response a little wren with russet breast
came hopping and searching over the leaves, and stood only a
few feet off, singing and bowing to me. Then she darted away
under the bushes, every now and again returning to continue
her duet: an intimate friendly little bird, whom I later identified as the quadrille wren (Leucolepis musica musica).

My work done, I walked through the razor-grass tunnels to
the other camp, which was alive with activity: the rows of
hammocks slung under the tarpaulins looked like curious
chrysalids; or if they had mosquito nets around them, like
Spanish galleons in billowing sail. The men swarmed about in a
variety of garments, ranging from striped shirts to long white
combinations, chatting in gutteral Arawak. Some were
engaged in making babricots to act as tables; Little Rufus,
preening his strong and beautiful body, whittled away at a half-
finished bow. Rufus Boyan, Albert and Elias were all weaving
baskets of mibi (aroid root) and mukru (Ischnosiphon—stems
of a tall cane with tufts of banana-like leaves at the top) to sell
in Bartica market at the end of the trip. I was sorry to see that
the baskets were strictly utilitarian with none of the old Indian
designs, merely a border design in ink-stained material. For

these Indian designs are not only beautiful, but reveal a mental world far removed from our own. Specific designs represent birds, butterflies, snakes, monkeys, savannah-grass, running water, wood lice, and so forth. Some are widespread, others confined to a single tribe or area. Yet no one could fail to recognise that these works came from South America—so strong is the psychological unity of everything that comes from that continent—and yet how hard this is to explain. The motifs come from the world around the Indians—a world viewed, it would seem, without fear. Never is there anything like the propitiatory art of Africa or the Pacific, or, indeed, ancient Mexico. There are no representations of evil spirits, no horrible masks to frighten away devils, for these Indians hardly believe in devils, have practically no fear of spirits, view life with an almost agnostic sanity. They are a guarded, calm, realistic, reasonable, and critical people. Their art appears to us placid and unemotive, perhaps leaning to the intellectual—and so, I would guess, it appears also to them. How then can one explain its family resemblance to the quite different art of Peru or Mexico, reflecting different beliefs and circumstances? Who can begin to analyse and describe the artistic nuances which unite the American Indians, and make them mentally distinct from any other people on earth?

In olden days the Indians wore magnificent feather head-dresses and ornaments. But today these have disappeared, except in remote districts, and they now seem uniformly quiet, inconspicuous, wearers of deep blues and reds, browns and yellows—the forest-dwelling equivalent of the many small drably dressed men who scurry about in the city of London—never the violent loudly-coloured shirts so popular amongst Negroes and East Indians. Perhaps they are in mourning?

Jonah and Jothan opened the food boxes and began to distribute the following week's rations. Soon we began to be puzzled, because as we had found the previous week, quite evidently less had been sent than should have been. But doubtless more food would be arriving before long.

In mid-morning a boat appeared from behind a small island close to the opposite shore. Despite all our wavings, it continued inexorably upstream; we had not been seen. Basil, looking boyish in blue and white pyjamas, leaped aboard the

Tacouba Express and gave chase. He brought back some mail but no rations, and the news that the launch was carrying supplies to a gold mine some way up river; also that our camp site was famous as the haunt of an enormous anaconda.

After lunch everything settled into quiet restfulness. Some of the men lay smoking in their hammocks. Others were washing clothes. I sat reading, stunned by the mid-day heat, the sheer power of the insolation. I felt as if I was being packed tighter and tighter with heat and light, until my head was taut, stretched and throbbing. My brain ceased to function, I laid the book aside and lay, listening to the sound of large ground lizards rustling in the dry leaves round the clearing, the swish of the water. Then a scarlet-breasted woodpecker hammered at a log in the forest, and suddenly the air was torn by harsh screams, like the sharpening of knives in front of a loudspeaker. They came from the top of a tree nearby from which peered down upon us a pair of gaudy black, cream and red birds, 'bultatas' or caracaras, who had discovered our presence. Somewhat intermediate between vultures and hawks, these birds take the place of jays in the Guiana jungle as warners of intrusion, but with a screaming unendurable as a road drill. They stopped as unexpectedly as they had begun. Then a pair of black and scarlet Heliconia butterflies started passionate love-making on a nearby leaf—the female sitting with wings closed (or occasionally, at moments of unutterable climax, opening and closing slowly) while the male hovered an inch above her, never touching. I reflected that their technique was one not described in the *Khama Sutra*—a courtship by fanning. When after an hour they had achieved not so much as a single contact a passing bird disturbed them, but at once they restarted this most delicate of titivations upon another leaf. There was something beautiful about such refined sensuality, the endless fluttering of the wings, like that of angels round the godhead in a Florentine primitive. Yet by human standards it was exasperating.

I never saw their consummation, for a gunshot from the men's camp followed by loud shouts of 'cayman, big, big!' aroused me. Albert Smith came running up and I took my gun and went after him. At the furthest men's camp a cayman had crept up to seize a man who was washing his clothes; but it had been seen and chased away. Now it lay concealed in a thicket of half-submerged bushes. I could see nothing there, but I fired a shot into the water, and there was a slight swirl—made I supposed, by a creature perhaps a couple of feet long; for after many months of the Guyana rivers I had seen not so much as one cayman, dead or alive, and I had almost ceased to believe in their existence.

Urged by the men, who said that the creature had now escaped out into the open river, I got into the boat and we pushed off. I sat on the roof, my gun loaded with No. 4 shot, designed for duck (all I had), and soon we were sweeping past the bushes under which it had lurked. A back-eddy and some minor whirlpools were coming out of the bay ahead, and the water was running fast—but there was no sign of a cayman.

Shouts from the bank, shouts from the men on board the boat—and suddenly, 50 yards ahead, I saw an enormous monster in the water, bearing down on us backwards, swept along by the current, barely paddling with its feet, which I could see clearly through the water. It had not seen us. Nearer and nearer it came. I took aim. It was almost alongside. More shouts, and the boat rocked violently as the men rushed to the side to look. I shot with the right barrel—I could see the marks appear like a rash round its eye. Up it leapt into the air, right out of the water, then plunged down deep, about 5 feet under, emerging again about 20 feet behind us at lightning speed. I fired again, and at once it rolled over, belly up, and was carried swiftly away on the current. We turned round and went in pursuit, anxious to secure it before it sank. Quickly we passed a rope around its neck, and towed it back to camp. As it trailed in the water I could see its legs twitching. Then, when we pulled it ashore, a horrifying rumble came out of its throat, it opened its mouth, and charged straight at me; but only a little way, before a couple of blows with the back of an axe finished it off.

Then the men proceeded to skin it. The still twitching skin, 9 feet long, was salted and dried, and stretched out to dry, and the white fatty carcase was tumbled into the river to provide a feast for perai and vultures.

As night fell, a bubbler frog under the bank began its nightly bubbling, producing a watery sound like the playing of a small fountain. All over the coastal plains of Guyana, in the rice fields, in the ditches, beside the sugar estates, by the roadsides

Elias weaving a basket

Jonah

Cutting through the Awaraballi bog

and in damp grassy places, these bubblers make the night pleasant with their pastorales. Once paddling alone in the dark down the Pomeroon River, I had heard one on a raft of bamboos, and flashed my torch on just in time to glimpse a tiny brown creature as it dived into the water. Now I decided to try to see this one properly. Like the quadrille bird, this frog (or toad) is easily led into a duet, so prodigious feats of bubbling were performed by both of us, until in the middle of a magnificent gurgle I switched on my torch—and just saw it jump. It was enormous! Next I turned my attention to a tympani frog whose resounding drum beats came from near my tent, in the dying leaves of a felled tree. By standing first in one place and pointing at the sound, then doing the same from another position, then searching with my torch beam at the intersection, I found it at last—a giant hyla with bronze eyes. Now I applied the same technique to other unidentified night sounds. First there was a noise like a piccolo playing a meaningless phrase at the top of its register. This proved to come from an olive-brown frog about the size of my thumb, with a pale fawn throat, who sat upon a dead leaf exactly its own colour. A tiny croak like a mouse being sick was the product of an exquisite toad of clearest lime green, with enormous stalked eyes and pale yellow, rose pink, and white splashes and markings on his body. He was an inch and a half long, with long legs, toes that had adhesive pads at their tips, and was sitting on the underside of a leaf almost within the circle of light of my tent. With a stupendous leap he shot from it on to a branch and away into the dark before I could catch him.

After supper Jonah and I sat drinking tea and chatting on the edge of the darkness, for round the pressure lamp flying ants were fluttering in thousands, while several big, dangerous looking wasps clung to the canvas of my tent. They had been working late, said Jonah, and had lost their way home. More attractive were two or three green katydids, or leaf-shaped grasshoppers, so hypnotised by the light that they offered no resistance when picked up.

I asked him about Arawak supernatural beliefs.

'Well, dey dont really believe in much nowadays, though some people talk about voices they hear.'

'But do you know anyone who has *seen* spirits?'

K

'A man told me that one day he heard someone following him and panting hard in a strange way, so he walk fast. He could hear shouting, so he ran as fast as he could, then ran back a little way to make a false trail, and hid beside the path. Along came something like a big black man, only all hairy, looking down and following the tracks, and as soon as it passed, the man ran back along the trail and cut way round to get away. Now those are the thing they call "Bush Dai-Dai"—just like a black man, only very big and strong and hairy. Some people are very frightened to meet one.' (Could runaway Negro slaves, whom the Indians had formerly helped the British and Dutch to catch, have given rise to this legend?)

'Then there is Jack o'Lantern. One day a man I knew was paddling up a small creek when he saw a light ahead, everything like a torch. So he draw in under a tree on the opposite bank and presently a man came along the shore with a pale face, and his eyes shining and casting a light up into the trees and all around. Well, the man crouch down in his boat and keep very still till the Jack o'Lantern pass, then he turn round and paddle out of the creek and back home.

'In the water they say they have mermaids, which they call Water Mamma. There are plenty of tales about them, and some of them are men. Down at Suddie there is a big bank of stones off the shore, and several times they say a big man was seen swimming there when the tide was running out. One day they caught him in a net and brought him ashore. He was in every way like an ordinary man, but he could not speak. They try to keep him, but he escape into the water and was never seen again.

'Then I know a party of young men who were camped one night by the river. One of them happen to put his foot down into the water just by the landing, and he touch something hairy lying there, so he ran back and told his friends. Well, they went down to see and one of them touched it too. It could not be a manatee for it had long, shaggy hair. As he touched it, it move. They were very frightened and didn't go near the water again that night, and the next day they left.'

Crawling on the ground towards the light came three ants so huge that for a moment I imagined them miniature demons. Dark rusty red in colour, they were fat and swollen with eggs, their taut abdomens large as marbles. They were queen parasol ants. Perhaps they had flown and shed their wings? Or they might have crawled from some nearby nest, drawn by the unexpected light instead of proceeding on their journey of fertility and nest founding.

In conclusion Jonah told me about a friend of his in the Pomeroon district. 'One day he notice behind a log an animal looking at him of a kind he had never seen before. It was between a monkey and a dog, and a very pale colour. Well, he fire and he saw it fall down. But when he go and look there was no sign of it anywhere about. So he always say it was a bush spirit.'

It was interesting to observe Jonah as he told these stories, which I have given as exactly as possible in his own words. He was a man unwaveringly true, and his attitude was one of scepticism. Yet here and there he seemed to hesitate, as if half believing. Perhaps it was the very simplicity of his tales, so close to everyday life, perhaps it was the eerie atmosphere of the forest, but I too was swayed.

The Indians do not seem a very imaginative race. They have no dreads of the unknown when in the bush, and so far as I knew Indian mothers do not frighten their children to prevent them from wandering and getting lost. (Indeed, treated as a responsible individual from the first, the youngest Indian child seems remarkably sensible compared with those of our own race.) Nor do the Indians have any foolish shame about fear—when they are frightened, they always say so, so I don't think their evident unconcern in the forest is bravado.

Saying good night Jonah walked out into the darkness and vanished towards the men's camp, a hundred yards away.

A bat swished through the tent—a vampire. They are quite common, and the men always slept with paraffin lamps burning in their tents, to prevent them from coming and drinking their blood, whilst I relied on my muslin net. I walked out from the pool of light under the canvas, and looked out over the river. The water murmured and sparkled, the wind moved the leaves of the trees overhead, and I looked up at their black silhouettes against the deep purple of the sky. The moon emerged from behind a dark cloud-bank and illuminated their branches, so that they seemed to stand out like white bones lying against black velvet. I shuddered at the thought and at this moment my oil lamp, which had apparently not been well filled, began to fade. This decided me to go to bed; and as I was about to crawl in it went out. I stood in the darkness, and at once became aware of the faint hissing rustle from the ground that I had heard before. Picking up my torch I shone it around. I could see nothing. The hissing came from behind the tent—and there the whole surface of the ground was alive, crawling with thousands of red parasol ants, each with a neatly cut disc of green leaf in its jaws, marching over the dry, shifting leaves with a million tiny feet and little clapping jaws. I followed their lines with my torch until I came to an old Kakaralli tree, up which they crawled—I could see them even 60 feet up. These ants are known to cultivate their mushroom gardens of decaying leaves underground—but here, perhaps to escape the flood-waters, their nest was evidently high up in the hollow tree.

The full moon looked down upon the edge of the clearing, and I found it hard to sleep. I dozed off, then awoke again as its flooding light entered the tent. The dry scuffling of the ants seemed louder than ever. It sounded as if they were walking right through the tent. I could hear the reed-like voices of small crickets, the tiny sounds which came from insects no bigger than a finger-nail. Occasionally a prolonged booming, like a motor boat racing over the water, from a giant frog. These noises, and an infinity of smaller ones, dissolved and faded from my attention momentarily, then were heard again, as the waves of tiredness passed over me. Above all was the continuous irregular sound of falling leaves, twigs, fruit, dropping in a steady gentle trickle from the canopy to the forest floor. Then a twig, larger than usual, dropped with a crash that aroused me from my half sleep. From the forest, a sheer wall 20 feet away, came the crackling of twigs, the shuffling of leaves, in regular stealthy procession as some animal walked through the jungle; perhaps only a mouse—perhaps a jaguar. I sat up and peered through the green net, trying to see through the pattern of light and shade of the clearing, so baffling, into those hollow dark patches beneath the trees. The wind stirred the net, and I turned, a little chill crawling up my spine. Then I lay down again and tried to sleep. Again and again, as I was on the point of slipping over the threshold into unconsciousness, some tiny significant noise would arouse me. In the dark hours, when one's resistance is at its lowest and one's imagination is playing at semi-nightmares, such little sounds can pluck at one's heart like the fingers of death—I could understand why some men feel their sanity slipping away at such times. Usually, I was rather fatalistic, but that night I could not sleep, although I dozed from sheer exhaustion; perhaps my conversation with Jonah had affected me.

Suddenly, at about 2.30 a.m., I awoke with a clammy forehead and a cold feeling of terror right down to the soles of my feet. Around me was the blackness of the tent, then bright splashes of moonlight for 10 feet on all sides, then the utter darkness of the jungle—and some one was walking around the tent. Tramp—tramp—tramp—tramp—tramp—, heavy, well-spaced footsteps—judging from the weight and length of pause between the steps, a very big man or beast. My scalp moved, and I sat as still as possible. The tent was open all around, and I strained my eyes over those white moonlit patches and into the black shadows—but I could see nothing. The footsteps ceased. Then again, inexorably, like a policeman on his beat, they started again, circling the tent. A cry would never rouse the men. My gun was wrapped up in a cloth somewhere—I had forgotten where. The footsteps changed direction. They came straight towards me. Something tiny flashed in the moonlight. Nothing more. On and on they came, remorseless, undeviating, filling the whole world, shaking me to my foundations. Then they passed right under my bed, right *through* me, turning me to stone.

At such moments one needs all one's philosophy. Never have I been more courageous. I grabbed the torch from under my pillow, leaped out of bed and shone it after the retreating Terror. Two red eyes glowed close to the ground. It was a colossal toad, 9 inches high. It blinked, then bounced away in measured hops, leaving the deep imprint of its bottom on the sand at each jump. Then it paused, and its head bobbed rapidly. It was eating something: ants! I shone my torch down —the ants were marching right under my bed. Worse, they had clipped small circles out of my green net where it touched the gound, mistaking it for some vast leaf, and were bearing them away, only to drop them a few yards off when they discovered their mistake. The ground looked as if strewn with green confetti. Hastily I shook the ants off my net, and tucked it in under my blankets, leaving a completely clear passage for them beneath the cot. Then I recomposed myself for sleep.

Five minutes later, or so it seemed, I awoke again and saw a beast evidently about the size of a Shetland pony standing beside my bed. It was looking straight into my eyes. 'Pooh!' my puzzled brain thought—'a figment of the imagination,' and I lay back and slept on. But in the morning a large mess like a pile of stewed fruit stood in the middle of the tent, where it had been sick. A labba,* said the Indians, pointing to its footprints: one of the largest of rodents; and I could expect more, for its path, regularly traversed, ran into the forest on either side, along the top of the river bank; the sort of track that jaguars follow too—when hunting labba.

The following day we cut inland from the camp to see if we could strike Arisaru. Soon to my dismay there was the glimmer of water ahead, and we began to wade yet again—to the knees, to the waist—in the dense undergrowth of a Mora and Kakaralli swamp forest. But for the certain knowledge that high ground must lie ahead I would have given up at several places where we had to swim. We crossed a succession of water paths which showed as moving currents amongst the still bog waters, swimming for many yards at a time, or balancing along slippery fallen logs with the aid of a long stick. Kunyow was my axe man, and following him I left the rest of the party, who had to go ahead in a straight compass line, and walked by a devious route through shallower places out of which grew thick masses of lily-like Spathanthus. I could not see more than 6 feet ahead through the thickets of sword-like cutting-edged leaves, and I was soon lost. I was amazed how Kunyow found his way, how sure he was of his direction. At one point we had to crawl on hands and knees under a colossal Mora tree many yards in circumference. Its buttresses had rotted and fallen away on three sides, and it was supported only by two spurs and a fragment of stump. It was quite hollow at the centre—and looking up inside I could see a spot of light far above. It gave a long shuddering groan, and a succession of creaks, which made my heart jump. Hastily we scrambled through.

* Paca.

A little way further there appeared in the water a smooth boulder of dolerite, protruding from the thick vegetation of the swamp. A shimmering sunbeam gilded its olive-green surface, and for a moment I stood upon it and gazed up at the sun far above, before plunging once more up to my waist into the water. It seemed of imponderable significance, a true sign of terra firma in the midst of soft, wet earth. A few minutes later and there were more of them. Then we were out of the water and walking up an incline. Here the men were waiting for us. They had come straight through the deepest part of the swamp, swimming and chaining the distance. Now they were clustered round one of the marker posts which we erected at every quarter of a mile. Upon it were cut two strokes: we had come half a mile in two hours.

But we were through the bogs and swamps. From here we walked up and down over a series of gradually rising ridges of slippery red lateritic clay, occasionally with rotten ironstone rock of honey-comb texture formed by the weathering of the dolerite. In places this weathering had gone further, and the ground was covered with loose crumbling piles of bean-shaped pebbles, easily crushed into clay by the fingers. Charred logs showed that fire had swept by not many years before, and the forests, newly regrown from it, were low and unimpressive. So steep were these hillsides, so slippery their water-running surfaces, that we made poor progress. With panting breath, clinging to roots and stems, we hauled ourselves up to the knife-edged ridge-crests and slid down into the narrow, boggy valleys between. We stopped for lunch in one such tiny valley, where a cascading stream wound between massive fern-clad boulders and banks of steep red earth and crumbling ironstone. Its waters were startlingly clear—the first clear waters I had seen in Guyana, where the streams are usually red or brown from decaying vegetation, when not turbid. Everywhere there was a thick luxuriance of moisture-loving plants. The ground was carpeted with Selaginellas. Clumps of Trichomaneas elegans raised delicate sprays of frozen ultramarine in the motionless air. The sun flung shafts of light on to the colossal reddish trunks of the Moras which rose around.

During lunch Kunyow dropped a line in the stream, pulled out a fish, wrapped it in a leaf and put it under his hat; then with his tin plate began to pan the gravels of the stream-bed and pound the largest lumps of quartz. We could see no specks of gold; but I took away one lump and a few months later an assayer told me that it contained appreciable quantities.

As we sat, there came a long-drawn-out noise like a roll of thunder, a devastating, continuing crash which smote the air and shook the ground, then withdrew, leaving a deepened silence. 'Big tree fall,' said Kunyow smiling: 'I t'ink mus' be dat same tree we pass under.'

Further on, the slopes grew steeper and rockier, the forest taller, with many noble Greenheart trees, and our progress was heralded by the ringing call of the greenheart bird, a cotinga about the size of a thrush: 'Whee!—whee—yoh!' 'Whee—whee—yoh!' it called; then doubled-voiced, would make an intimate pigeon-like 'Roocoo, chrr, chrr', which for some time I could not believe came from the same bird.

We crossed several more hyaline streams and at last came to a place where, above a small dell, gigantic rocks were piled in confusion. From here the ground rose sharply. Cautiously we moved forward, climbing rocks as big as cars, as big as houses, which lay poised in this colossal scree, all intergrown with ferns and banana-leaved Heliconias with spiky vermilion inflorescences.

In a long nightmare we scrambled upwards on our faces, our fingers worked into every hold, and soaked to the flesh, for down the slope and covering every rock was moving a thin trickle of water. Weary, I lay on a rock and tried to measure the slope with a compass. It was 60°—and ahead it grew steeper, while far above a great cliff brow overhung, from which the rocks seemed to have fallen, broken off by wind and water. We clutched at the soft and treacherous Heliconia stems, at the crawling lianes and snaking roots, aware of appalling gaps between the poised boulders. Many had only recently fallen, and were held up by trees and branches. Some were split and cracked, others balanced so delicately that we dared not climb on them, for fear of disturbing them and crashing with them into the depths. Higher and higher we strove, slipping, falling, and rising and slipping again, panting for breath, red in the face, streaming with sweat, up this terrible jumbled slide.

At last I stood with Kunyow on the topmost boulder of the

scree. Ahead stood an almost vertical face of smooth, damp clay, running with water, and so hard that I could make no impression on it with my fingers; and above it the cliff, over-hanging and seemingly impassable. Lying on my face I wormed upwards for 20 feet until I could grasp a single prickly root which afforded a hand hold. To this I held for a while, and rested, drawing breath. Between my feet I looked down—it was like a picture of Chaos.

Five feet above, on a slight ledge, was a small tree whose roots must have plunged straight into the rock, as I could see no sign of them. Eventually I was able to clutch this tree, and to worm my way up by means of cracks until I was grasping it firmly. I tested it and found it secure, then drew myself up to it and swung out and around it over a drop of more than a hundred feet clear, on to another small ledge. Above this there was a rock scramble which earlier in the day I might have called unclimbable, but which now seemed easy going; and another 60 feet brought me to the narrow ridge which formed the sum-mit of the mountain.

Here, when the men—who like mountain goats had swarmed round the sides of the cliffs—had rested, I had a few trees felled. At once a spectacular view began to appear over the plain of the Essequebo. First I saw the great river itself about 3 miles distant, and followed its course as it writhed through the hummocky expanse of tree tops. The jungle roof, a billowing ocean of greens, stretched away as far as the eyes could see— until it washed up the flanks of the Andes: the mightiest ocean of trees in the world, the Pacific of forests! Perhaps there were suggestions of hills in that far pale shimmer where green melted into blue. It was impossible to be sure.

Above the tree crowns an eagle floated, soaring round and round in wide circles, carried by the same trade winds that moved the coffered ranks of clouds. Butterflies bobbed over the blossoms of flowering lianes and trees—pale mauve flames of Futuis (Jacaranda), white soapsud masses of Shirua (Nectandra).

In the farthest visible landscape on our left, some 10 miles upstream perhaps, I detected an unusual colour, a faint hint of stubble in the appearance of the forest: an Ité swamp, perhaps? Anyway, something I had not seen before.

We continued the line down the far side of the mountain,

down a steep clay slope bearing fine forests. But we were exhausted and it was late, so after an hour we abandoned our task for the day. We had come altogether one and a half miles from the bank; and the last mile had taken us six hours.

The following day we returned. Wading through the swamp we came upon the wreckage of the huge decayed Mora, up whose hollow chimney-trunk I had looked: it had indeed been this tree that we had heard falling. I clambered up on the prostrate bole, and gazed at the opening left above. I felt as if I were at the bottom of a deep well as I saw the blue sky far above, the jewel-sparkling leaves around the edge. A glittering macaw fled across the gap with harsh screams; a toucan hung like a cross for an instant; and an enormous tarantula surveyed me from a tree-trunk a few feet away.

We climbed the mountain to one side of the crags and cut back to where we had ended our line. Beyond was a lovely glen where a beautiful river glided in crystalline cascades over mossy rocks between thick sedges. The rocks were red stained, the pools were deep, and in them small fish flashed.

On the far side, dry red leaves carpeted the hills and a tall forest reached to the sky. We walked fast on gentle slopes of firm brown sand through the mysterious aisles of the trees, haunted by the ringing cries of greenheart birds. Here was a forest, perhaps never before visited by man. Godlike Mora-bukea trees, buttressed with resplendent dark red bark, raised massive crowns in a lower firmament beneath gold-skinned Greenhearts, sweet-smelling gales and silverballis, bitter-barked manyokinaballi—thousands of columns rising into the air for mile after mile . . . until we descended the last of the foothills into a bog of Moras, snake-rooted corkwoods, and silvery Turu and Manicole palms (Jessenia oleracea; Euterpe edulis) growing in a mire of deep, wet peat—'pegasse' as it was called locally.

Walking became difficult, for this rich, soupy stuff was in places many feet deep. Except when standing on a root or buttress we had to hop on to fallen palm leaves, sticks or tacoubas, jumping onwards before we sank. This was a wood-moor, the tropical forest's equivalent of the blanket bogs which cover the hills of Scotland. Where the ground is under water for long periods of the year, even in this hot climate the decay of vegetable debris is slowed down, so that thick peat forms. Somewhere below it there must have been an impermeable layer, perhaps of laterite or weathered granite. Eventually we came to a little stream which crossed the bog upon a bed of white sand. This marked the end of our line—our first full line of $3\frac{1}{2}$ miles—and here on firmer ground we rested awhile.

9

The Cayman's Lagoon

For several miles above Arisaru we could make no landfall. The mountain was evidently an isolated hump, and my days were spent reading and musing on the roof of the launch as we travelled from one unsuccessful probe after another. I had begun to notice an increase in the intensity of my day-dreaming, even when I was occupied with work. Characters from the books I was reading became more vivid, and I was aware of powerful tides of feeling inside me, waxing and waning. I am sure that partly it was the simplicity of my existence, the fewness of stimuli, that gave my inner life this added importance —together with the hallucinatory landscape through which we floated—where webs of colours and lights wove and unwove with the strands of feeling in my brain. Sometimes I felt an apprehension of some great change, some revelation to come— as if I were on the point of solving an important problem. And several times at night I woke suddenly from agonised dreams of which I could remember nothing—except this same sense of impending disclosure.

We made our next camp a few miles upstream on the eastern bank, where the river, here very wide and evidently shallow, came curving round from the west. With trees on either hand for wings, draped lianes for curtains and the wall of trees behind for a backcloth, our clearing was like a stage facing the river's diffuse landscape of half-submerged tree-crowns: green clouds afloat on the shimmering water, backed by waving grey ostrich plumes where a dense woodland of Awaraballi palms stretched its horrific ranks a full half-mile along the opposite shore. An old hollow Kakaralli (which would certainly drop in the opposite direction if it fell, Jonah assured me), and a hog plum tree in young fruit stood beside my tent. Bush cow (tapir) and labba footprints and trails suggested that night visitors might be as frequent as at Arisaru.

That night as I lay in bed a tremendous bellowing shook the ground—muffled, agonised, like the cries of an entombed giant. Caymans! They seemed only a few feet away. As soon as it was daylight I set out to find them, cutting inland behind my tent. After only a few yards the ground sloped down in a long mud beach to a tree-filled lagoon, its shore marked by cayman's footprints large and small. Next day we went fishing there—for the lagoon, an ox-bow now cut off from the river, was alive with trapped sun-fish, and as we sat the caymans crept up in the gloom, only their large innocent eyes showing above the water, and tried to take us by surprise. One, over 9 feet long, tried to rush me with gaping jaws when I was off guard. A lucky shot from Basil stopped it just in time. It had an abnormal extra limb protruding from the right hind leg. Others seen included some very young ones a foot or two long, which seemed to indicate that this was a breeding place. My interest was in curing the skins, which were very beautiful: black above, white beneath, and speckled along the sides. But I was discouraged when Jonah said that the skins of this species were too thick for handbags or shoes, or even to cure properly. Basil kept them rolled up to sell as curios, but he and the other men were largely after the teeth—easily pulled out as they fitted like dunce's caps on the heads of younger replacement teeth growing below—which were readily saleable as charms against snake-bite. Often, within half an hour, a shot cayman was completely toothless. I suggested that this might reduce the saleability of the entire skins, after which Basil left a few teeth at the front.

'These bucks are a superstitious lot,' commented Lord in a low voice, as we sat side by side on a log watching a skin being stretched and salted. He gave me a lugubrious confiding smile to indicate that we were above such activities. He was at an 'all thumbs' stage, making ludicrous mistakes, then withdrawing into a moody, abstracted condition to impress us that he was thinking deeply while the rest of us just floundered in the jungle.

"But aren't the people at the coast just as superstitious?' I suggested. He gave a nervous laugh, unsure quite how I meant this.

'Maybe. But it is a matter of education. All this bush-knowledge these bucks boast about is only memorising a few names. I had to memorise thousands of words in Latin and French! How can *you* respect such people?'

'You're too intelligent to say that,' I said. You know that Jonah and Jothan or Big Rufus are as intelligent as any of us —but their intelligences are specialised because of living in the bush, their eyes, and noses and ears are more highly trained.'

Lord looked like a mournful bloodhound, his jowls and eye-pouches sagging. He sniffed. 'It does sound terrible, what I said. But I did not mean it that way. I was thinking more that what we have to fight in Guyana is this sort of superstition.' He cheered up. 'I mean, I was brought up also to believe all this nonsense about caymans' teeth. You know for a while I was frightened of every old woman because my mother used to tell me stories about the old witch who drank children's blood at night, and made them thin and die. Everybody in the coastal villages frightened children with it to make them good.'

'That's a wicked thing to do.'

'Exactly. She was something like the vampires in Europe. The only thing to stop her was a chalk line—she couldn't cross that. Even my mother and my aunts and other people used to talk about her. And remember, superstition breeds itself—only the other day an old woman was in court for drinking children's blood, to make her young again. And there was a white child murdered for the blue of its eyes, and another one to boil down and rub on a race-horse to make it win—just as a white child is goin' to win in life. That is why I think most people should *not* get a vote—it is nonsense to think they know what politics is about. Universal suffrage without qualifications! It make a thinking man despair.'

Down river the floods were beginning to abate and we were able to wade inland further than before along several lines. One day, wet and somewhat miserable as usual, I sat chewing my lunch of 'bakes'—puffed up dough cakes fried in deep fat, but now cold—when Lord sat beside me again. He was completely drenched with mud while the rest of us were tidy, and evidently thoroughly angry that he, a superiorly educated man, should be such a hopeless bungler in the forest compared with a group of Indians.

He looked at me soulfully. 'You know, Mr. Guppy, I am not a Negro at all. I am a "Red" man.'

'What does that mean?'

'I have white blood—my great-grandfather was an Englishman from England. You can see my skin—it's clearer than a real Negro's.'

'Are you proud of being a red man?'

'Yes—because red people have more energy than all these niggers and bucks and Indians. They are the doers in this colony—even more than the white man. But you would never know this about me, because I have bad features.'

'What bad features?'

'Well . . .' he hesitated. 'Thick lips and a dark skin.'

'But don't you care at all for your Negro side?'

'Of course, but I am ashamed of it. The laziness of the Negroes and the lies they tell. Do you know they have black people's magazines in America which pretend that the Negro has a history as big as the white man's? It makes me angry because I know it is not true, so why should they pretend?'

'It depends what is meant by great. Without a written past, how can you know anyway? There is wonderful African art, from which European artists have learned. And in Guyana the Negroes seem to be the intellectuals, more interested in cultural things than any other race.'

'You cannot understand—the black side in me is so very different. I belong to two opposite cultures. I want to go to Africa and see my fellows there, and what they are really like. I want to help them to get educated and meet the world. I want to know what it is like really to be a Negro in Africa. Every educated black Guyanese would like to know that—but he also fears what he will find, because already we know we here are different.'

'But you would secretly prefer to be a white man?'

'Of course, if I could be accepted—because white men have all the advantages. Partly it is education, but also I think it is because they know how to work. Most people here think about nothing but sex and sport. And education itself after all—it is about white people. Shakespeare, Joyce . . .'

'Don't you think that in time a true black civilisation or a civilisation of mixed-blood people will arise in the tropics?'

'Yes, that is sure—yet now, still, we are looking to Europe and America for leads—have you read *Ulysses*?'

'Yes.'

'It is a most enjoyable but dirty book. A great work of literature that everyone out here would like to imitate. I do writing myself and I realise its greatness, but I fear its sensual influence. We Guyanese have to watch ourselves, because true civilisation is impossible without sublimation.'

'Probably true. But I think of it as a very naturalistic and true book, full of sadness.'

'Yes, but everybody picks out only the mellow, smellow, smellonious buttocks type of bits. Pornography and lust are enjoyable, but they dissipate the ability for continuous effort. In the old days religion would hold a man back, but modern freethinking men have to fight lonely battles. That is why I think marriage will grow more and more important as religion declines.'

'That's an interesting viewpoint.'

'Sex is the greatest danger to the African. If he suppresses it he becomes a prig and a dictator. If he lets it free, his life is dependent on it, he can't do without it, and it uses all his energy. That is why polygamy is important!'

'I have heard that some of the local religions believe in very free sex?'

'That is correct, Sir. There are some sects that worship in a completely animal way.' His face glowed. 'The worst is the "No Underclothes" people. They assemble in a large hall outside Georgetown, and they sing hymns and dance till they have froth running out of their mouths. Then all the lights are put out and they have to take off their underclothes and be naked before God.'

'What about the wish-come-true man—do you know about him?'

'There is more than one, Sir. That is a whole religion. If you pay ten dollars your wish will come true within three days. Mostly people wish about love and jobs. It is a religion for the man who wants to get on in the world.'

'What about the Ethiopian Church?' I had seen a most beautifully clad procession, headed by one Bishop Mar Loukas, in the streets of Georgetown.

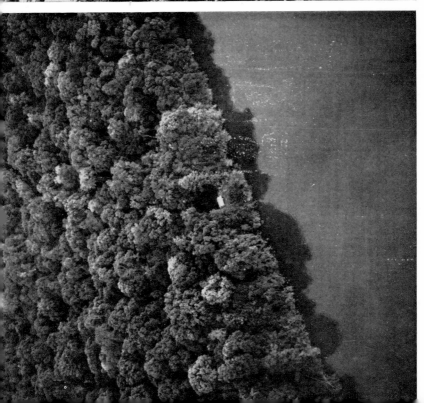

The camp opposite Omai seen from the air and the river

'They are growing, because everybody turns to Africa, and of course to Haile Selassie and the Abyssinians most of all, because they have always been free.'

'But they are not Negroes! They are supposed to be a different race!'

'Yes, but they are Africans.'

Half a mile more of wading brought us to another creek where tall Ité palms spread their fans along the bank.

'Does this mean more savannah ahead?' I asked Jonah. He pointed at the water and said, 'No. Dakama forest. Wherever there is Dakama, you will find water like that.'

I had heard of Dakama (Dimorphandra conjugata), a leguminous tree said to grow to enormous size, but seldom found as far north as Bartica. The water was certainly of a colour I had not seen before, like liquid damson jam or blackcurrant jelly, a really rich, dark colour even when held in the hand. I drank some, and it had a sour taste.

Beyond here we walked on level white sand overlain in places by peat, among Moroballis, Apoucouita, and other trees of boggy soils. Then rapidly the aspect of the countryside changed to that of one of the rarest and most impressive vegetations on earth—the herculean Dakama forest. I was bowled over by it: there was little undergrowth and few seedlings, so that one could see clearly its extraordinary features— the enormous size of the individual trees, which were commonly 4 to 6 feet in diameter, 10 to 18 feet in girth, and rising in great scaly, black-barked columns to loose colossal branched umbrella crowns 160 feet above. Almost no other trees were present, and these vast stems sprang from hillocks of fallen leaves and twigs 6 to 8 feet high, which had accumulated around the base of each trunk, evidently since each had been a seedling; giving an undulating landscape of immense coppery mole hills, each with a tree-giant at its summit.

Even between the trees the leaf-litter was often 8 feet thick, as we found by digging in the hole left by a fallen tree's roots, turning into rich, wet, black peat before finally we came down to sand lying thinly over clay.

I examined the leathery fallen leaves, golden brown, oval in shape, and fully 9 inches long and 6 across. What a weapon! With showers of these the Dakama smothered all competition,

L

taking over areas of forest until it occupied them completely.
Why then was mature Dakama forest so rare? Was it because
the trees were easily blown over? Here, obviously, they were
very shallowed-rooted. Impervious clay lay just below the sand,
and the ground was criss-crossed with recumbent colossi. Like
the leaves, these were very slow to decay, so that in a hundred
feet we had to scramble over fifteen, several more than 4 feet in
diameter. Yet between these logs grew the present forest—so
clearly wind-blowing was not the answer. Puzzled, I climbed
along the logs, jumping from one to another (it was easier to
travel this way), and for more than a mile we continued so until
the line was finished—seldom touching the ground, marvelling
at the incredible spectacle of this forest.

Of course, this made it even easier than usual to lose the cut
line—especially as there was so little undergrowth to be cleared
—as I soon realised when the usual return race for the boat
began. By now I was careful, especially when out of sight of
anyone, to watch for the tiny signs on the ground, trees, and
twigs that indicated the path. Failure to do so meant being
lost in a minute in the maze of leaves. It was late—we had only
about two hours before sunset in which to get back to the boat
—so after missing the line several times as I negotiated fallen
logs, I kept close to Justin, the axe man. By the time we
reached the swamps, the light was beginning to fade. We
waded, swam and floundered, and were the last to arrive back
at the boat—except for Lord, who was usually first, as he took
pride in having been a notable runner at school.

We waited, worried, and halloed again and again. But there
was no reply. We banged a Mora buttress with the axe. Nothing.
Lord evidently had lost his way, and now night was falling. He
had last been seen far back in the Dakama forest, racing hard to
get ahead of everyone else. It was dark already.

'This is serious,' murmured Jonah. 'Let's hope he clever
enough not to go far.'

'We must get torches and lanterns,' I said. 'We'd better go
back to camp and return.'

'Yes—better let the men eat—they have had a hard day,' said
Jonah. 'Then we can return and find him fresh. If he stays still
he will be safe. But if he tries to find his way, we may never
reach him.'

So, leaving a man at the waterside in case he should arrive, we set sail. Horrific tales that I had heard of men lost in the jungle came back to me as we journeyed, ate, and returned. Even Kunyow, an experienced bushman, had been lost, turned aside by floods. Without a compass Lord could never traverse the swamps. At night snakes, jaguars, and other dangerous creatures would be on the move—but even worse would be exposure to damp and cold, hunger and fear.

Basil and I chatted as he steered us by the stars and the dark silhouettes of the forested shore.

'Even from Bartica men gets lost. Last year a man go out to get sawarri nuts and he lost for six weeks. Dey find he by Potaro landing, 100 miles away. He was alive, but he lost his mind. All that time he must have lived just on nuts and wild fruit, because he drop he knife, and nearly all his clothes gone. Another man dey find dead only 100 yards from de path, an' 3 miles from a village. Other people jus' disappear. Best thing Lord could do is try to climb up in a tree fork, above the ground.'

It was decided to work in two shifts, and six volunteers set off first, carrying all our torches and lamps, banging on buttresses and shouting as they went.

After two hours we could hear them returning—and with them was Lord, wet, shivering, cold and hungry, and only just recovering from his despair. He had been found 2 miles inland and half a mile from the line, in the middle of a tangled corkwood swamp. He had lost the line, and had run on instead of stopping and searching. Then he had followed a creek, thinking it would lead him to the Essequebo. But it had wound away inland and disappeared into the floods. Bewildered, he had started to make himself some sort of dry perch for the night, when he had heard the men banging on a tree. Then he had struck on a corkwood buttress again and again with his cutlass, until at last they had heard and found him.

The following day on a line only 2 miles above the camp we emerged about half a mile inland on to a slightly rising plain of soft, powdery, silver-grey sand. There was a cheer from the men when they realised that at last, so unexpectedly close to the river, we had struck through to the true white sand peneplain that must everywhere lie behind the swamp.

On it grew an almost pure forest of cylindrical brown trunks:

Wallaba trees typical of white sand, rising from the ground with hardly any buttresses. Amongst them were a few columnar Baromallis (Catostemma spp.), and here and there a few Cassia apoucouita, against whose iron-hard wood our cutlasses rang loud as we slashed our way. Their pale yellow flowers lay in thick drifts on the ground amid a thin growth of young Wallabas, through which we could see far ahead. The forest was light and open, and pineapple—like Bromeliads, typically found only on high branches—grew low down or even on the ground.

From the air I had viewed other regions of white sand—which in places may be hundreds of feet thick—and had seen the fern-like pattern of rivers eroding their way into it over the underlying clay layers, of springs emerging in lines of gulley-heads along the sides of its rolling hills.

These white sand areas received the same rainfall as their surroundings, but rainwater falling on them sank straight through, so their forests had to withstand much drier conditions, and belonged to another climax series which we classified as 'Xeromorphic Rain Forests'. Now, as we walked forward, this erosion pattern began to unfold on the ground. The water in the creeks we crossed was of a vivid iodine colour, characteristic of the drainage from these sands because it is full of dissolved tannins from fallen Wallaba leaves.

Then slowly the forest began to become more open, giving place to low woodland with an undergrowth of bracken, rather like a Scottish birch wood. Lying on the ground were numerous charred logs, evidence of a forest of large trees that had been swept away by fire. Through a succession of glades we went, haunted by a small bird which made a restless sound like a jangling spring: 'twanga-wang-a-wang'.

'Dakama 16 inches! Dakama 40 inches,' called out the caliper men—and a few colossi began to appear, perched high on their mounds of accumulated debris, while the ground became as springy as a mattress. I expected a new view of the previous day's titanic landscape but the trees were mostly twisted and misshapen, sometimes half bent over. Then, of a sudden the forest ended and we were walking through a dry sand heath with coarse grasses and small scattered trees, with ahead of us a scene like one of Paul Nash's Battle of Britain paintings. As far ahead as I could see, grim and silent, ranks upon ranks of enormous dead trees raised their silvery branches against a cornflower-blue sky—dead Dakamas, all burned out by some terrible fire.

I climbed one of the living trees on the edge of the desolation, a fig with small green inedible fruit. From its branches, 20 feet or so above the ground, I could look for miles in every direction. As far as the eye could penetrate the area of burnt forest stretched ahead; but on either side, three or four miles away, it was bounded by dark walls of high forest, rising on the left to the flat top of Mount Arisaru, which lay formidably flanked by precipices, like a great aircraft-carrier along the horizon. This then, doubtless, was the puzzling countryside that I had seen from its summit, when these burnt tree skeletons had looked, in their thousands, like a field of stubble.

I climbed down, and picked my way forward through the fallen tree skeletons. Among them a new vegetation was growing up, a high shrubbery of young White Cedar trees, bushes of Melastomes and Malpighiaceae covered in pink scented flowers, and in the glades between, open savannah-like stretches of knee- and waist-high grass-like plants, mostly Xyridaceae with three-petalled flowers, primrose yellow, or of an unbelievably intense sky-blue—bluer than the chicory of chalky waysides—forming fields of colour bending gently with the wind. Foot-deep water from the recent rains flowed delicious and clear or stood cool and beautiful between these grassy clumps.

Growing up from the crowns of the fallen trees (in which doubtless they had lived when they were still standing) were numerous extraordinary aroids, mostly Anthuriums and Monsteras, which, expanding in the unlimited sun and moisture now available to them, had developed gargantuanly into small erect trees of their own, 10 and 15 feet high, with stout trunks curiously pock-marked by the scars of their fallen leaves.

We sat and lunched on a silvery log. It was a curiously peaceful scene, damp yet sunny. Bibulous bunyahs bubbled in the bushes, or flipped their yellow tails in the line of trees from which we had emerged. Dragonflies hovered in the sunlight, and mouse-big black and sulphur bumble-bees cruised among the Xyrid flowers. From the size of the young trees and other plants I guessed that the area had been burnt in 1940, a notable drought and fire year in Guyana. The fire had not only killed the Dakama trees, but had destroyed the thick layer of litter and peat upon which they habitually grew. In Guyana's rare drought years forest fires were frequent, sometimes caused by lightning, more usually by the spontaneous combustion of drying out peat. All the water that now flowed around would formerly have been held in those 6- or 8-foot-deep layers of decomposing vegetation typical of Dakama forest, while now it flowed over clay 9 inches down.

Dakama forest had previously been described as a form of Xeromorphic Rain Forest (like Wallaba forest), but I now see that it was often part of a peat-forming landscape process—of a putative Bog Rain Forest series. Most Dakama forests hitherto described had been in the eastern part of the country, where the tree typically formed a low scrubby woodland, quite unlike the magnificence of its mature form. There it grew on white sand that was thin—and eroded away almost to the impervious clay beneath. If such low Dakama forests were not destroyed by fire then their litter would eventually begin to hold water and produce peat—at which point the trees could develop into their gigantic form. Dakama woodland, therefore, was to begin with part of the Xeromorphic Rain Forest series, but by changing its own environment, it moved from one series to another, and turned into part of the Bog Rain Forest series: but giant Dakama forest might also develop direct from other Bog Rain Forests in which Dakama grew, by smothering the seedlings of the other species. In the present burnt area, for example, as could be seen by the enormous numbers of young White Cedars and Maddaburi with which the area was covered, it was obvious that a White Cedar bog was evolving. Perhaps, after another few hundred years, the Dakama might return—if other factors had not altered in the interim. Meanwhile a new succession had started—Xyrids, Malpighiaceae, White Cedar, and Maddaburi. There were no young Dakama present. But once they came in and established a foothold, they could certainly become dominant again—smothering the ground in thick layers of slow decaying twigs, leaves and trunks, eliminating the competition of all but their own seedlings. Yet this weapon with which they destroyed all rivals also made them uniquely

vulnerable—to fire, in times of drought, when their litter
became dry. Undoubtedly this was the reason why few mature
Dakama forests have ever been seen (or indeed exist)—despite
their potential total dominance of boggy areas. They were like
some conquering horde incapable of establishing a lasting
dominance over the defeated.

Our last venture from the camp by the Cayman's Lagoon
took us upstream several miles. It was a morning of rolling river
mists with dense white clouds sweeping downstream, enveloping the camp, leaving the leaves and canvas dripping. In the
launch, drenched with dew, we steered by compass and
current over the calm oyster-grey water, only occasionally
illuminated by a probing sunshaft, while from the unseen outside world came the howling of monkeys, the screeching of
parrots overhead as they fluttered along in twos and threes.

Slowly the air cleared, the sun shone down from a cobalt sky,
and we found ourselves close in by the grey wall of Awaraballi
palms. They rose in a high bank from water 10 feet deep or
more, with the outer, younger plants almost completely submerged: an impassable barrier of terrible thorns 100 yards deep
and over half a mile long, consisting of this single species in solid
growth, save where a wisp of liane struggled through here and
there. On the long, grey-green leaves iguanas sunned themselves,
plunging like arrows into the water as we drew near.

Further upstream we dragged the boat through the solid
barrier of green which rose from the water, chopping branches,
small trees, and spiny palms with cutlasses and axes. In the
gloom within was a many-years-deserted camp site, its muddy
beaches indented with the footprints and central tail-lines of
wandering caymans. Mora and Kakaralli trees formed a high
roof over the miserable stumps of smaller felled trees, the
mouldering old tent poles and collapsed fragments of palm
thatch. We found a model of a banjo carved out of now rotten
wood, and one or two old bottles:

> 'Tis now the vampire's bleak abode,
> 'Tis now the apartment of the toad;
> 'Tis here the painful Chegoe feeds,
> 'Tis here the dire Labarri breeds,
> Conceal'd in ruins, moss, and weeds.

As Charles Waterton said of his own former jungle home in Guiana.

A large yellow and brown tortoise wandering near the trail was picked up by Kunyow and hung from a tree by a twisted piece of liane. Tortoises had the advantage over other wild game that they could be hung on a tree by the shell, or turned over on their backs and left alive until a supply of fresh meat was needed. Then they would be smashed against a stone or log, the head cut off, the still wriggling mass of flesh cooked and eaten. The very red beefy-flavoured meat was delicious—but after seeing one or two killed in this way, I could no longer bring myself to eat them.

A quarter of a mile inland deep water stopped us and we returned to the boat. Kunyow, the Castillean nobleman, sat in the bow, his tortoise at his feet, and produced strangled tootings from a broken bottle he had picked up at the abandoned camp, and whose bottom he had knocked out. At once a pair of macaws in a tree overhead took up the challenge, and to this duet of enraged sounds we pushed out into the river. Then louder than all came another noise—the drone of an engine. Another boat? But this was overhead: floating over the jungle rim came a little red and yellow single-engined two-seater seaplane. It dipped low as it saw us, swung round in a wide circle—a hand waved—and continued following the river upstream and out of sight.

I was stupefied. Where had it come from? A Dakota flying to the far interior, or a Grumman Goose from B.G. Airways, I could have understood. But I did not know that such an aeroplane existed in the country. Could it be the property of a rancher or a trader returning to the Rupununi? Lebourg from Dukduik had spoken to me at the Bristolburg of his plans to fly a group of prostitutes to the mining country along the Brazilian border—could this be his plane? But it was too small for his purpose—it was simply a pleasure plane. I envied the pilot his freedom, his carelessness aloft. But I resented his detachment from my jungle world. I felt that the seriousness of my life in it and of what I was doing was challenged by such frivolity. It was like the sight of a Rolls-Royce being driven through the slums of Calcutta—out of its proper context, and disturbing, even insulting to the inhabitants.

That night as I was about to go to bed we again heard a distant engine. As it came nearer we flashed torches and were answered by pin-points of light a mile or so away across the river. In our loneliness it was wonderful to hear the sound of other travellers. As the lights drew nearer we raised flickering flambeaux above our heads, and out of the darkness, like a ghost rolling over the jet black water, came a large open boat packed with sleepy men, balata bleeders and miners—a wild, rough-looking lot. Grappling hooks and ropes were flung out and they tied up. They had rations for us, and the cases and drums were quickly unloaded. In the uncertain lamplight dark sweating faces and torsos gleamed oilily. Old friends waved and shouted greetings. Men swarmed ashore, and for a while the camp was lively with laughter and joking. Then quite suddenly they were all gone—for they planned to spend the night 20 miles up-river—and the camp was empty and quiet again. The engine faded away, lights were snuffed out. All we were left with was a pile of stores, a parcel of letters, and an unsettled excited feeling—a sudden yearning to be back again amongst men.

10

Gold

With smooth engine we swung up the narrowing river. Hour
after hour the monotonous scenery flowed past. Mount Arisaru's precipitous sides faded behind. To each camp that we
left we remained attached by a thread of possible return, our
emotions suspended between its certain shelter and the possibilities ahead.

'Oh my! Omai!' shouted a man—'I go drink rum and dance
over dey tonight!'

Straight in front of us, amongst a jumble of hills, was the
unexpected scintillation of a whole hillside of galvanised iron
roofs. From the name on the map I had imagined a miserable
hovel or two, like Rockstone; but this was huge, obviously a
flourishing mining camp—almost civilisation. As we drew close
I could hear the hum of engines, the sound of a radio.

Perversely, I felt depressed. Instead of the verde walls of the
river banks I should have opposite me a bustling clearing, harsh
in the sunlight. Tin roofs, lorries revving, dance music—I
detested the thought. My men would become restive, and so
should I; I should feel the urge for human society, and lose my
solitude without finding companionship. I directed the boat
into all the little bays and creeks on both sides of the river, in an
effort to find a camp site where I would not be able to see Omai.
But the land was all low-lying and swampy, except directly
opposite. So there we drove in to a dark mud beach, where
dusty leaves above our heads proclaimed the falling water-level.
A wisp of lichen-like river bats—mere flickering phantoms,
scarcely credible as flesh and blood—flitted away as we
climbed roots and buttresses up the 12-foot-tall near-vertical
bank—to a level terrace of hard earth, a perfect camp ground.
While clearings were being made I strolled up and down the lip
of the cliff, surveying the mine. At the river's edge the little red

and yellow float-plane of the previous day was moored to a
wooden ramp, high up on which stood a Grumman Goose
amphibian. Beyond this was a large tin-roofed building, open
on all sides, while scattered over the bare hillside were many
pleasant looking little thatched houses.

Across the water came an aluminium canoe with two
Europeans in it. They hailed me from below, and came scrambling up the cliff—an occasion, I felt, when drinks like molten
lava should be tossed down the throats of all present to set a seal
on friendship. Instead I invited them to share my tea. I con-
vinced them that my purpose was forest exploration, not the
establishment of a secret brothel for their employees, as they
had feared, and we parted with invitations to visit one another.
But inwardly I resolved to continue my solitary life.

The Kakaralli trees which stood all round the camp were in
full blossom and filled the air with fragrance and a delicate
snowstorm of white and yellow flowers. I would look up into
the dark glossy leaves and watch as the flowers came tumbling
down in hundreds. From the roof of my tent came a continual
soft swish as they descended upon it and slid down the sides.
They covered the ground, and Boodhoo had to sweep them
aside into drifts so that we could walk to and fro without
crushing them. In the under-storey trees termite's nests hung
like tremendous footballs. When low enough the men slashed
them with their cutlasses, and said 'Lazy! come out and do
some work!' as they watched them scurrying out to repair the
damage. Under my tent a line of evidently underground-
dwelling termites emerged from a tiny hole, and then disappeared again a few feet further into the earth—unlike most
termites, which build an earthen tunnel as a protection against
light and enemies whenever they have to travel along the
surface.

The following morning a sound like distant artillery awoke
me just as leaves were becoming black silhouettes against the
grey river. Then I was aware of a curious fetid smell—and
Basil came rushing up in great excitement to borrow my gun,
for a herd of five or six hundred peccaries was coming towards
the camp! The men had smelled them earlier, and had been
about scouting on their down-wind fringes. Food was again
very short, because of the discrepancies in the rations sent us,

and if we could kill one or two it would make a great difference.

I roused myself, handed over the gun and some cartridges, put on a pair of gumboots, picked up my cutlass, and raced into the forest. The cloying odour of the pigs was borne in powerful gusts upon the air, while the rumbling was growing so loud that one could distinguish the noise of individual trampling feet and clashing tusks. It was still dark, but suddenly ahead I saw a torrent of coarsely hairy forms and flashing teeth galloping towards me through the undergrowth. These were the big white-lipped peccary (Tayassu peccari), long feared as one of the most dangerous animals of the South American forests, with a reputation for concerted attack, decisive use of razor-like tusks, and for waiting in bristling groups around treed hunters. There was no time to consider their reputation, however, for by this time the herd was upon me, and I was upon them, with waving cutlass. At close quarters the stench was terrible—but the animals, being lower on the ground, were running much faster than I could, weaving in and out of the undergrowth, and in a moment more I had lost sight of them, though I could hear them all around and thundering away into the distance.

A few seconds later the men came streaming past in pursuit, guns and cutlasses in hand, blue cotton shirts flying. The pigs had taken alarm before they had been close enough to shoot, and it might be hours before contact could be made again. I listened to the sounds of the chase circling away far off, as I made my way back to the riverside and along it to the camp. Half an hour later came three shots in rapid succession, then a fourth. Three huge pigs, each weighing nearly 100 pounds, had been shot—by Albert Smith and Leno Thomas who came staggering in with them across their shoulders. One, a boar, had had a large circular patch of flesh containing the scent gland removed from its back, lest the scent contaminate the meat.

It was several hours before everyone was back, and mid-morning before we could start work cutting inland behind the camp. Soon came 2-feet-deep water, thick sedges, and undergrowth full of a bush-sized species of Kakaralli with velvety claret-coloured flowers. A tapir fled on the right with heavy crashings, leaving behind his deeply incised hoof-marks and piles of green dung. A swamp deer sprang away through the shrubbery; a tinamou rose like a rocket at our feet—and in the distance I could hear monkeys crashing through the tree-tops. Overhead, brilliantly pendant from the branches of a tall tree, was a cluster of macaws. Even more than at Arisaru, we were in a dry world where animals were abundant. But while that had been an isolated mountain, this was the edge of an upland area stretching to the Potaro, the Pakaraima mountains, and beyond into Venezuela and Brazil.

Behind the low levee bank that terminated this swamp lay a vegetable fantasy—a bog of Maddaburi trees (Clusia). When young these trees produce roots like the ribs of a crinoline around them. Then the central roots die, and the trees are borne upwards on their circle of stilts, which finally may be 6 to 8 feet high and 3 inches thick, forming a structure like an old-fashioned parrot cage, from the top of which the tree—usually symmetrical, with precisely arranged rosettes of pointed leaves and pink and white magnolia-like flowers—rises another 30 feet or more.

Beyond this bog a gradually rising plain of brown sand bore the most magnificent greenheart forests I had ever seen. In every acre there were over thirty greenheart trees above 12 inches in diameter, comprising 53 per cent of the trees of that size, and they were all tall and perfectly shaped, a wonderful sight as the afternoon sun streamed in almost vertical pencils through their foliage. The undergrowth was sparse, and I could see perhaps a hundred feet or more into the shimmer of leaves. A curious haunted feeling comes from never being able to fix one's gaze upon anything definite. In the forest everything is different, yet the same; the mind has no point of attachment, and one exists as if lost in fog, steering by compass, slashing trees to give identity to one's course. A stream or gully forms a reference, seized upon with gratitude, and so now was a huge rock standing a little way off the path amongst the trees. It was eerie to see there, a silent mass of primeval fluid earth injected through the crust and now weathered, shattered, rising out of the sand. I felt uneasy till I had walked around it, probed it for devils and spirits, seen if it was inhabited by anything more disturbing than echoes.

On the opposite bank, behind Omai, where mountains rose out of the alluvium and the white sand plain, and curved around in a thousand-foot-high ridge, there were innumerable irregular knife-edge spurs running towards the river which our lines had to cross. They were of dolerite, with slippery slopes of red lateritic clay, forming a landscape quite new to me. For many days we struggled up their breathtakingly steep sides on hands and knees, or hauled ourselves up clinging to lianes and bushes. Wherever the slopes were gentler, and on the brown sand plains and gravel terraces on the riverward side of these mountains, we would come to stretches of forest dominated by Wirimiri trees (Eschweilera Confertiflora), showering rapidly-decomposing deep red flowers on the earth.

Many were the vegetable mysteries that present themselves in these hills—one day we found an Eschweilera of a species new to science which we called the 'Broad-leaved Kakaralli'. It had rough bark and unusually elegant, slim buttresses; and its leaves were large and ovate, unlike the smaller pointed leaves of its cousins. Just beyond it grew two giant legumes, Dicymbe altsonii, known as the 'Clump Wallaba' because it forms an enormous bole surrounded by minor trunks. In one tree this central bole had died and rotted away, and the subsidiaries, now each of great size, formed an immense coppice springing 140 feet into the air. Their presence indicated that we were on the edge of a new vegetational region, that of the Pakaraima mountain. There this tree, according to Jonah, formed almost pure forests upon the white sand—forests in which a man must feel like a beetle walking through a hazel coppice in England.

There was every reason to believe that the Guyana lowlands were being invaded by plants from two directions—from the Pakaraima mountains to the south-west, and from Amazonia and Brazil to the south, from whence were coming such species as the balatas and the prickly Awaraballi palms. The lowland area in which we were working had apparently been a shallow sea in late Cretaceous or even more recent times, when the Pakaraimas, now far inland, had formed the coast, while Arisaru, the Omai hills and other mountains had been offshore islands. Guyana contained more 'endemic' species of plants— plants found nowhere else—than one would expect in part of a continental land mass, and they were thought to have evolved upon such isolated island areas, and to have spread into the lowlands when these eventually emerged from the sea. Indeed, some were still spreading, such as the Greenheart; others, such as the Wirimiri and the Clump Wallaba, appeared to have spread only a little way, while still others remained neither multiplying nor decreasing upon the hilltops upon which perhaps they had originally evolved. Some of these isolated trees were thought perhaps to be among the most ancient species of flowering plants existing, survivors of forests that had been relatively undisturbed since Cretaceous times, for the Pakaraima mountains form one of the oldest known comparatively unchanged land surfaces. Their great masses, like Mount Roraima, are true 'Lost Worlds' bearing an unique flora and fauna of endemics, where if anywhere one might hope for clues to the origins of flowering plants—of which little is known.

On one steep lateritic slope I found a small undergrowth tree which neither I, nor any of the Indians, had ever seen before. It had a dark, smooth trunk clothed with stout thorns (rare in the jungle, except in palms) from which, when slashed, white milk poured. We searched for flowers or fruit but could find none, but from its milk and leaves guessed it must belong to the Apocynaceae. Four years later I found and identified other specimens of this tree—on the Wai-Wai expedition, at Shiuru-tiri, in northern Para 300 miles south. It was a Lacmellea. Another equally isolated and mysterious tree stood upon a small hill east of Omai. It was of mighty dimensions, with a buttressed trunk 30 feet in circumference that rose out of sight above the general level of the tree-tops to a fine mist of leaves and branches 180 feet above the ground. There would have been no possibility of obtaining specimens of its leaves had not parrots, far out of sight in the branches above, torn off twigs and leaves and dropped them abundantly upon the ground below. In his entire life Jonah had only once seen another specimen of this tree—at the Penal Settlement, Mazaruni—and we never saw another.

How could such trees exist so isolated? Were they the remnants of a formerly more extensive population, now almost extinct, or outriders of some yet distant vegetable invasion? Whales in the ocean inevitably become extinct when their numbers fall below about 500, for difficulty in finding a mate; similarly among plant species there must be a critical number below which they can no longer survive. This, however, may be very small in the case of plants which are self-fertile, and it made me wonder how common self-fertility, cleistogamy, and apomyxis might be in these jungles.

These laterite hills, with their speckled light and shade, Indian-red earth, falling pink flowers and bird songs, were full of unexpected little streams in deep-walled gulleys. Often our course took us along these streams towards their sources. The gully walls would become higher and steeper, even in places overhanging. Occasionally the whole gully, stream and all, would shoot up vertically in a precipice 40 or 50 feet high, as though someone had taken a deep semi-circular bite out of the hillside, and sometimes we would have to climb round and over two or three of these sudden walls of clay and rubble. Eventually, we would reach the source, where from the base of the final semi-lunar precipice clear water flowed out from the earth, often above a pink impervious layer of bauxite of the lurid colour of false teeth gums.

The actual ridge summits, where rusty ironstone often out-cropped in decaying masses as on Arisaru, were usually covered by low shrubbery and tangled festoons of bush ropes. Curiously enough, the trees on these dry slopes were often identical with those in the peaty, waterlogged Manni bogs. Perhaps it was absence of competition that allowed certain highly adaptable species to flourish in both places: slim Sarebebeballis, Aromata (the fish poison tree), Parakusan and Manobodin and Cassia apoucouita, whose trunk looked like a consolidated mass of vines, with holes right through from one side to the other.

There were a number of such 'ropy' trees. What could be the advantage of this curious type of trunk? I sometimes wondered whether such trees had evolved from lianes—there were several lianes closely related to the genus Cassia—or from parasites like the giant figs, which surrounded their victims in a mass of gradually fusing stems.

Near Omai we followed one little stream, its sandy banks rich with delicate plants, purple leaved Nautilocalyx, dew-spangled filmy ferns, Marantaceae and wild gingers. Then two deep ditches, partly choked, struck out from the stream side— clearly the work of men. Along them we came to an old clearing where great white piles of quartz dust shone in the sunlight, abandoned years before when the gold in the gravel had ceased to pay. Underfoot were the collapsed remains of batelles, tent posts, decaying palm thatch. We paused for a moment, watching the fairy-like dance of sun on quartz, each pile of which radiated an intense light like a heap of diamonds, making the cavernous darkness of the trees around seem doubly profound. It was like a stage set for *A Midsummer Night's Dream*, with sunbeams playing and butterflies dancing over the red-bracted flowers of Cephaelis, the vermilion-glowing spikes of congo cane, the purple berries of Melastomes, borne atop rich thick foliage like jewels proffered on the out-stretched palms of green hands. No sound broke the mystery save the gurgling of the stream and the greenheart birds shouting in the hills around.

This opening was like a lens through which the jungle gazed up at the sky, and through which the sun and moon could look down into its sadness: into that continent of almost perpetual darkness which was our work place. Even the Indians do not live in the forest. They make large clearings which change its character, or dwell by the riverside. Soon these forests will be destroyed or tamed like the once glorious northern forests, now degraded into timber crops. Their mystery will be gone. There will no longer be that same wonder which made me pause at the sight of a broken saucepan, telling of a man's brief life of a few months here.

A little above this clearing, where the stream flowed twisting out of a deep ravine, we found a place for lunch. Exhausted by the steep hillsides and the mental effort of learning the names of unfamiliar trees, I lay on the cool sands that spread at a bend in the stream. After I had eaten I took off my clothes and swam, whilst upstream Justin Joseph and Jonah fished for yarraus. Kunyow caught a number simply by chopping at them with his cutlass. Then a quick slash upwards from the wrist, and he decapitated in flight a tiny bird that flitted past. 'Good for bait!' —he smiled at my querulous look, tucking the bloody body into his shirt pocket. The water was starred with the blue flowers of a Petraea vine, whose panicles hung high up in the trees like bunches of grapes; as I floated I could watch the little flowers come spiralling down between the epiphyte-laden branches.

In half an hour's collecting I found eighteen distinct species of ferns from the rich carpet that covered the many ironstone and dolerite boulders of the stream-bed—mostly delicate and

M

beautiful species of Trichomanes. One grew on an old prospectors' notice, painted in black and white on a rusting tin can
hammered flat—one of several loosely nailed on the trees or on
once stout posts in the ground—claims for so many square feet
of ground. Its owners were probably long since dead, but their
names lived on in the lonely woods:

JUPITER JACOBS

&

STANILAUS MONTGOMERY

Lic. No. 2031 A

Nov. 6, 1921

With the continued dry weather kabaura flies had become
numerous, and despite the use of 'Shoo!' my ankles were so
swollen and blood-blistered from their bites that they over-
lapped my shoes, while my groin and waist were so reddened by
the bites of Bêtes Rouges that they looked as if I had been
whipped. Mosquitos and sandflies had also become a terrible
nuisance, and in the evening I was driven to wearing thick
wollen socks and long trousers tied at the ankles, while each
night I went through the routine of removing pests from my
body. Fortunately, Kunyow had constructed a little jetty out
into the river from which I could bathe. There also I would go
whenever I felt oppressed by the weight of leaves around and
overhead. I never failed to find refreshment sitting there, just
watching the gentle flow of tea-coloured water and its cargo of
insects, leaves and flowers. One evening, descending the notched
tree-trunk that served for a ladder, to throw buckets of water
over myself, I noticed a pair of bright eyes looking at me from
below the platform. I paused, threw a stick into the water, and
a small cayman about 2 feet long flipped its tail, gave a miniature roar, and sank from view. A moment later it reappeared
among some leaves dangling in the water; so I called Little
Rufus, and we shot several toy arrows at it which glanced off
but drove it away.

   This little incident luckily put me on the alert, for a few
days later when I was again about to step on to the bathing

stage, I noticed a curious light in the water, like a chequerboard just below the surface. It was not very obvious, but it was puzzling, so I stopped. It was the back of an enormous submerged cayman. Its back and tail projected several feet to one side, and underneath the sticks of the landing stage I could now see its unblinking eyes fixed on me. I climbed to the top of the bank again and threw a lump of wood, which struck it square on the back. It at once sank, and swam underwater to a mass of foliage which trailed in the river. I fetched my gun and shot into the mass. There was a moment of wild tumult amongst the leaves and branches, then the cayman surfaced about 50 yards out from the shore, and swam away upstream, looking as large as a motor boat. For the next few days it hung around the camp, cruising off shore at night, its eyes shining like two rubies whenever I shone my torch over the water. Sometimes it lay in hiding under the bank by the men's camp, but never very close; sometimes under my landing stage. Then a week later to my relief it disappeared and did not return.

Every Sunday morning as usual I supervised the issuing of the following week's rations of salt beef, salt fish, rice, dried peas, frying oil, biscuits and salt. We were supposed to receive a fresh supply each month, together with petrol and oil, and to have about a week's supply of everything always in hand. But in fact we had received over a fortnight's rations less than we should, and considerably less petrol than we needed, for the flooded condition of the forest had meant a lot of cruising up and down finding dry places to survey.

Each week Philbert, Jonah, and I had checked the rations again and again; and we had thought of every possible explanation to account for the discrepancies, such as that variations of atmospheric humidity had allowed the salted or dried foods to dry out, and so reduced their weight and volume. But nothing of this sort could account for the hugeness of the missing quantities, which by the end of the expedition amounted to one month's supplies—one-third. Some crass individual, quite likely in the office at Bartica, was being negligent. But for the success of the huntsmen, by now we should have been starving.

Now on this Sunday morning there was no food whatever to distribute. We had only enough to last until the end of the day, and the men were on the verge of rebellion. I had sent letters begging for food on every boat that passed, but we had received none. Fortunately, we now had the mine opposite us, and I steeled myself to go across and see if I could borrow—an odious task, for in the interior nobody, even a large mine, has a great deal to spare. It was particularly awkward because I had not yet been over even for a short visit.

We had listened for several days to the sounds of the radio, of the cars and machinery, of the voices which sometimes floated across a mile of waters. The little gaily coloured seaplane had circled the camp, the Grumman had roared its foaming way in take-off and landing on the water in front of us; and various furtive canoes had slipped across from the mine and spent the night on our side of the river. I could tell that the men were happy, for after dark their fires would flicker late, and faintly on the breeze there would come a slow rhythmic song from their camp—a melancholy arabesque on the night air, accompanied by a pensively plucked guitar. But I had been too tired in the evenings after work to join them or to go across, and I had also valued my tranquillity.

Now I made up my mind that I should have to go at once rather than ask the men to wait until the morrow, on the chance of a boat arriving with more supplies for us. But just as we pushed off, we saw on the far downstream horizon a faint silken line moving away from the shore, the first indications of a boat's wake. The silken line enlarged into a string of beads pulsating outwards, and then around a bend the boat came into view. Half an hour later it arrived, the camp was swarming with balata bleeders and pork-knockers, and we were saved.

I wrote yet another indignant note about our supplies, gave our visitors one of our wild pigs for their evening meal, and then they were off again, while we settled down at once to weighing, checking, and issuing what had arrived. To my surprise and dismay we had yet once again been sent short measure—but this time we had proof, in the form of an immediate check against the invoices, which were inaccurate. In a couple of weeks' time I should again be in a difficult position. Someone, somewhere, was probably making money out of our distress. I wrote yet another furious note and resolved to post it from the mine.

From the roof of the launch I watched the bare red cliffs, the black protruding boulders, the glaring aluminium roofs, as they drew nearer. New settlements are seldom pretty, but in the tropics they can be hideous as scar tissue. Here the felling of trees had exposed a raw red soil now covered by rank razor grass. Forest Indian settlements are soon surrounded by pine-apples, cassava, hibiscus and other flowers and shrubs. Their palm thatch is no more out of place than the dry leaves of the jungle floor. But Omai, in its superb setting of river and forest, was an area of devastated countryside, a midden of rusting petrol cans, broken bottles, oil-stained gravel. It was an exploratory mine, the first large-scale attempt to see if the reef-mining of gold (instead of alluvial washing) would pay in Guyana. Until that question was resolved no time was being wasted on beautifying it.

I tied up alongside the little rocking seaplane, and walked up the wooden ramp leading to the hangar of the olive-green Grumman amphibian. Along its side in yellow lettering was painted 'British Guiana Anaconda Gold Mines Limited', for this was a subsidiary of the then largest mining company in the world—Anaconda Copper.

'Hi, it's the botanist!' called a voice. 'We thought we were never going to see you!'—and all at once I found myself amongst a group of friendly people in their clubroom, having drinks, chatting, laughing, throwing aside the moroseness which my solitude had engendered. My new friends, mostly Americans or Canadians with a few strongly Americanised Guyanese, invited me to lunch and to spend the rest of the day with them. Their informality was heartening after British official circles. Within an hour my worries seemed trivial: difficulties were there to be solved, not magnified and made into a way of life.

After lunch the Manager, Jack Knaebel, showed me around the mine. We descended 300 feet by lift, and on our way I noticed that weathering of the solid rock had taken place down to 60 feet below the surface in this hot and humid climate, instead of at the most 2 or 3 feet, as in England. At this depth what looked like solid feldspar crystals were soft as butter, the granite itself merely clay containing sand grains. Then we got out into an under-world of deafening drills, tangled ventilator pipes and flaring lamps under a low, dripping, rocky ceiling. The air was saturated, the ground covered in dark pools of oily, muddy water. I wore a mackintosh and a helmet with a carbide lamp, from which flared a naked finger-like flame backed by a circular reflector. There was no actual gold to be seen, but little veins of gold-bearing quartz ran through the darker coloured dolerite. We walked to the drill face, where in ear-splitting semi-darkness a group of men stood behind the bucking machine, smoking cigarettes which they lighted at the helmet-flames. Knaebel shouted over his shoulder an explanation of what was going on. They were drilling in three eight-hours shifts towards what was hoped would prove to be a dome of richer auriferous rock, that had been revealed by vertical sample-holes.

Up above again, the sun was eye-blasting at first, after the darkness underground. I was taken to see the crushing and separating devices which sampled finer and finer specimens of the rock, ending up with powder. Then the assayer's shop where this powdered rock was fused in ovens, and finally the little buttons of pure gold from each sample, which were carefully weighed, and from which were calculated the yield. In this type of mining the veins of quartz, which were here exceedingly rich, were counted in with the other non-auriferous rock extracted, for it was the overall yield which mattered.

When the tonnage of rock per day which it was necessary to handle for the mine to pay had been calculated, the total amount of suitable rock in the area would be estimated to see if there was enough present for the mine to be able to operate long enough to make a profit. Costing, said Knaebel, was very tricky—for many factors were almost unpredictable, such as rates of exchange and the price of gold.

On the surface by the crusher were large piles of rejected rock of poor quality. A few minutes of scrambling, and Knaebel handed me a lump of quartz as a souvenir. On it was a little trace of metallic gold the size of a pin-head, while scattered through the lump itself were probably fine particles of gold, too small to see. At night, he said, the men would come secretly down to these mounds to search amongst the masses of grey stone for such pieces of quartz with glittering pin points.

We next drove up to a high point overlooking the workings, then returned to Jack's house for drinks. Like all the staff houses it was a small wooden building, thatched for coolness, simple in shape, practical in design. The single large main room at the rear exactly accommodated an army tent with fitted groundsheet and gauze walls, forming a damp- and insect-proof enclosure, entered through a rather close-fitting fabric sleeve. It provided a complete self-contained unit in which were the beds and cupboards, books, radios, all the perishable furnishings of a home. In front was an open pillared wooden verandah with fern baskets and flowers, deck-chairs, basket chairs and tables; while under the house was a shower and lavatory. Each home was well sited, with the maximum of privacy—from the balcony one could look up and down river for miles each way. I looked for my camp—but the forest appeared immaculate, inscrutable, save where a fallen tree sloped out over the water and a faint blue smoke haze hung low over the trees.

I spent much of the day in the company of the miners off duty—sentimental toughs full of old ballads, tear-jerking songs and obscenities. Superficially Jack appeared much like them, but away from them he stopped play-acting, and something else showed. Far from being incoherent and semi-literate, he had a highly organised intelligence, a wide variety of interests and tastes. He loved his life with its vagabond trappings, its freedom and adventure, and he cultivated the outward behaviour of the people he had to work with because while he could understand them, they could not understand him. But within him all the time was a cultivated mind, and even more, some poetry. I realised that I had a potential friend from the sensitivity with which he had guessed what I would want to see and know. But how could I return this understanding? How could I break through my pathetic sense of inadequacy, of poverty, of junior status—all the lack of self-confidence that my job had given me—and meet him on equal terms?

The red and yellow seaplane was his, and when the fierceness of the day was over he took me for a flight. He appreciated that this would be no mere pleasure, but would give me an understanding such as nothing else could of what I was doing. The plane was a little Aeronca, brilliantly coloured, spotlessly clean, smelling of aluminium and lubricating oil. It was so delicate and flimsy-seeming that I was afraid of pushing my feet through the floor when I got in. Harold Curtis, the company's pilot, swung the propeller and we raced away across the water, then rose with amazing lightness into the air. It was a revelation to float carelessly, sinuously above the green parsley beds through which for so many weeks I had been struggling on foot. Wide turns, steep banks, long side slips—I had never before realised the joy of flying, used as I was only to the unbending tedium of airliners. The world was a bubble and we floated in its centre, bathed in irridescence. Seen through a thousand feet of cobalt blue atmosphere, the forest beneath looked at first like a billowing mattress upon which one could have bounced. Then as the sun sank and the shadows grew longer it was transformed. The crowns of the taller trees rose illuminated from the darker background, sculptured delicately like a field of magic cauliflower heads. The flowering Futuis shone with the clear mauve incandescence of the heart of a gas flame, the trysils along the river bank with their plumes of white flowers were like mounds of dark green ermine, tasselled white. Distance smoothed the ripples from the water—and that silver mirror in the dark pile of the carpet was the Cayman's Lagoon; that slight collection of matchsticks fallen by the river's edge our last camp. Arisaro showed like a raft above the forest horizon to the north-east, while south and west, in the far distance, through gathering mist, what a magnificence of jumbled mountains! Chains and peaks, precipices, gorges and canyons, long spumy waterfalls, blue in the shadows of the valleys, yellow above in the setting sun: the Pakaraima mountains, stretching from the summit-cube of Eagle mountain beyond Kaieteur, to Roraima and the borders of Brazil and Venezuela.

Above them, the now setting sun was like a golden yolk in a glitter of resplendent clouds and veils of mist. The sky was molten, running with a thousand fires. Away from all familiar scales proportion was lost, and I felt surrounded by a terrifying chaos, a microbe witnessing the birth of a new star. Night was falling even in the upper air as we slipped down to the dark coiling river and ran splashing up to the ramp.

There followed an excellent dinner, drinks, music in cheerful company. I was exhilarated and happy as late that night I stepped aboard my boat to shouts of 'Come again! Come as often as you can!'

11

The Muniris

A few days later, on a Sunday morning I went fishing with Jonah, Basil, and Justin—for that evening I had invited some of my friends across for dinner.

We landed at a muddy line cut a few days previously on the eastward curve of the river downstream, a short way inland from which was a maze of swamps and waterways where a tortuous river doubled and redoubled across the low-lying plain. As I was balancing my way over this creek along a slender, twisting tacouba there was a thud of hooves followed by a shot, then a long crashing as a swamp deer rushed away from us. Basil had shot its fawn, a pretty brown creature with white spots, pathetic as it lay crumpled on the ground.

'If you rub it agains' de trees and you wait here, you goin' get de mother too,' said Justin.

'No, I don' wan' wait for long time. Leh she come back, an' if I find she when I return, den I go shoot she. But I ain' goin' a wait,' was Basil's reply.

As we crossed the river for the fifth or sixth time, we smelt wild hogs again then heard their grumbling. At once Basil and Justin decided to go on either side of the beasts, then charge in and slay them with their knives.

I told them to drive the pigs towards me as I wanted a good photograph, and stationed myself near a buttressed Mora behind which I could dodge at the last moment. I was just adjusting the camera when the entire horde burst like a broadside of cannon-balls from the bushes a few yards away. I jumped desperately up a little undergrowth tree. Huge boars, sows, tiny piglets rocketed past around and beneath me, whilst I felt the tree bending under my weight. Gently it deposited me on the ground as the last pig bolted past—then men and pigs were lost in the distance. The chase continued for half an hour without success, then we reassembled and went on, enlivened by tales of how Basil had actually laid hold of a pig, while Justin had chopped one (though not enough to inconvenience it), all demonstrated with leaps into the air, thwackings of cutlasses and shouts of excitement.

At this moment Jonah stopped: 'Good place here. Big haimara hole.' For we were after the enormous, ferocious, but deliciously white-fleshed haimara (Macrodon trahira).

With critical eye I inspected the spot he had chosen: midway between two hairpin bends (we were almost surrounded by water) the swift current had excavated a deep pool undermining roots and releasing stones, before swirling round in a powerful backwash and on past a little sandy spit.

First we laid about right and left, clearing a space in the undergrowth in which to manœuvre, and making a great deal of noise. Then, selecting a couple of young Yarri-Yarri trees (Anaxagorea sp.), a small straight-stemmed species with whorls of twigs at intervals like a Christmas tree, and tough, springy, aromatically-scented wood (said by experts to be even better than Greenheart for rods), we cut ourselves a pair of 15-foot poles. To each we tied 10-foot lengths of stout cord with a thick 18-inch wire leader bearing an enormous hook, big as a man's hand, and large enough to catch a shark. Then we baited each hook with a ragged tennis ball of blue and red freshly-bloody trumpeter bird meat.

Thus prepared, we marched to the very lip of the bank, flung in the baited hooks, and dunked the flesh slowly up and down so that a good infusion of blood and meat would mingle with the water. Then we issued our challenge; we struck the water hard a couple of times with our rods, poked them in and swished them round as if we were stirring soup, and flicked the surface with the tips.

This will scare every fish around! I thought, gazing down at our baits, held just visible 18 inches down in the brown water, and inwardly comparing our methods with those of a trout or salmon fisherman.

But crude though our procedure seemed, it worked. Within seconds a big grey body came hurtling up from the depths and my rod was almost snatched from my hands. My companion flung down his rod and stood with cutlass in hand, ready to give help should I need it. It was sheer physical combat—for above all I had to prevent the haimara from getting under the bank and becoming entangled among the tree roots. Sometimes the rod, 2 inches thick where I held it, was bent almost at right angles, its tip deep beneath the water for moments on end, as if I had hooked a rock—but a moving rock. Then the savage monster, 4½ feet long, and stout as a barrel, would break the surface, thrashing and rushing from side to side, before plunging below again in jagged rushes.

Then, when it realised that it was thoroughly caught—and before either of us quite knew what was happening—in a final act of desperation it *charged*. It flung itself right out of the water directly at us, its enormous mouth agape with arcs of white teeth as big as tin-tacks! We leaped aside as it thumped to the ground lashing and snapping, then ran in striking at it with cutlasses. It was moments before we could collect ourselves sufficiently to strike an accurate blow and kill it. Not since I had tried to recapture an escaped conger eel in a small boat had I known such alarming fish company. It must have weighed 30 pounds or more.

Within an hour we had caught six more of these monsters, all from this same 'hole'—we tried, without success, elsewhere—and I began to realise that our clumsy methods must reflect a very exact knowledge of the ecology and behaviour of the haimara.

For the haimara, after all, is not interested in eating flies. It is a lurker and pouncer rather like a giant pike, and it eats other fish, and birds, and mammals that fall into the water. Furthermore, it does not live in crystalline streams, but in murky, silt-laden water where sight is certainly less useful than hearing or smell in making its captures. So our tramplings on the bank, like a herd of animals, may only have alerted it; and our 'challenge' could well have resembled the struggles of some creature fallen in the water.

Laden, we returned to the boat, to find that Basil meanwhile had shot three trumpeter birds with one shot, by waiting until they walked into line. What with these, the fawn, the haimaras, and a sucking-pig shot earlier, there was more than enough fresh food for our party and for all the men, and several fish left over, which Basil began to salt down and dry in the sun as we sailed back. For this unexpected excess I was exceedingly glad, for I was beginning to be haunted by a constant fear of running out of food.

The previous day I had received a somewhat sharp note from Taylor:

To A.C.F. Survey Party:

Your shortages of food and petrol can only have arisen through wasteful measuring and improper use of the launch. Please correct both these matters. I would remind you that the launch is government property and not to be used for pleasure trips. You have now received adequate food for a further month. Let us have no more of these complaints.

Assistant Deputy C. of F., Georgetown.

I was in no mood for such pleasantries, particularly as by now I had twice borrowed a week's supplies of rations from the mine to keep the expedition going. Far from having a month's supplies in hand, we were a month short—and unless more arrived on the morrow I should have to borrow yet again. At no time could I get straight, for even when I received supplies I had to pay them back to the mine.

Night after night the sun set in magnificence that defied the usual descriptive terms. Sunset became the day's chief event, an incredible rhetoric of colour given gratuitously to the billion trees and animals of the forests. Men travel thousands of miles to see the Aurora—perhaps one day they will come to Guiana, where this night, as I brought my guests across, the river ran with the blood of a thousand fire-dragons slain in the upper atmosphere. Unable to speak we sat on the lip of the river watching their twisting bodies being devoured by tides of celestial fire, until darkness was complete, save where a few monstrous forms still floated red or ashen in the sky.

Of a sudden sheet lightning flickered on the horizon. It seemed to portend the coming of a new rainy season. Dry weather was supposed to last until late November, but in the interior the seasons were incompletely known. If the rains came before the river had fallen a further 8 feet or so, we should not be able to complete our earlier, flooded, lines on our return journey. But perhaps after all this was only fair-weather lightning, and the violent rain squalls which sometimes hit us were only local occurrences?

One of my guests was Tom Dolan, the company's secretary, a little neatly dressed man with a humorous face who loathed Guyana, the forest, everything about the country. His voice rose in a despairing wail: 'See that grawse—it's alive with creatures! I scream every time I look into it! All my life I've lived in New York, where things like that didn't exist, now just when life is beginning to blossom the love of the unknown makes me come out to B.G., the land of Bête Rouge. A crutch bleeding on a field of Bête Rouge should be the coat-of-arms of the colony.'

We sat down at a babricot-table of thin saplings covered by a huge red bath towel by way of tablecloth.

The cutlery and crockery I had borrowed from Omai, and I had arranged my bed as a sofa by covering it with my Mexican hammock-blanket. Boodhoo and little James excelled as waiters. It was extraordinary to sit and have a meal in such style under a tarpaulin by the light of an incandescent petrol lamp, listening to the gentle swishing of Kakaralli flowers as they fell in steady streams on to the canvas. For amusement I had written out a menu card:

The Edge of the Forest, Essequebo River, British Guiana

MENU
October 17

Fried Haimara (*Macrodon Trahira*)
with buttered capers

———

Haunch of Roast Venison of *Coassus rufus*
Roast and boiled potatoes

Fried plantains
Tinned peas

———

Palm-cabbage salad of *Jessenia bataua*
with olive oil and vinegar

———

Fresh Forest Fruit: Balata (*Mimusops balata*)
Spondias mombin plum, and wild cashew
(*Anacardium giganteum*)

———

Nescafé

Tom glanced at this. 'Jesus, this is better than Government-house in Georgetown (not that I've been there).'

Tom knew to the day how long he had been in Guyana and to the day how soon he would be leaving. 'From then on Central Park is going to be the wildest place I ever step into, and that not often. Christ-alive! In New York when the toilet goes wrong you press a button and a man comes round from some shop on the corner and fixes it. Then he *goes*. Out here its different, he stays—he's your *pal*. You meet him every day; you drink with the bastard because there isn't anyone else to drink with, and you listen to him while he tells you how the damn thing works.'

We sat drinking coffee under the blossom-dropping trees, in our little arena of light. The air was an ethereal mist of wandering sounds, detached relics and dissonances. Probably such a hidden sound-atmosphere surrounds us all the time, but louder noises claim our attention, unless like now there were none. It is hard to explain what such nearly total silence is like, for in civilised lands we never experience it.

In the jungles I have heard aircraft engines being tuned up 30 miles away, and a steamer's hoot when the boat was 20 miles off. Indeed, my men told me that by the hooting of this steamer the Indians of the whole Pomeroon region told the day of the week, and had time to get to the boat before it left the following day—so far do ordinary sounds travel when freed from the competition of other, more immediate noises. Now, amid this delicate web we could distinguish the sighing of the little waves of the river through the leaves of half-submerged trees, the swish of falling flowers, the footsteps of insects. We drank, told stories, laughed at Tom's obscenities, and it was time for bed. I took my visitors across the river and returned, bearing with me a letter from the Forest Department which had arrived by the day's Grumman plane, care of the mine.

It was late. I was tired. I opened the letter:

To A.C.F. Survey Party:
    Send me the launch's log book by return Grumman Flight from Omai. Your discrepancies in rations and wasting of petrol are viewed here extremely seriously. The Acting C. of F. and I intend to visit you to inspect work done and to

uncover the causes. Please understand your pleasure uses of the launch must cease forthwith.

Asst. Deputy C. of F.

I felt totally downcast. The joy was knocked out of my work. I had signed on to work for three years with this third-rate organisation, and I had two years still to go. I could not afford to buy myself out. It would cost at least £800 to repay my year at Oxford at the expense of the Colonial Service, and that to me then was an unattainably large sum. Viewed in retrospect, I can now see clearly what I should have done—sent off a stinging letter and carried on as I saw best. The Forest Department would never have been able to replace me—certainly not at short notice—whereas I should have been able to get a job anywhere in the world. But the whole bullying hierarchical framework of British life then—public schools, sports, competitive examinations, Civil Service grades, etc.—which so overawed my colleagues in Guyana, had undermined me. I knew my worth—my originality, my critical mind, my creativeness, as well as my ability and conscientiousness at work. But they counted for almost nothing in officialdom. My miserable life in Georgetown was suddenly made plain. Among these trees I saw in miniature the structure of the world. I compared myself with one of those saplings that waits deep in the jungle, gathering strength, until the day comes when it can shoot up, break through into the sky above—in the true world. But the Colonial Service was making of men a plantation where the slow-developer held back the average, while the over-vigorous was cut back to size. I determined to leave: but how? I had to save every penny I could, and meanwhile sit my time out. It was an unbearable prospect.

Such turbulent thoughts were seething in my brain as we headed up-river in the morning to do our last line from Omai. Not that they were as clearly defined as I have related. I am extroverted in appearance, but in fact the opposite: a problem produces in me withdrawal until I can arrive at a solution. And now I saw none. I just sat in a state of deep gloom, carrying on by rule of thumb.

After two hours' battle through rocky channels we tied up to a riverside root and climbed ashore in a place where the sickly-sweet smell of damp earth and rotting leaves combined with the fragrance of rushing water. We were just below Crabbu falls, up through which we would have to take the laden boat on the morrow.

As we cut inland, that same geological formation which caused the falls produced a display of topographical virtuosity which soon reduced us to panting exhaustion: bogs of soupy black humus into which we plunged waist deep, alternated with slippery hillsides, thick gravelly terraces bearing enormous Clump Wallaba trees, even expanses of bare sloping rock.

After a mile we had to stop and rest; and a little further we had an early lunch beside a pleasant streamlet in a steep-walled ravine which ended abruptly at an overhanging vertical wall of damp sand and clay consolidated by tree roots, from the base of which the water issued above a mossy bed of pink clay. High overhead was the mouth of another gully, like a hanging valley in the Alps, and to reach it we struggled around the sides and up the walls, then along a narrow knife-edged ridge. A quarter of a mile more and we gave up for the day beneath a velvety-barked Purpleheart tree. We would have to return to complete the line from our next camp.

Back at camp I changed and prepared to go across to Omai to dinner, to say farewell to my kind friends—and to borrow a fortnight's ration for the next leg of our work. A big barbecue had been prepared under the stars. There were quantities of good things to eat and drink, including mutton specially flown from the United States and roasted on skewers over a huge wood fire in a pit. There was dancing and merrymaking round the fires on the hill, above the dark still river over which the jungle hung, while the moon, full and enormous, floated overhead. Everyone was very gay, singing and talking about good times in the past. There were tales of mining in the Arctic regions, of Kodiak, Nome and Hudson's Bay; of Bute, Montana, and the early days of the Anaconda Copper Mines, of Peru and Mexico and adventures on the River Xingu; but most of all there were old-time miners' songs and stories of their homes and families.

Perhaps such welters of sentimentality are crude and easy to laugh at, but it made me realise how desperately everyone here longed to be away from these wilds, how they wanted to forget for a moment that it was a foreign and unsympathetic land, in

A saprophytic gentian

Fungus (*Ramaria* sp.) on a decaying log

Ascending to the tree house

Broad-leaved Kakaralli

which they could never be at home, and that at its best camp life was only a shadow of existence.

Then, when I was leaving, I was put into a position which I still remember with shame. My hosts asked me as a final farewell if I could take them for a trip in the launch to see the river in the moonlight. I hesitated, then stammered some excuses. Without flatly disobeying the instructions I had received only the previous day I could not do so. I would gladly have hired a launch had any been within reach, so that I could entertain them. I felt very bitter, I was placed in a false and humiliating position; and the organisation for which I worked, and of which I felt myself representative, was shown up as incompetent. I had written letter after letter, and even sent a radio message from the mine, but still every time I came across to visit my friends I was forced to beg. They knew that it was not my fault, and their kindness and tact I shall always remember. But under the circumstances I was over-sensitive, and I could not relax with them as happily as I longed to.

Nowadays, of course, I would not have hesitated to use the boat, but it takes time for one to learn to stand by one's own judgement, and it was my first experience of this sort. But what I regretted more than almost anything was that through these humiliations I had missed winning a true and warm friendship with Jack Knaebel. On my third visit to Omai he had been in an expansive mood, ready to take me to his heart. But I was utterly depressed and unresponsive, and made all the wrong answers, abstracted by worries. I understood what he was feeling. As boss of the mine he had to stand apart, not make favourites or special friends. He had detected in me someone of sympathetic character and similar interests. He knew my problems, but regarded them as trivial, solvable, not things to become emotionally involved with. From his standpoint he was correct. But I just didn't have the confidence. I lost a friend I would like to have had. Only chance can repair such a misunderstanding, and the chance did not occur. When we parted it was with cordiality, mixed in my case with gratitude, but not with the friendly companionship that might so easily have been.

From Jack's plane I had seen the silvery patterns around the falls and rapids upstream, the black heads of rocks tossing water from their eyes like flowing hair. But I had seen no clear

N

channel. After discussion with the captains of the various boats
that had passed, a few of the men with years of water-sense
were certain that we could get through, so we left, taking with
us some extra rope and pulleys from Omai.

Close on mid-day, out of the silence and lowering melancholy of the endless black-green forests and the endless sluggish
brown waters, we suddenly came into the rapids' thunder-
shaking atmosphere: shelving red and brown rocks of evocative
forms, the rush of falling water, the twitching of white wood on
shoals, the cool smell of spray and decaying paku weed.

To our right the mainland was steep with dense forest in
which Jacaranda trees raised feathery umbrellas of violet
trumpet flowers. On the left the river was strewn with rocky
islets covered with shrubs, whose twisted white stems showed
through their leaves. On a sandy beach a family of giant otters
leaped and rolled and played—until they saw us, stopped,
pointed their noses into the air for a minute, and trotted out of
sight. Only the tense muscles of the men, the straining eyes
which watched for hidden rocks, indicated our danger.

As we struck the fast water there was an obliterating sense of
urgency, of physical tension—yet of relaxation, for we had
delivered ourselves totally into the hands of engineer, steersmen,
and bowmen. Kumaka hole, which we passed first, was impressive, with tall monolithic rocks standing like gate pillars above a
sinisterly smooth rush of water; beyond, clear water amid an
aerial ballet of primrose-winged butterflies, from which
suddenly a great green grasshopper fluttered and landed
beside me on my tyre, like a thick juicy leaf standing there on
the black rubber.

Then came Crabbu falls: a mile-long string of curiously
jointed flattened discs of granite, like the tors of Dartmoor,
riding above the undulations of the waves. We passed through
with no difficulty, coasted along beside Smith's Post Island—
named after some long-dead prospector—then followed a long
gentle curve of the river round until we were once more sailing
southwards. Now on our left we noticed signs of former camps
and settlements, a contrast to the morose, uninhabitable flood-
lands we had left. Coconut trees waved in the jungle, and at one
place an orange tree showed itself. We were on the edge of the
gold and diamond prospecting fields of the Potaro, still by no

means thoroughly explored, while only 30 miles further south the fabulously rich Siparuni area had hardly been touched.

Abruptly we were sailing over night-black water: the waters of the Potaro itself, rolling into the muddy brown Essequebo. On it the occasional flecks and piles of foam were from the falls at Tumatumari a few miles up—while further up still, this same water had for an instant hung over the void, then thundered 840 feet down into the Kaieteur Gorge in what is surely the world's most beautiful major falls. In the Pakaraima mountains there are numerous small falls that are much higher, including the world's highest, the Angel falls; but none with such perfection of form or setting.

Opposite the Potaro mouth a solid bank of clay gave a fine view up and down river, and here we stopped and made camp. A small, half-smothered lime tree, bearing a solitary fruit, indicated that men had lived here before.

It was a lovely afternoon. I sat having tea, looking out over the river in the fading light. I was sorry to have left Omai and its reassuring sounds of other human life. Yet it was good being alone again with the silence that I valued, which allowed things buried inside to show themselves. I was gently humming that theme from 'Tapiola' with which I had started the journey, thinking of the work ahead, when I reached towards my cup of tea—and stopped. There, trying to crawl up the saucer was an enormous ant. Nearly 2 inches long and half an inch high, it was charcoal-black and sparsely covered in coarse brown bristles. It had huge jaws, and from its abdomen protruded a powerful pointed sting. It was a muniri, or Neoponera. Ants are believed to be descended from wasps or wasp-like insects, and these, the most primitive living ants, are virtually wingless hornets, and not merely the most formidable ants in the world, but among the most formidable of all insects. One of my men had known a dog die when stung on the nose by a muniri, and I had been told by several people that the most intense agony they had experienced in their entire lives had been caused by a muniri sting. It was on the cards that one day I too might put my hand down without looking, and feel that 2-inch black menace twist round under my fingers. But fortunately they were not common, and I always took the greatest care to avoid places where I saw them.

Muniris live in nests in the ground usually containing some ten or fifteen, though sometimes there may be many times that number. They are solitary workers, going out from the nest singly and wandering in the forest in search of food for several days at a time. When they walk in line, the Indians say they are carrying water to their nests. Once I had seen such a line, and sure enough, held in each jaw was a large drop of water. A single one of these ants, such as the one in front of me, might be met with anywhere.

Drawing back from the table slowly, I watched while this huge specimen—the largest I had ever seen—probed the tea cup, its movements slow but certain like those of a heavy laden commando climbing a ladder. There was about it something horrible and impersonal which, together with a slight jerkiness of its limbs, reminded me of a robot. I could hear the almost mechanical clattering it made. Then it dropped down and ambled slowly over the canvas top of the camp table, stopping every now and again to examine a crumb.

Just as it reached the edge of the table a foot from me, Jonah happened to pass.

'Look out, Mr. Guppy!' he called, and flicked it off the table with his cutlass blade, then sliced downwards to cut it in two. But he missed, and the ant was off, moving with astonishing speed—and *squeaking* like an enraged mouse.

Jonah chopped and missed again. I took the cutlass from him, and this time its body was buried in the soft soil, but undamaged, so strong was its armour-plating. It shook itself free and started running again. Two or three times I struck, and each time the blade was deflected. It became panic-stricken in a clumsy, terrifying way, and begun to run about in confusion like a miniature armoured car gone mad. It emitted a strong smell and reedy squeaks. Finally I severed head from thorax, and crushed it upon a log with the blade of the knife.

'You must watch out for those,' said Jonah. 'There are plenty about, and they are bigger than usual—the worst kind. The men have already killed two or three. It was one like this that kill my nephew, when he was twelve years old.'

A minute later, and I saw another—emerging from a tiny hole in the ground under my bed. At once Jonah and I dragged the bed aside and set to work digging out the nest. As we dug the ants ran out thoroughly aroused, emitting their thin sibilant squeaks, 's-s-s-s-s' in the highest register, while their jaws made little clacking noises. The noise could be heard from several yards off and was quite frightening. Chopping right and left with our cutlasses we killed fifteen. But perhaps there were others out hunting? To prevent them returning we scraped the earth all round the nest and round the tent, so that they could not follow their own scent trail back.

Then I moved my bed to the far side, and to make doubly sure that no returning forager could get inside, I tucked the mosquito net in all round off the floor.

Even so, next morning an ant had found its way in and was clinging a few inches from my head. It had probably been on the bed when I had made it. Shaken, I held the net to trap it, got out and killed it. Close search revealed two others in my tent. In their jaws gleamed tiny drops of liquid—they were 'droughing' water, said Jonah, and must still have a nest near.

The sun's rays streaming low overhead flung the shadow of our bank away across the water as I breakfasted. The blue of night slowly lifted and dissolved in the morning air, draining away upwards. Faint black specks indicated a cluster of rocks just below the mist-filled Potaro mouth—and there, beyond the hump of Yesi Island in mid-river up-stream, seeming infinitely far away, distant mountains showed pale and wan. For a while they were sharply outlined in the sky, making me draw my breath with excitement, because they told of new landscapes further south. Then, as the sun rose, they were lost in the dancing atmosphere.

In mid-morning, while working at the men's camp, Philbert Thomas was stung on the finger by a muniri. He had grasped a twig, and the ant had been on the other side. Philbert was about thirty-six, exceedingly strong and bred in the Indian tradition of stoicism towards pain. I had extracted a deep splinter from his hand a week previously, and however deeply the knife probed it had been exactly like carving a piece of wood. When I had applied iodine I might have been rubbing a grease-spot from a chair-cover for all the emotion he showed.

Now, however, he was sweating profusely, trembling, and breathing deeply and slowly. I made a ligature round finger and wrist, cut into the wound and treated it with calamine lotion and antiseptic, and made him lie down. By mid-day his hand was as big as a grapefruit, and he was twisting in his hammock with the pain.

Jonah tried to cheer him up: 'I see a man with a big weal on the hand—*forty* days after a *muniri* bite he!'

The ants were beginning to get on everyone's nerves. We searched around, and found yet another nest in a hole at the base of a small sapling. When we shook the tree accidentally an ant emerged, so we dug the nest out, and killed about ten more. Some stood their ground, hissing and squealing defiantly. Others ran fearlessly forward to attack.

'I never see any place like this for muniri,' said Jonah. 'Not in the whole of my time in the bush.'

When camp-making was finished the next afternoon, I detached myself with difficulty from reading Proust (whom I had just began) and we cut inland for a mile. There was no sign of the corrugated landscape of gully and ridge that I expected: instead, long level stretches of brown sand and clay, broken by a broad winding stream—doubtless that in which, lower down we had caught haimara—beside which the men set spring-traps for fish, as it was only a short walk from camp.

Next we saw a troop of Kwata, or spider monkeys (Ateles), in the tree-tops. The largest monkeys in Guiana, black in colour, they grow to the size of a small man. Little Rufus was very much afraid of them, for he said that they would come down and kill him if he were to shoot one; while Jothan remembered an occasion when, high up a balata tree which he was tapping, he had been surrounded by five or six of them. They had shaken the branches and made faces at him, and had seemed on the point of attacking, when he had managed to slip down to the ground and get away.

Jonah and I had almost reached camp on our return, walking a long way behind the rest of the men so that we could collect plants, when we heard the flop of dropping fruit ahead, and the subdued chattering of another troop of monkeys—ring-tailed capuchins. No sooner did he see them, than Jonah stood very still and motioned me to do likewise. Then he made a curious wavering whistling, which started low and rose till it was so high-pitched as to be almost inaudible. He produced this noise by whistling while simultaneously bubbling his breath through a mouthful of saliva. He did it again and again, quite gently—and the effect was extraordinary. The monkeys stopped what they were doing and leaned down scrutinising us, trying to make out where the noise came from. They shook the branches to attract attention and elicit a response, while we continued to stand like statues. Presently they began whistling in reply, and clambering down the trees. They came lower and lower until some were only 15 or 20 feet away, and a few feet off the ground. Then they paused, anxiety on their faces. There were about twenty of them: big males, youngsters, females with babies riding on their hips. They stared intently at us, obviously very much puzzled. A mosquito came whining through the air, towards my face: I blew it away. At last one old male came down to the ground, and edged towards us, with hand out-stretched to touch Jonah. We scarcely breathed. A baby, clinging to his mother's waist, pouted his lips and gave reedy squeaks of alarm. Just as he was about to be touched, suddenly Jonah stamped his foot, threw up his hands and shouted 'shoo!' At once all the monkeys gave piercing screams—their rage and terror were indescribable as they scrambled up the trees. Safely aloft, they beat their chests, chattered violently and shook the branches till the whole forest seemed to be quaking. Small branches, epiphytes, fruit, fell down or were torn off and thrown or dropped in all directions with no semblance of aim. We shook all the small trees we could find in order to annoy them yet further, and for a while pandemonium raged. Then the monkeys lost interest and resumed their exploration of the tree-tops. Once in a while one would remember us and shake a branch in a sudden gust of anger, or drop a fruit, but gradually they melted away through the jungle until we heard them no more.

Jonah said that by continuing whistling with sufficient patience and keeping totally still, he had lured these monkeys right up to him on the ground, filled with curiosity to find out what he was. They had plucked his clothes, pinched and tickled to see if he were alive and why he was not like other monkeys, he said.

'Why then did you not do so this time?' I asked.

'There were too many of them. I was afraid.'

Monkeys are seldom molested by the Indians, except when

there is no other bait available, of if there is nothing else to eat. Or sometimes a female carrying her young ones may be shot and the surviving young ones reared as pets, or to be sold.

Back at camp in the evening, I nearly put my hand on yet another muniri ant which had climbed up my chair arm. Foragers were evidently still returning to the destroyed nests.

But I began to doubt this explanation as the days went by, for each day we continued to find other ants. I had to shake out my shoes and shirt, examine all my clothes before putting them on, scrutinise the chair or log or ground before sitting down, for fear of an agonising injection of poison and a couple of days in bed. No one else was stung, but our nerves were thoroughly strained. I thought of moving camp, but it would waste time. Also this was one of our most beautiful camps, and one of our most rewarding, because the forests around were so rich in new plants and in animals—of which the muniris were only un-attractive examples. And there was the excitement of feeling that this was our furthest south, the edge of the upland region of the Pakaraimas: early morning and evening, when the air was free of day's muslin haze, brought with them those mountains in the sky, wonderfully speaking of marvels beyond our reach.

12

The Tree House

Among my books was R. W. G. Hingston's *A Naturalist in the Guiana Forest*, an account of the Oxford University Expedition of 1929 which made pioneer studies of forest structure and ecology. One of its photographs showed a man far up a tree, climbing by spiked boots. This was Jothan Fredericks, my third-in-command—and he was very proud of it. He loved to describe how he had built the tree-top observation posts for that expedition, and what a marvellous tree climber he had been in his youth—and indeed still was. Now, on our first Saturday at the new camp, our work—preparing herbarium specimens—was done early, and he stood diffidently outside my tent, scratching his left instep with his right big toe.

'Sir,' he said, 'I have found a very good tree we could climb. We could build a platform for you in it very easy. It is about a quarter mile down the trail.'

Picking up my cutlass, I walked along behind him and a group of the men. The tree was a slim young Wadara (Coura-tari). Its crown stood clear above the rest of the forest, the branches splaying out in a regular cone just above canopy level at about 120 feet. In them were numerous epiphytes, and several lianes whose tangled stems hung in loops to the ground well clear of the trunk, which was slim and tapering, without evident protuberances.

Jothan swung a dangling liane in his hand. 'It would be easy to climb to the first branch with a belt, even without climbing irons. If we could use the rope and pulleys we borrowed from the mine we could fix a seat to draw you up.'

'How long would it take to do?'

'Not long, perhaps a day if it go well.'

I had expected him to say much longer. Such an opportunity seemed too good to be missed—it was depressing always to work among the damp and decay of the forest floor in a claustrophobe's nightmare of flickering sun-flecks and clutching twigs, never able to see more than a few yards in any direction, pressed down by the tonnage of vegetation. Strictly speaking, building a tree house was not part of my survey work. But it would be valuable in the long term for me as a botanist to examine a vertical slice of the forest at close quarters—an experience few botanists had ever had. Jothan and one or two others were on salary, the others were paid by the day, and there would surely be no objection even if my dreary departmental bureaucrats heard of it, so long as it cost them nothing in time or money.

Jothan was obviously anxious to show his paces, and Julian James was willing to help him. Best of all, Julian had brought a pair of climbing irons. So I decided to go ahead, if all the work could be done on a Sunday or in spare time.

First we constructed a trestle stand to get Jothan above the tree's 8-foot buttresses. Then, with the end of our big borrowed coil of rope attached to his belt at the back, and another smaller coil over his shoulders, Jothan climbed up the trestle and passed a length of rope around the trunk and in and out round his belt, forming a secure band which allowed him to lean backwards some 9 inches clear of the tree.

Then he began his journey, looking like some curious frog or looper caterpillar jack-knifing upwards over the coarse bark. Every half-dozen steps or so he would pause while he adjusted or tightened the belt around the tree a little. Then he would continue, moving first the belt upwards with his hands, then his feet to a new and higher grip.

In a few minutes he was lost to view in the screen of lower branches, so that I had to move aside to see him again. Halfway up he paused lengthily, and we wondered whether he was all right: he was detaching an Anthurium—it fell with a mighty rustling, slithering, and spattering of debris.

In half an hour he had reached just under the first branch— and here his difficulties began, for it was too thick to climb over. Again and again, without success, he cast with the end of the small coil of rope. Finally he made a big and heavy knot at the end, and whirled the rope round and round. This time it went over—but the end hung out of reach.

One of the men shouted, 'We go pass you up a stick, Jothan—pull up de line!'

A fifteen-foot Yarri-Yarri pole was cut and cleaned, except for the whorl of branches near its base, which were left short, to form a sort of grapnel. This was tied to the end of the long rope which remained on the ground, and Jothan drew it up, and with it pulled the line to him, and secured the loop so formed to his belt—all of which entailed a good deal of leaning and twisting about. I paced up and down, sweating with anxiety.

Next Jothan tied the other end of his short rope to the Yarri-Yarri stick, so that it formed a sort of harpoon, and flung the contrivance right through the cone of branches above him, so that it fell and hung on the other side of the tree. By manœuvring himself around the trunk and leaning out holding on to a root, he was able to grasp the stick again. He undid the rope-end from it, dropped the stick, tied the rope end securely around his waist, released his climbing rope-belt around the tree, and proceeded to walk himself up the trunk and into the crown. I simply did not look.

'Big monkey up deh—go get gun man!' shouted up Little Rufus; while a more juvenile voice called:

'Watch he no trow down crap!'

A faint chuckle could be heard from the tree-top, far away and out of sight.

Then Jothan called down: 'We want plenty long big stick and bush rope. Send up fast!'

While Julian James started climbing the trunk to assist him, the rest of us began to cut a series of poles 3 to 4 inches in diameter and some 15 feet long, and tied a bundle of them, together with our smaller pulley, to the rope-end Jothan had paid down to us in pulling up the Yarri-Yarri grapnel. The other end of the rope we passed through a bigger double pulley, which was then tied to a young Kakaralli tree and doubly secured to another stout sapling a few yards further off—leaving us still some 30 feet of rope on which to haul.

Jothan tied the pulley, when it reached him, to one of the smaller branches fairly high up in the tree-crown—but near the centre, so that loads lifted could be guided in among the branches. Our next bundles consisted of poles lashed together with a quantity of bushropes, together with all the other ropes we had. Then a crosspiece of wood was tied into a loop at the end of the line to serve as a seat, and Justin Joseph prepared to ascend. He was all smiles, but my heart began to thump when I saw what I was in for. I suffer severely from vertigo, and already in my imagination I could feel my legs buckling under me as I tried to crawl into the crown above. But there was no escape—I would certainly have to go aloft if others did.

When Justin was a few feet up, the seat began to revolve. His smile vanished.

'My, I bad frighten!' he called down.

'Hold on de bush rope, eh, man,' called Jonah.

By grasping the long straight roots that fell down just clear of the tree trunk with one hand he could hold himself fairly steady as in a series of jerks he was hauled upwards. It was a relief to see him at last safely astride a branch. Two more men went up, while those remaining below kept them supplied with materials.

By mid-afternoon the house was ready.

'Tree house very comfy!' called down Jothan.

There was no escaping. With quaking heart I steeled myself, and got on to the horrible little swing-seat. Holding tight to the ropes above, which I twisted round my arm with one hand while I grasped a Clusia root with the other, I indicated that I was ready.

Creak! my breath was out of my body as I flew up a couple of feet unexpectedly. More jerks, and I swung, totally helpless, 10 feet up.

'Hi!' I said. 'Go easy! I want to see everything as I go up.'

I had my camera on my knee, and calmed myself as I pointed it down at the men and clicked.

Then I was on my way again. At 20 feet I passed through one layer of tree crowns, that of saplings and undergrowth species, and already the forest around me was lighter. At 60 feet I was among the spreading branches of the main under-storey, and the shadowy ground beneath me was already almost completely hidden by a mass of sun-flecked intermediate leaves, forming a sifting semi-solid screen below. I was beginning quite to enjoy myself, absorbed in the interest of all I saw, though unable to see very far in any direction.

A few more feet and I was nervous again, for the forest became lighter and sunnier, and looking up I was appalled to see the distance I still had to go. At 100 feet I could see through the tree-crowns to the tangled pastures of the canopy—then a few more jerks upwards, and strong hands grasped me and swung me inwards to a safe landing on a very solid-seeming platform. I got out, staggered drunkenly, and realised that the whole tree was swaying in a strong wind.

Holding on, I looked around, reassured by the stout construction of our house. It consisted of a funnel of strong sapling stems that had been lashed around the inside of the splaying cone of the Couratari branches, forming a wine-glass shaped structure, up the insides of which it was possible to crawl for some 10 feet on all sides. Cross-pieces narrowed the mesh between the main bars, a platform had been laid across the centre, and a subsidiary ladder ascended 15 feet further to a branch in the middle. It was amazing that half a dozen men had been able to design and build it so well in so short a time. Their delighted faces were all about me, smiling at my evident pleasure—though this was in large part a reaction of relief at being at least temporarily safe.

I relaxed a little, and began to look around. I was afloat on a magic carpet slightly above the general level of the canopy, which spread away in voluptuous green billows on either side. Above, the branches of the Wadara—laden with orchids, bromeliads, aroids, mosses—curved up into a blue sky in which tiny cloud-puffs sailed and a king vulture circled. Around and below the green tree-crowns rolled, spangled with flowers and seemingly solid enough to walk on. Half a mile away stood another emergent tree—a pillar above the greenery. Elsewhere nearer trees obscured the horizon annoyingly.

Yet in those nearer crowns was the life I had come to see. Two fat splashes of scarlet twisting round a branch revealed long tails—scarlet macaws! and the tree, a fig, was full of them, feasting on the ripe fruit. A further tree contained hanging nests of the big black and yellow moriche oriole—while over the meadow of golden blossoms spread below me (a flowering tree-crown, or only a liane in bloom?) a medley of butterflies darted like liquid fire. As I watched a Morpho hecuba came sailing over the tree-tops on rigidly-held 8-inch wings of golden brown and dusky blue, an emerald humming-bird shot by like a bullet, and a brown Anolis lizard with big head and whip-like tail dashed along the twig on which I had hung my camera and snapped up a fly, saw me, nodded as if in greeting, and puffed up his throat into a red balloon.

To the casual traveller in Guiana the forests appear almost empty of larger animals, and of course we had seen even fewer than usual because of the floods down river. Yet in fact this boundless three-dimensional labyrinth of plants provides a myriad niches, crammed with one of the richest assortments of animal life to be found on earth.

To consider the mammals only: on the ground roam tapirs, armadillos, giant anteaters, pumas, jaguars, jaguarondis, ocelots and other smaller cats, wild dogs, deer, agoutis, pacas, capybaras, opossums, herds of peccaries. Yet the most typical animals of Amazonia or Guiana are not ground-living creatures as in Africa, Europe, Asia, Australia, even North America— but arboreal beasts: the sloths, which hang upside down from branches, and which have green plants growing upon them so that they look like lichenous knobs; and the amazing prehensile-tailed monkeys, found nowhere else on earth—capuchins, spider-monkeys, marmosets, sakis, howlers, owl-monkeys, to name but a few. Two-thirds of the mammals of this region are arboreal, including coatis, porcupines, kinkajous, lesser ant-eaters, squirrels, tayras. . . . Then there are birds in almost infinite variety: tinamous, toucans, curassows, guans, trum-peters, oil-birds, trogons, barbets, puff-birds, cotingas, sun-bitterns, parrots, umbrella birds, chatterers, humming-birds, tanagers, troupials, honey-creepers; reptiles and amphibians— boas, anacondas, bushmasters, coral-snakes, iguanas, tortoises, escuerzos, surinam toads, bull-frogs, tree-frogs; marvellous fish in the rivers; insects—butterflies, moths, mantids, katydids, ants, flies, bugs, lantern-flies; spiders, crustaceans, molluscs, infusorians, worms of every conceivable phylum. And of all this multitude of living things the greater number are never seen at all unless one has keen eyes and nose and ears—and patience.

Life is most abundant in the tree-tops, then on the ground, least in the middle. Hingston, for example, found that three-quarters of all insects in the canopy were leaf-hoppers (which lower down were relatively uncommon), whereas moths were most abundant near the ground. As for man—he is only a rare biped, never the master of these forests, merely one of the larger of the animals which survive in them. Nowhere are there high human forest populations as in India, Burma, or West Africa. Over large areas his effects may be discounted even today, while in thousands of miles there are no human inhabitants at all, and other populations are much more important influences on the ecology.

I began to wonder how long I could spend in my tree house. Every ascent meant four to six men pulling, and one of the expert tree climbers, up above, to swing the seat in towards the platform. Rather than keep those below out of action, I decided to limit myself to two hours on this first ascent, and I shouted down: 'Leave us up till about half past five! Come back then.'

Then with only Jothan beside me I set to work to observe all I could in the time left, so that I could get some idea of the inter-relationships of the parts, and of what were the important factors that created this enormously complex social whole.

First I examined the tree we were in. Every inch of the upper surface of its branches was covered with epiphytes, largely bromeliads with yellow sun-reflecting leaves, a defence against dessication in the fierce heat, light, and relative dryness up here. In among them were orchids, mostly very tiny, with 3-inch flower stems.

In the sunlight of the forest roof the various flowers are visited by certain quite definite animals. Bright red flowers attract humming-birds and butterflies, which perform much of the pollination that in temperate climates is done by bees, here uncommon. Similarly, dull purplish flowers are said typically to be visited by bats, white flowers by moths. In the lower levels ants and beetles become important pollinators. If ripe fruit hang long on a tree, birds or monkeys are likely to eat them and disperse the seed. If they fall as soon as ripe, in the dry season rodents and deer are the animals involved; but if flood waters cover the land, they may be distributed by water, or pass through the guts of fishes. So it is that similar-looking trees, growing side by side, may yet differ in vital respects in the ways in which they utilise the total environment, affect the other living things in it, and are competitive with one another. The climate is favourable to growth, the total number of possible roles is enormous, and the sum of roles performed by each species is its niche. It seems very unlikely that any one species ever occupies all the roles of another, which could account for the large number of different species which have evolved being able to hold their own; while competition between individuals of the same species is probably fierce—hence the diversity of species, and the fewness of individuals of each. All this was strongly reminiscent of the picture of human diversity found in a large city—and suggestive that the same sort of factors accounted for both. Following this reasoning, complex, mature societies would be relatively unaggressive; simpler, but crowded societies particularly so.

Jothan gently squeezed my arm and pointed. In a distant tree the branches were stirring. Brownish-yellowish figures could just be seen among them; a pack of ring-tailed capuchins —perhaps the same as those we had seen before. Fascinated, I watched as, shaking the branches, jumping and swinging, they passed from tree to tree until they were all out of sight.

The sun was low, and over the forest roof came the dread-filling chorus of far off howler monkeys, reverberating over the miles of loneliness.

It was dark when I finally descended, excited, nervous, and also a little disappointed—for it would need months to begin to get some idea of this rich new world. I had not been able to afford a pair of field glasses, and I had no means of trapping the life in the various levels, without doing which I could get no proper samples of what was living in them. Furthermore, it was as frustrating as a child's first understanding of the freedom of birds, to have to remain passively in one tree, and not be able to swing about and travel laterally like a monkey!

At six the next morning I was up, hurrying through the chill, damp jungle, resolved to spend at least an hour in the summit before we went off to work. Jothan and Little Rufus ascended first—then I. To my amazement they were almost invisible when I drew level—mere silhouettes against the whiteness of a thick mist-blanket that covered the canopy. The Wadara was dripping, sparkling with huge droplets, lighted by a fleecy golden sun just edging above the trees.

At the riverside the day had been clear. Yet on the far shore

Tacouba walking

Dragging an eight foot cayman out of the river

Sunset on the Essequebo

there had been clouds resting on the trees. I had seen this phenomenon day after day, and had thought that in the cool of the night clouds had floated down to rest, as happened some-times in very heavy rain. But now I realised that these tree-top clouds were a product of the forest itself, caused by the condensation of water-vapour transpired by the trees whenever humidity reached 100 per cent, as just before dawn, and later dissolved as the sun rose.

The calls of birds came through the mist, and slowly the whole world turned from buttercup yellow to cottony white. Toucans were in a neighbouring tree, yelping and crying. But there was little to see, only a visual magic as the heavy moisture of the forest's night-time breathing swirled upwards.

From my tree house during the following days I watched the sun rise and set, saw great parties of white-headed sakis and ring-tailed capuchins combing their way through the summits, swinging along, babies clasped round their mother's waists, unsuspecting of my presence; heard a bell-bird tolling in the branches *below me*, saw a harpy eagle make its strike, saw the evening flight of parrots—and one day watched, amazed, while three unceasing avenues of primrose-yellow Pierid butterflies poured past in migration.

Downstream our lines re-encountered the breath-stealing topography of interlocking ridges. Amid them one day we were confronted by a broad creek of a new and distinctive colour, its water red as chrysanthemum petals where the sun flecked it, greeny-brown like oil in the gloom. What change of vegetation could this portend?

The further bank was an overhanging 20-foot-high wall of clay covered in filmy ferns, mosses, and a few stalked tree-ferns. Up it we ascended by a zigzagging crack-like gully, until, puffing with exertion, we reached the top—and in front of us stood a truly gigantic tree, whose black, heavily-rusticated trunk rose like a Dakama's from a pile of large leaves. Its bark slashed the colour and texture of pink ham, and around it there hung the most ethereal perfume. It was an Arisauroballi (Dimor-phandra davisii), a close relative of the Dakama, known only in a small area around the Potaro and the upper Mazaruni. It was the first I had ever seen.

o

A whole forest of these black giants stretched ahead of us on almost level white sand, and we could see far into it, for there was no undergrowth beyond an occasional seedling. It was a fantastic scene—scented springtime overhead, where plumes of white flower-spikes tossed amid the newest pale green young leaves, and autumn below, with the sun blazing down on a plain of pancake-sized, crisp, fallen leaves. The trees were shallow-rooted in peat and thin sand over the clay, as I could see from one or two lying prostrate with smashed crowns and still clutching roots, evidently blown down in a storm. Light-heartedly we walked on through this great natural hall of thousands of columns—the most beautiful of all the forests I had ever seen.

Then, the work done, we returned to the boat, where I sat on top reading Norman Douglas' *Siren Land*. I felt happy, but emotionally confused. At one point Douglas described a chianti, and the flavour of chianti appeared to me so strongly that I looked up, nearly cried out loud when I saw where I was, and felt like throwing myself off the boat in frustration.

Suddenly I hated the jungle. I longed passionately to be away from it, among familiar things and people. The men were smiling to me, offering me a split-coconut to drink, but they were alien. They, and the landscape, had sunk into my mind—but not into my deep heart. Everything around contradicted my memories, the things I read about. I was captive in a spiritually incomprehensible world.

Back at camp I read Proust in the fading daylight. Then I lit the Coleman lamp whilst wasps, moths, and grasshoppers fluttered about. I felt desperate. I had deceived myself into tolerating a place and work which could never really satisfy me, by turning them into something deeper and more meaningful. Reading, music, and introspection had become a substitute for living and loving. Perhaps Tom Dolan's single-minded longing to escape had liberated my suppressed feelings? Now that I saw my own situation clearly I could hardly endure it.

I had thought at first that reading Proust was like looking into an aquarium and watching brilliantly coloured fishes play. Now I felt as if I were the captive fish in the aquarium, so much more real than my world was Proust's. Books, sunsets, dawns, the marvellous spectacles of the river and the forest, threw a

veil over the void. They had become to me like the cinema to an
addict, a means of making life bearable. But I could not live an
emotional life with my eyes alone. I needed involvement with
other humans.

And just for the sake of a living I could not continue to waste
my time in other people's ways. I had to be creative outside the
scope of my job, to keep myself developing. There were many
things that others could do as well as I. What I wanted was to
do the things that only I could do—to cultivate my originality.
I remembered what a friend had once told me: 'Be sensitive to
boredom. When you are bored, give up what you are doing. It
is a sign that your brain is turning to things that are really more
important to you.' Unfortunately, I was so lacking in ego that I
was always ready to adapt to others just to assuage my loneliness, ready to be self-deprecatory even when I knew I was
right. I wanted to attain self-sufficiency, even though I knew it
was an icy substitute for involvement. I thought of Aggie—if
only I had a girl! The men had girls to whom they wrote, but I
had none—only that one far away in England, who had not
written for five months. I had no love life, no sex life, not even
the illusion of meeting that they give.

The work of the expedition no longer required initiative. I
had established a routine, and now when necessary Jonah,
Jothan, and Lord were all able to supervise the surveying and
do all the field work, except that which was purely scientific.
We had had not a single delay, not a day lost, except as the
result of the floods. And even in the worst flooded forests we
had done parts of several lines, sometimes as many as five in a
day, so that we still had time in hand. Health had been excellent
thanks to the advice of my doctor friends and the sulfa drugs
they had given me, I had been able to treat successfully all
ailments brought to me—not even a single case of the notorious
'bush-sores', which may spread and last for weeks, had turned
septic.

I smiled when I compared the situation at Bartica, where the
office was incapable, evidently, of even getting our food
supplies to us competently.

I then became slightly more cheerful, as I thought of the
studies I had made of the forests. Not only had I collected a
quantity of botanical data, and developed original ideas of how

the vegetation should be classified, and the analogy between human and plant societies, but in doing so I had extended my critical approach to reading and thinking. I am naturally slow in my handling of ideas—I need time and calm in which to examine, sort, and clarify them, and even then I am liable to overlook important details, at least for a while. I have to consider and reconsider before I am sure of anything.

Much as I had loved Cambridge, and particularly Trinity, and then Oxford, where I was at Magdalen, my intellectual habits had not been formed there really, but between the ages of fourteen and sixteen and a half, when I had lived in a small village in Perthshire with my mother, virtually cut off from the outside, wartime world, and after that at school, up to the age of eighteen. In the first period two kindly and learned neighbours, one of them a naturalist, had taken me up and had guided me in my voracious reading, particularly of old scientific works purchased on day trips to the second-hand bookshops of Edinburgh and Glasgow—Darwin, Wallace, Bates and Belt, Huxley and Waterton—solid Victorian works of measured pace. Then after I had persuaded my mother to send me to school, and in two terms had passed all my various examinations, I had spent my remaining school years as a sixth former, studying biology. But as there was no biology master at my school this had meant going by bus to Plymouth twice a week to study at the Marine Biological Station there under Dr. Ashley Lowndes. Working virtually as his assistant, I had covered a far wider field than the usual curriculum, on long walks with him into the neighbouring fields and woods, investigating liverworts, mosses, and algae, or trawling round the Eddystone lighthouse in the station's research vessel, or taking high-speed ciné films of ciliary movement. After this individual attention, this deep probing into the subjects on which he was working, Cambridge, by contrast, seemed a violent cram-course for the honours degree. Much as I loved the place and the friends I made there, my work had suffered, for while there were so many new things to learn, everything was done too hastily. Then at Oxford I had kicked my heels taking an elementary course at the Imperial Forestry Institute, while in my spare time reading all that I could lay my hands on about the ecology of tropical forests. Why had I gone on? Because at that

time the Colonial Forestry Service seemed the only route by
which I could study tropical jungles, and because I was too
poor to opt out. Yet this inability to proceed directly towards
my goals had confused me. What I myself was, had got submerged. When all was said, perhaps this extended period of
isolation and calm in the forest was what I needed most?
Perhaps it was enabling me to re-find myself and establish my
own methods of thinking and solving problems, which I had
begun to see were in part by testing highly speculative analogies,
in part by translating everything into visual blocks which I
could move around. I had found this much out about myself;
also, that if slow, I was at least perservering. With these
consoling thoughts I went to bed.

We had now completed all our lines, fixed, pressed and dried
all our herbarium specimens, spent many hours in the tree
house, and the following day we had the afternoon free. Should
I spend it aloft in the tree house, I mused as we lunched? In
all I had already spent the best part of an entire day in it, and I
felt that it would be unlikely to yield much more in a single
afternoon. Jonah suggested a trip up the Potaro to Tumatumari
falls, the highest point to which the river launches reached: they
were known to be magnificent—a great wall of falling water in a
semi-circle across the river, around which all goods had to be
portaged. There was reported to be a small landing place there
with a shop or two—I imagined the little wooden houses
nestling amongst broad-leaved bananas and palms, and the
rainbows and spray of the falls; the rice and split peas in barrels,
the bottles of rum and beer, the brooms and brushes, mangoes
and sweetcakes, gumboots, buckets, cutlasses, boxes of salt beef
and tinned foods—everything for simple needs; and the vendors
from the bush squatting outside.

On the other hand the place might be derelict, like Rockstone, a mere landing for the goldfields further inland. In either
case I felt I knew it in advance and I had no idea how far away
it was—it was off my maps—perhaps a trip of several hours.
Besides, all the men would want to go there. Those I would have
to leave in camp would feel disgruntled; while those I took, if
there were a rum shop, might be hard to prize away again. So I
decided instead to continue south up the Essequebo for an hour
or two, to investigate that mysterious bend behind which the

distant morning mountains rose—for pleasure, out of curiosity, to collect plants, and to see what further changes I might notice in this botanical borderland. On the morrow we would start down river again.

Only a few men wanted to come on this trip. The remainder busied themselves about the camp, packing up so that we could leave early, and dismantling the pulley and ropes from the tree house. It was a relief to travel slowly, to sit quietly in an uncluttered boat watching the banks, free to land where we wanted, to swim if we found a shallow beach free from the dread quadrumvirate of perai, sting rays, alligators, and electric eels. I felt soothed by the peacefulness of the scene, the lack of definite objective or commitment.

First we landed at the far end of Yesi (Arawak for tortoise) Island, a tiny hump just visible from the camp, and the last thing on the edge of my map. Small bright fish darted in the shallows of a shingly beach, beyond which, up a steep sand bank imprinted with iguanas' and turtles' feet, a few spiny palms fringed a dense tangle of trees and lianes.

Then we sailed south again over the smoothly rippling water along a majestic leftwards curve, with the afternoon light glancing over the level olive floor and dark dense walls of forest —and above the farthest curve a wedge-shaped hill, air-bloomed a delicate smoke colour. The sun was declining, the light becoming more golden, the greens softer, darker and more velvety. The clouds overhead were beginning to coalesce or dissolve into their sunset forms. The wind was a delicate breeze, the water gently lapping; then as we turned slowly to the east, I could hear a louder rushing above the engine noise—and the river spread before us into a broad lake crossed by a bar of wooded islands and rocks through gaps in which it poured.

As we came up in the shadow of the central island I was amazed by the colour of its rocks—they shone with a brilliant blue lustre, the blue of tempered steel or a Blue Gillette blade.

We landed on a tiny half-moon of sand sloping steeply into deep water, and I hastened to examine them. To my astonishment, nearer-to they proved in fact to be of a dark chocolate brown. But over their vesicled and pock-marked surfaces (they were volcanic) a double iridescence flashed—of red sometimes, but predominantly of this steely blue, which was perhaps a reflection of the sky.

It took us a good ten minutes to struggle through to the other side of the island, only 15 yards away, for between the interstices of the sharp-edged rocks rose the unbelievably dense gnarled vegetation typical of rapids. For when they are above water, sun and moisture are abundant, and the struggle for growth on them is fierce. Then the river level rises 20 or 30 feet, and deep below the surface go all these raging vegetable battles, perhaps for months at a time, once or twice a year. Obviously only the toughest plants can survive such conditions, and a peculiarly knotty, twisted growth of trees, scaly, barbed lianes and herbs results. In order to penetrate at all I wormed my way like a snake close to the ground, chopping here and there with my cutlass; sat upright for breath a little further; then bent double and slashed through the last solid yard till I could stand, perspiring and covered with fragments of bark and leaves, in the very centre of the islet. Then I crouched down again and continued to the far shore.

To the south the great lake stretched for another 2 miles, ending in a curve where the river swung westwards. Beyond, perhaps, would lie another curve, or the water might stretch away into ultimate blueness between straight walls. If we continued, perhaps we would find a new kind of tree or flower or butterfly, perhaps nothing. It was getting late.

On a spray of small leaves, 25 feet aloft, sat a small hawk, looking down on us and uttering a scream every now and again until Everard Thomas wantonly shot it. In the warm shallow water beside the rocks sunfish splashed, and the men fired arrows at them without success, using a toy bow and arrow which little James had brought.

I walked from end to end of the chain of islands, until stopped by the deep rapids at either end. The coolness of the water was maddening—I wanted to plunge in amongst the slapping waves and wash away the sweat and vegetable debris of the day. But the rocks were much too sharp to risk being banged against, and downstream would be perai. So instead I waded out as far as I dared, collecting Podostemonaceae of a species different from those in the other falls we had passed, with much smaller flowers of a tender green showing just above the water line.

In the potholes and vesicles of the blue rocks sand and gravel had collected, and this the men carefully scooped out and washed, hoping to find diamonds or grains of gold. I did the same, but found only quartz pebbles. Then Justin brought me a stone about three times the size of a pin's head, with a rather greasy surface but one or two sharp edges, which he said might be diamond.

'Yes, that's a diamond,' said Basil.

'How much do you want for it?' I asked.

'Five dollars,' said Justin.

'I haven't got that.'

'Then a big haimara hook.'

'O.K.'

The sun was about to set, and looking westwards across the golden ripples of the smooth sliding water I saw a lighter patch in the darkening forest upstream—where a large river was flowing into the Essequebo: the Konawaruk, famous for diamonds and gold.

We set out back to camp in the stillness of late sunset. The water was a mirror of jet, the forests on either side walls of black velvet with fantastically cut edges, the sky a bowl of nile-blue porcelain. Rings of silver floated on the water where fish rose for flies. The roaring of the falls faded, and we were lost in darkness only faintly lit by the amber and crimson fires over the forest on our left. They faded to lemon yellow, lingered and went out, whilst the sky darkened to purple shot with brilliant stars. The reflections of the stars floated like grey tears on the water beside us.

13

Sandbanks and Green Fish

Next morning I smoked the inside of a tin to give it a dull surface, filled it with water and dropped my stone and a few others in to compare their refractive powers. Whereas the others became almost invisible, like ghosts against the soot, my little stone shone brightly, so I wrapped it up and put it with some camera lenses into my haversack. Then, as the men were loading the boat for our return downstream, I walked a few yards up the trail with my camera to photograph a cauliflorous flower, which sprang directly low down from the trunk of a small Duguetia tree. As I moved around, adjusting my tripod so that it stood level, getting the flower focused and composed in the view finder, I was suddenly aware of the now familiar squeaking of muniris—only many times louder than usual. There, almost at my feet, at the base of the little tree, was a swarming, demented mass of Neoponeras. There were at least fifty of them, standing on their hind legs and hissing, or rushing round and round in circles. More were pouring out of a hole in the ground. They were marshalling themselves, working themselves up as wasps do before launching an attack in my direction—and I knew how fast they could run when roused. I seized my camera and fled, stamping hard to shake off any on my shoes. It was a great relief to reach the boat and push off. Until that moment I had not realised the strain that these ants had been.

Three immense otters bobbed up ahead of the boat and kept us company until one lolloped up the bank with a big perai in its jaws, and the others followed. A capybara stuck its head out of the water then plunged in alarm; an ocelot showed briefly on a riverside log, marmosets whistled from low branches as we rounded a bend. Strain though they had been, perhaps the muniris were but a sign that I had struck lucky, in finding this particular area where we had seen more animals than anywhere else—one of those rare patches of forest, seemingly no different from any other, that teem with life. That such patches objectively exist is confirmed by what the Indian hunters say. As many of the larger forest animals are omnivorous, food chains appear more complex than, for instance, in the great grassland regions. Perhaps the animals move around from patch to patch as different species of tree in different forest types come into fruit, as well as into hills and down again as the floods come and go? No one knows. I wished that I had been able to investigate.

We were now on our way back to civilisation which, in the shape of Bartica, we should reach in about a month's time. An hour after we had left camp we looked back and could still see grey smoke from our morning fires spiralling faintly in the air. From now on we should be on familiar ground. Suddenly I realised that in the excitement caused by the muniris I had lost my 'diamond'—I had taken it out of my haversack with a lens, and left it on the ground. It was too late to worry about it—I just could not face turning back, which would have wasted two or three hours, for a stone I had exchanged for a fishhook. So I composed myself and sat on top of the launch reading *Siren Land* again, comparing Norman Douglas' populous countryside, full of voluble peasants, crumbling temples, palaces, churches, with its rich history stretching from today back to a legendary dawn when mermaids played on its shores and Odysseus sailed by, with the almost unrecorded and unpeopled historyless land around me. An occasional broken bottle or flattened tin might speak of marginally livelier days. A few scratched rocks and pieces of crude pottery of uncertain age told of a past whose glories may be faintly echoed in Indian legends, but of which we know almost nothing. A few bricks remained of the Dutch occupation, a few names of the French. Waterton, Schomburgk, Barrington-Brown had passed here, and other famous travellers from Raleigh and Humboldt to Bates and Beebe had written about nearby places, and memories of their writings might provide tentative associations. The whole area could be traversed in a mere two days by boat, or flown over in twenty minutes. And yet, whether I liked it or not, to me it was more important than those much-tilled classical fields of Douglas. For here in this quiet landscape I had lived alone, silent, thinking, for two months. The swamps, rivers, sunsets, camps, the tall overhanging trees whose twigs and fruit had rained upon my canvas roof at night—all were now part of my being. The amorphous-seeming forests had become a host of societies, and had altered my outlook about my own world. The expedition way of life had come to seem natural—and we had almost turned into one of the features of the landscape.

I looked forward now almost with nostalgia to revisiting the earlier scenes of the expedition. Yet, as we continued down river it was like entering a new land. During our week at the Potaro mouth the river level had fallen fast, and the whole aspect of the lower river had changed. Many of the small rocky islets which I remembered had coalesced, linked by newly exposed white sandy beaches; and when we came to Crabbu falls, the granite tors stood high out of the water around us. We crossed to avoid the dangerous Tigre rapids only, to our dismay, to find Kumaka hole unrecognisable. There was no stopping or turning round: the water was smooth and black in a rock-walled channel, sliding fast round a bend ahead from which we could hear a tumultuous roaring. A fallen tree leaned far over the bank, smothered in trailing lianes, obscuring even what little would otherwise have been visible. The roaring grew louder— we all stood up as we rounded the bend, I on the roof, the men below, and strained our eyes ahead. Running at high speed we passed through a positive valley of towering rocks between which the river surged, bumped once lightly on a hidden boulder, and then we were through on a tide which swept between two islands, into smoothness.

Our old camp opposite Omai was now inhabited by a grey-bearded Neptune-like old Negro fisherman with an invisible girl friend. Her lurid pink drawers hung drying on lines among the trees, but we never saw her, for she was subtly spirited away from the camp in the night when we were asleep.

In the morning I went across for a last look at the mining camp, and was invited to stay for lunch. Then, with yet more borrowed rations, we followed the long swing of the river downstream all afternoon. As it expanded a long vista opened ahead—and stretching from side to side lay a barrier of purest shimmering gold, an enormous sandbank exposed by the falling water. On the left, it came right up to the wall of Awaraballi palms; to the right a channel remained open barely a quarter of a mile wide through which the diminished river flowed.

Our old Cayman Lagoon camp opposite the Awaraballis was now perched high on a 20-foot cliff above us. Two men clambered up to it along a fallen tree and lowered ropes to us in the boat; then steps were cut in the clay cliff-side, and we disembarked. Underfoot the earth was dry, baked hard by a month's sun. The ground under the hog-plum tree was now scattered with sweet yellow plums, and there were many more signs than before of visiting rodents or other animals. With only a little sweeping up and cutting of sprouting stumps and weeds the camp was soon ready for use again.

Whilst this was being done I walked up and down along the cliff top.

In front, across a mile of rippling water, lay the sandbank—dun coloured, white, gold, or even a fleshy pink according to the mood of the skies. A new sound filled the immensity of air and water. Formerly there had only been the wind in the trees, the faint stirring of the river, unobtrusive bird songs, and sometimes the howler monkeys. Now harsh whirring cacophonies, inappropriate and unexpected over a tropical river, came from tiny white specks wheeling in the air: terns, come inland to nest. Sometimes they flew by in pairs swooping low to the waves and then high up and up, in endless chasing games.

Then, looking down into the olive-green water I saw two beautiful fish just beneath the surface, like slim translucent green ghosts: arawhannas, fish of very ancient family and amost prehistoric appearance. They swam lazily, gracefully, like green rippling knives, by snake-like undulations of the body and not by means of fins. Upstream and downstream they cruised, sometimes side by side, sometimes far apart, scouring the wave tops for fallen insects, which they snatched with a sideways twist of the head.

One day, when we were again short of food, Basil threw out a baited hook to attract one of them, and when it rushed up and mouthed the bait (they seldom actually swallow a hook) I shot it with my 12-bore from above. At once it turned over and began to sink slowly: we only just managed to scoop it out of the water with a butterfly net. Three inches or so of water must have broken the force of the shot considerably, for they had not penetrated its scales, though they had scored it down both sides. Indeed, it was only stunned and began to revive, so we killed it with a cutlass.

I examined it with delight, for it was one of the most beautiful fish I had ever seen. About 4 feet long, the body was like a bean pod in shape—slim and straight-backed, with flat sides going down to a knife-edge below. The tail tapered ribbon-like to an acute point, and there were no prominent fins. The whole fish was covered in circular scales as big as silver dollars, edged at the rear with bands of pale pink and silver. Above, the general colour was a deep lovely sea green, shading below to silver, so that it was nearly invisible as it swam among the wavelets. But its most extraordinary feature was its mouth, which opened in a slit across the top of the head, like the flap of a mechanical scoop, adapted for snatching floating guava or lana fruit, insects or fry from the surface. Behind and slightly below were huge, round, black and silver eyes, fixed gazing upwards. The flesh was delicately flavoured, the bones few, long and white, and it made a meal for everyone, for almost all of it was edible.

Like the more famous arapaima gigas of the same family, which is the largest freshwater fish in the world, this fish has spread into Guyana from the Amazon basin, and is now slowly moving down the Essequebo. Savannahs form the watershed between the river systems of Guyana and the Amazon, and in the rainy season these are flooded so that a man could sail up the Amazon, Rio Negro, Rio Branco, Takutu, and Ireng, across the savannahs, then down the Rupununi and the Essequebo to Bartica and the sea. By this route there has been a migration of the Amazonian fauna into the main rivers of Guyana. River porpoises have already spread right down to the mouth of the Essequebo and, apparently by following the coast, up into the Courantyne. Whether there has been a contrary migration of species from Guyana into Brazil I do not know, but it seems likely.

Later, when it was dark, an opossum following the 'bush-cow' path that ran along the riverside cliff ran straight into the lighted circle of my tent, sat up apparently blinded by the glare, and stretched its forelegs up into the air, as if invoking heaven. Then off it went in a circle, and a few minutes later I heard it blundering about in the darkness under the hog-plum tree, making so much noise that I rushed out and chased it away.

Every time a plum dropped on the stretched canvas of my tarpaulin it made a noise like a sharp, short explosion. Whenever a gust shook the tree it was like being in the trenches, and at first sleep was impossible. Huge bats hung upside down in the tree and the sound of their guzzling was at times disturbingly loud, as was that of the ghostly army of labbas, accouries, adouris, red snakes and other beasts beneath. My torch beam illuminated eyes not only on the ground and in the branches, but half-way up the trunk as well. Right through the night the terns seemed to continue their screaming; and in the grey dawn light around 5.30, as breakfasts were cooked and coffee was boiled, they were still up, wheeling and crying in the sky over the sandbank, their harsh voices emphasising the loneliness of the miles of river and forest.

We set out muffled in the whiteness of towering mist banks, sometimes with little glimpses over the calm lilac and grey water, towards the Awaraballis. It had been unthinkable to attempt to cut through their ferocious ranks before, but now that the water was lower I decided to try. Gradually the sun drew aside the cotton-wool curtains, pulling them upwards in gleaming dissolving masses until they vanished completely, leaving nothing to obscure the finely textured blue above.

Near-to the sandbank looked like an optical illusion, with its tiny 4-foot cliffs overhanging the water, its scalloped bays and miniature undulating hills and dales. Along its shores were a series of raised beaches—indicating the successive levels at which the river had paused in its fall. Where sand and water actually met it was difficult to see, for the transparent water revealed every particle, at the same time half-reflecting the wavy sculptured sand above. We turned into a wide bay and drove ahead until the boat slid to a standstill. Then we jumped overboard and waded ashore.

Far ahead over the blazing sand, black specks, the nearest some 200 yards away, began running even before we were aware of them: turtles, keen-eyed beasts, come ashore to lay their sun-incubated eggs in holes in the sand, and now toddling as fast as they could to the water's edge. With a sudden unpremeditated exuberance, we were all away running as fast as we could over the open windswept plain to catch them. No words can describe the joy of this moment. For the first time in two months I could move, could swing my arms and legs without striking something. My heart, my lungs, my muscles, stretched; my brain was empty except for the ecstasy of this wild race which we were all running, chasing the ridiculous stumpy turtles as they legged it for the water.

When we were 30 yards from it the nearest turtle reached the sandbank's edge and flopped into the river. I drew up, panting on the little cliff top and saw it breast-stroking away under water. Then it popped its head up for an instant a long distance out, and we turned away breathless and happy, and flung ourselves on the sand laughing. It was sheer liberation to lie there with a land horizon 3 miles away instead of 10 feet, under an open sun instead of a screen of leaves, with free wind blowing in our lungs, instead of a soup of mosquitoes and water vapour.

We picked ourselves up, and shuffled along the undulating plain of loose golden grains, following the queer parallel lines of the turtles' footsteps with which it was criss-crossed, each step 6 or 8 inches from the ones behind, in front, and at the side, forming a series of little squares as if made by a machine. The tracks wandered up and over the delicate waves of sand; and we walked beside them prodding the sand with a stick to find the soft loose places where the eggs were buried. Justin was skilled at this, and he found two caches, one of twenty and the other of eleven eggs: white, shaped like hens' eggs, but smaller with hard calcareous shells, unlike the spherical leathery ping-pong balls that sea turtles lay. In Guyana these turtles are found only in the Essequebo. But, like the arapaima and the arawhanna, they too have come over the watershed from Amazonia.

The palms formed a solid wall half a mile long, emerging from the water of a series of lagoons behind the sandbank. Almost everywhere they were obliteratingly dominant. Only at two places along their entire length did we see even the leaves of a vine emerging.

At one point where they grew straight out of sand I set Jothan and the other men to cut inland, while Jonah, Justin, and I continued examining their outer edge. In most places the now-stagnant lagoons were half choked with small palms with fan-shaped leaves, unlike the feather-leaves of the Awaraballi. Then I realised that these were young Awaraballis, and their leaves not true fans, but caused by cohesion of the leaflets, at least at the tip. Some of these 'fan-leaved' seedlings stood on the bare sand, but many were only just showing their leaf-tips above the water, so that for the greater part of the year the young of this palm must live submerged, one of the most aquatic of all palms. It was roughly at the high-water mark of debris that the change to the adult feather-leaf form took place, and I wondered to what extent a fan-shaped leaf-tip was suited to underwater life—for most submerged plants have finely divided ribbon-shaped or at least flexible leaves, whereas the young leaves of this palm were stiff, prickly and cutinised, and of a heavy dark green.

So far as I knew this palm swamp was unique in Guyana; and no other solid and exclusive growth of them has been reported by any traveller or botanist.* Elsewhere it is a plant growing only in clumps or singly. But here some combination of circumstances had allowed it to burst out in this magnificence of nodding grey-green plumage and menacing armament. It is probably of recent origin, for Astrocaryums are a variable lot; and it seems to be spreading rapidly outside its present range in the upper Essequebo and Demerara rivers, wherever there are silt banks and inundated lands.

Along the line which the men had cut we pushed cautiously into the interior of the palm wood. Immediately under their shelter the soil changed from sand to a thick, springy mould derived from the decomposition of the many generations that had occupied the site. Although the dense-packed crowns were only 40 or 50 feet above the ground, it was very dark and the air was close, filled with the damp odour of decay. In contrast with our recent explosion of feeling outside, in here we felt smothered by the jumbled fallen and leaning palm-trunks, the debris of leaves and spathes. We had to guard even the movements of our hands, for everything, even the mould on the ground, bristled with spines. A fall would have been serious, for

---

* Since this was written I have been through a great deal of the territory in which this species of palm is found, and have seen no other woodland of this size.

though many of the spines on the ground were rotten and harmless, thousands of others remained sharp at least at the tip, and would have driven deep into one's body, or passed through one's foot.

Then the ground undulated down, and soon the palms were rising out of deep, murky water. As we pushed onwards, the water slowly rose up to our armpits. The bottom was covered with fallen trunks, leaves, midribs spathes, in varying stages of decay; and above water the foliage was swathed in masses of scrambling razor grass, which cut our hands and faces as savagely as the spines stabbed. Step by step we felt our way forward, our feet protected only by thin canvas shoes, our bodies by the lightest clothes, holding our breaths lest we overbalance and become human pincushions. One spine ran half an inch into the sole of my foot, but I dared not stop to extract it.

At last, some 60 yards from our entry, the palms stopped abruptly, giving place to the shrubbery of second growth, and the soil changed from mould to a sticky clay. As we collected together again Justin raised a hand bristling like a piece of a porcupine. I worked on it for twenty minutes, but many of the spines were half-rotten and we were still digging out broken-off bits two days later.

Beyond, after a narrow flood plain, lay gently rolling brown sand upon which grew magnificent, tall columnar trees bearing a lofty canopy. Sometimes one could see as much as 30 yards between them. We walked along at good speed, quite silently over a floor of moist leafy humus, until we came to a steep-sided valley in the bottom of which a stream glowed like a giant ruby, as the sun struck down into its tannin-stained water. All round it thick peat lay over the sand, full of rotting twigs and logs, from which ferns grew in tufts, while huge aroids perched like a display of hats on the limbs of the vast Mora trees. Strewn everywhere were the yellow fallen flowers of a Cassia.

Here we ended our line and lunched, watching the wine-coloured water flow past; then walked back to the sandbank with Basil in front, the yellow combs of a pair of powis he had shot bobbing along over his shoulder.

We sat down in the shade of a few isolated Awaraballis which

P

stood on the sandbank, looking like extras in a film saga of Biblical times, and gazed across the sand to the wind-whipped river with its sapphire-sparkling waves. Around a distant point downstream came a small boat I had never seen before, rolling heavily and emitting big puffs of white smoke which stood above it momentarily, like billowing sails, before dissolving.

Always I felt a wild leap of apprehension at the sight of a boat. Visitors, passers-by, news of the outside world, were disturbing: fear was mixed with my excitement as I opened my letters, hope rising, despite all efforts to suppress it, that one would bring some possibility of escape from the Colonial Service. While, if there were no letters, I would be bitterly downcast. So much for my emotional independence when put to the test—but now I had a special reason for uneasiness, for almost any day I expected Smeed and Taylor to arrive. I knew that the work had come up to my own personal standards—Jonah and the other men had often told me that we had worked on under conditions in which other expeditions had given up. I was anxious to show Smeed that I had done well, and I intended to give him a warm welcome—and to win his friendship if that were possible. I hoped that living in proximity for a while might achieve this.

Taylor, unfortunately, was in charge at Bartica and so responsible directly or indirectly for the shortages of food on the expedition. I was therefore worried lest it was his intention to discomfort me if possible, to draw attention away from this. Both men rather liked playing the God-like superior, and my rather ironic disposition made me see this perhaps a little too keenly. But I was determined that hostilities would never begin.

We saw the boat stop at the camp. Could it contain my superiors? Then, after ten minutes, to my relief it pulled out again. It sailed slowly past us, its load of balata bleeders waving a greeting over the water. The men emerged from the forest, paused dazed by the glare, then spread out over the sand searching for more turtles' eggs. Then we set sail in a breeze that blew the tops off the waves and sent them spattering over me as I sat on the roof.

Among the letters that had arrived was a communication from Taylor: 'A.C.F. (Survey Party)—prepare camp properly for arrival of Acting C. of F. and myself on November 3rd or the following day to inspect the work of the Survey party. Asst. Deputy C. of F. (Bartica).'

There was also a small note to the effect that certain conditions of the men's pay had been altered as from the beginning of the trip, which meant that their pay would be reduced by about three days' wages. The men had no written contracts—most of them could not write—but they had agreed to specific terms. and they had worked well: they rose long before dawn, their day's work started at 6.30 or 7 a.m., and mostly it would be 5 before we returned, dead weary to camp, when they still had to cook for themselves. At times their work was both hard and dangerous. I did not see how it was possible justly to alter their terms of work half-way through the job. Most of them were saving their wages for their wives and families, so that even a small reduction would concern them greatly.

I wondered if I should tell them now, or wait and argue their case when my chiefs arrived. It would certainly be easier not to tell them, as they would be bound to take offence. If they walked out, as they so easily might, it would mean the end of the expedition—and I wanted to complete my work.

My ways and those of these men had somehow coincided, and between us there had developed a warmth where to start with we had had little in common, except that we belonged to the same species. I had never been in a position of command before, and I never pretended to superiority, except by virtue of my job. I had never asked them to do anything unreasonable, or that I was not prepared to do myself, nor had I ever overstepped ordinary good manners in speaking to them. I respected their integrity. They were the sort of people who think before they decide: canny, astute judges, quick to detect trickery, weakness or stupidity.

Before accepting their jobs they had come and gone, chewing the matter over, asking questions. But once they had agreed to terms they had stuck to their side of the bargain. I felt my bosses should do the same.

So I decided to tell them and seek their co-operation to carry on our work until my chiefs arrived—when I should be on their side in pressing to get the order rescinded. So I called them together and explained the new terms. As they listened, their

faces hardened, their fists clenched, and when I had finished
there was much muttering.

Sandy spoke up in a bitter voice: 'That's very bad, Sir.
Twenty-five years I work for the Forest Department. I always
get fair treatment till now.'

'Nothing like this ever happen before,' agreed the old timers.
Young Levi and Rufus said nothing, but listened to what was
said, conscious that something important was happening, and
that presently they should have to declare an opinion.

Said Philbert: 'Also never before we had short rations like
on this trip, and always measurin' to make dey go far. Every
time before we had rations to spare, and at de end of de trip
dey share out. Now dey don' even sen' 'nough widout borrowin'.'

I told them that in a week's time my boss would be visiting
us, and that I would bring their case before him and support it.

At this they became calmer. Sandy then said: 'If it was anyone but you, master, I would take the boat and gone, but with
you I go carry on like before.'

They stood around for a while, talking and grumbling
together, then went off in a group. I could still hear their
voices as they disappeared among the trees along the path.

Next morning as I was shaving, I heard loud shouting from
the men's camp. I hurried across and found a group clustered
around one of the small under-storey trees. Clinging to the fork
of one of its branches, below a termites' nest, was a little furry
animal, somewhat like a long-haired dachshund with a long
bushy tail, and blank fearful eyes like small black buttons. It was
a tamandua, or little ant-eater. It clung desperately to its
branch, and gently swung its pointed snout around to look at
me, uttering not a sound.

Amidst a shout of laughter, one of the men threw a large lump
of wood which struck the branch just above its head, causing it
to recoil and tighten its foothold. Then another man set to work
with an axe at the base of the tree. In a rage I forbade him to
continue, and told them that I should be very angry indeed if
any harm came to it. They all looked sheepish and sulky—for
capturing it, playing with it, perhaps torturing it a bit before
killing it for its skin, would have relieved the boredom of camp
life. However, I insisted they should leave it alone, telling them
that it was a harmless and interesting creature. When I

returned an hour later it was still there, looking down cautiously with its infinitely desolate black eyes. That evening it had gone.

Next morning three small caymans watched us as we skirted the scalloped, wavy edge of the great sandbank. As we drew near two submerged and disappeared, but the third remained gazing boldly at us with saucy eyes. So we changed direction and raced towards him: he sank, till only his eyes and nose showed like a trio of floating walnuts; then, in a sudden flurry, dived when the boat was almost on top of him.

The water in the lagoon that lay between the sandbank and the shore was moving, suggesting that an unseen river opened into it among the trees ahead. I decided to sail up this river, hoping that it would lead into the lake that had previously terminated one of our lines, or enable us to by-pass it. We stopped the engine for fear that sand would be sucked in by the pump, and poled steadily along till we drew abreast of the opening of a deep, almost circular bay. At the head of this a turtle plunged into the water. At once I stood up on the roof and saw it, like a large dart-board, swimming gently under water towards us. I pointed, and in an instant the men were overboard, forming a semi-circle to cut it off. The water was only about 3 feet deep, and I could hardly believe my eyes—for suddenly it doubled and accelerated, and shot to and fro, fast as the swiftest fish, in a series of zigzag manœuvres which threw everyone into confusion. Then it was away, heading for the open river, with a faint surface ripple marking its now deep under-water flight.

The channel varied much in depth. Where the water was deep the sunlight was lost in its darkness, and only the motes and specks at the surface were illuminated so that the river appeared as if dusted with pale yellow; where it was shallow the sunlight struck through to the sandy bottom, and the water glowed an intense port-wine red.

After 100 yards we turned back, for the river was too narrow and winding for the boat, and coming out, landed on the sand-bank. We then walked until we came to dry land alongside it where I sent the men to cut inland under Jonah and Lord, the Negro ranger in training; then I, with Jothan and Elias, re-turned to the boat and set sail for a point further south where I wished to examine and photograph one of the forest types that fringed the sand.

As the boat slid to rest in shallow water I saw vague menacing forms flit away over the bottom: giant stingrays, some almost 4 feet across, others small as dinner plates. We stopped along-side one monster who stirred in his murky bed and then settled down again. Through the water I examined him. Coloured to match the sand but a little paler, the eyes and spiracles on his back made him look like a big circular ghost, with his long tail half hidden.

With bow and arrow Basil shot the creature, then grasping the arrow, which projected waving into the air—for the water was only 2 feet deep—he held it firmly against the side of the boat whilst the ray lashed to and fro with its terrible poison-barbed tail, whipping sand and water into a turmoil. Then quickly he jerked it on board where we killed it with a cutlass before it could do any damage. It was a large fish, weighing 16 lb. or more, and its poison-mucus-coated barb was 8 inches long. The sight of these fish made us all shudder, for we realised how lucky we had been, jumping carelessly over the side in the shallows. Barrington-Brown describes what could have hap-pened to any of us:

My interpreter, William, was unfortunate enough to step upon one, which, being of the colour of the bottom, was not observed. It drove its spine or sting into the side of his instep, producing a jagged wound which bled profusely. I immedi-ately put laudanum on the wound and gave him a strong dose of ammonia. In a quarter of an hour after he was writh-ing on the ground in great agony, actually screaming at times with the pain which he felt in the wounded part, in his groin; and under one armpit. His foot and leg were so cold that he got one man to light a fire and support his foot over it, per-sisting in trying to put it in the flames. I gave him two doses of laudanum, one shortly after the other, without relieving his sufferings in the slightest degree. After three hours of intense pain he became easier, but had returns of it at intervals during the night. For a week he was unable to put his foot to the ground, and the wound did not heal thoroughly for six weeks.

The boat was aground and we had to wade ashore. Moved to caution I took with me a stick and walked slowly, prodding the silty ground ahead and watching as in dozens these soup-plate-like fish shuffled away across the bottom. According to Indian legend they originated in the Rupununi River, a large tributary of the Essequebo, from Mocca-Mocca leaves plucked and scattered in it by the ancient hero Inchkinang, as a means of preventing his younger brother following him to the floor of the Mighty Ocean in search of the Giant Snail. In fact, like the Arapaima, the Arawhanna and the river turtles, they seem to be of Amazonian origin.

After our work, while waiting for the men who had cut inland to return, we tried to stalk several turtles—black specks on the sands half a mile away. There was little cover and however slowly and cautiously we moved forward, we were always detected. Sun and sand were hot, and weary with unsuccess we gave up the chase. I decided to bathe whilst the other three went searching for eggs. I selected a shallow cove with a narrow entrance, through which I should be able to see a cayman even if it approached submerged, and after a careful scrutiny of the bottom for stingrays, I slipped in and lay contentedly in the warm water. It was an extraordinary relaxation to lie naked, swim a few strokes, splash in the shallows, dig into the soft sand of the bottom and lie half covered, like one of the rays.

Across the mouth of the little bay the wind was blowing the water into choppy, steel-blue waves. Baroque clouds began piling up, and when they crossed the sun it was suddenly chilly above water. With a few warning drops, heavy as lead, rain descended in ice-chilly showers. I submerged and lay quite warm with only my nose out of water. I was thinking, trying to compose the mixture of loneliness, despair, disillusionment, and enthusiasm which surged, alternately dominant, within me these days. If only I could settle for one mood—but I was not my own master, or able to shape events coherently.

I noticed through the rain a large, round, hairy object swimming softly towards me through the straits. It opened big sparkling eyes, and proved to be Elias, who had decided to bathe too. He stopped a few yards away, very respectfully, and we started chatting. I had noticed his beautiful natural manners, his kind and gentle ways, and his magnificent physique:

his smooth, golden brown enormously strong body would have overjoyed any sculptor. He exuded simplicity and good nature and seemed in every way a happy man. Yet now he told me of his life in Georgetown, where for the first time he had encountered spitefulness.

'Mr. Guppy,' he said, 'I is from Santa Mission on Kamuni Creek—do you know that side?'

'Yes,' I said. 'It is one of the most beautiful places I have been to.'

'I was always happy till I left there. Then I grow serious. You is the first nice master I work for. Mostly dey don' care at all. First I come to Georgetown to work as house boy for an engineer. I do my best to please him, and he kind to me. That made the other servants jealous. They break things and say I done it. They mess up my work and say Elias lazy.'

'How horrible.'

'I get so miserable I leave. My master beg me to stay because he know de truth. I go back to Kamuni, but I miss Georgetown bad.'

'What do you miss most?'

'De pictures. I used to go every night.'

'Didn't you get bored with them?'

He smiled to show how impossible that was.

'No. Whenever I gets money I goes to Georgetown for a few days, and every night I goes.'

Here was a man used only to the jungle, whose only possessions were a hammock, a cutlass and a canoe. It was hard to imagine what impressions would remain in his mind. I could not guess, and he could not explain. But I sensed that the screen presented a mythological world of such wonder that real life was meaningless in comparison.

'After what you see there, there is nothing. So I just works to keep my wife and children. I'm a happy man, I don't care— except for go to Georgetown.' He smiled again.

'What do you do now?'

'Two years ago I move near Bartica. I build a house on a small creek. An' I gets jobs when I can. I glad to come on this trip, to save money. No drinking and spending with other men, like mos' jobs. Also I make basket, to sell when I get back.'

'How do you sell them?'

'A man in Stabroek Market, in Georgetown, sell them for me —good money. After I return, I don't work for a few months, I go jus' live with my wife and children. I might do some wood-cutting, and grow vegetables—I got a good field. Also I go hunt and catch fish. Nice life. No need for money.'

Somehow he had preserved himself. He still found his happiness in the forest Indian's life—when he could escape from the need to earn money. It was almost a civilised man's dream—but for us the chains get tighter, the moments and places of possible escape dwindle.

The rain ceased and as the sun broke forth the men returned and we embarked, laden with turtles' eggs and with one neatly filleted stringray. It was cooked and eaten by Basil that evening, but remembering its unpleasant appearance alive foolishly I did not try it. The eggs on the other hand were delicious, with a slightly chalky flavour and texture. Those that we did not use we put in a box of sand where they would keep fresh for several weeks. Those which had tiny dark spots showing through their shells, a sign that they were developing, were eaten at once.

Below this line we were back in the alluvial plains, formerly impassably flooded, now a mushy landscape through which fast-running creeks of black water coiled between steep mud walls. Sometimes in them small arawhannas rippled lazily, suggesting that they bred upstream.

Returning along one such line, a sudden chill smell—and from the south-east black clouds appeared, obscuring the sun and coagulating into islands and continents. Thunder rolled with a crash that shook us, and as we hurried blue lightning flashed overhead and heavy drops came pouring down, thrusting the leaves and twigs aside, pelting the ground around us, shaking the ferns, making the dead leaves dance.

Quickly I stripped and put my shirt in my haversack to keep it dry. We stumbled along hardly able to see, holding palm leaves over our heads in the grey rain-mist that filled the air and roared in drum rolls over the trees. The cold was bitter, the wet winds whirled against my back and bones. Then the sun suddenly blazed out again and set the last few falling drops a-glitter, the leaf-tips sparkling. Dry again in a few minutes, I resolved in future to carry a spare white cotton vest for extra warmth against the possibility of another soaking—for this storm seemed to presage the break up of the fine weather. And, indeed, every day after this electricity piled up in the atmosphere and thunder growled about overhead. We hurried to complete our work, fearful lest the impending rainy season prevent us.

Caymans now swarmed on the river. Their snouts cruised along as dark specks on the water, and at night we heard them splashing and roaring. The lagoon behind the camp had become a great deep hollow, almost dry except at the far end where the trees drew back, leaving a pool open to the sky. Here a few goggle-eyed foot-long babies still splashed fiercely, survivors no doubt of larger broods mostly eaten by the cannibalistic adults, or which had escaped to the river by some opening amongst the trees.

After our days on the sandbank this formerly delightful camp now seemed like a prison. How I hated the enclosing jungle! The harsh barrier of leaves and twigs, the face-enwrapping spiders' webs—and now, after each rain, the thick mud underfoot, the wavering humid air, the sweet smell of crumbling logs and decomposing leaves, the great crawling millipedes that accompanied decay. Bête Rouges, ticks were on every living leaf—and under the dead leaves scorpions, centipedes, cockroaches. Everything was so complex, while on the sand all was simple, clean, washed, newly emerged from the waves. Perhaps crocodiles, turtles or iguanas walked the sandbanks at night, perhaps stingrays sidled in their shallows, but they were visible, in the open. So when the time came to move again I determined that we should make our next camp on a sandbank. Our old camp at the foot of Mt. Arisaru had been particularly attractive, and that was where we now were heading, but I was intoxicated by the thought of having an unobstructed horizon of river, forest, and sky, of being able to take a stroll, or go for a swim in warm shallow water. Yet although the river level was still dropping fast, to be safe from sudden floods we should need a bank at least 6 feet clear of the water.

The flat slab of Arisaru appeared ahead, ringed round with vertical precipices hundreds of feet high, picked out by the slant of the sun. The river narrowed suddenly to less than half a mile—and in it to my delight, jutting out from the bank, was a plain of yellow-brown sand, dotted with the rotund figures of turtles beginning their mad race to the water's edge as they saw us approach.

'Overboard! Overboard!' shouted the men, as each one flung itself frantically into the water.

But the sandbank was only some 3 feet high. I pointed out the flocks of terns twittering round it, and sitting in little depressions in the sand where they had laid their eggs, their tails and wing tips sticking out behind—looking like fleets of tiny fishing boats with sails furled and masts lowered. If the birds had nested, I suggested, surely they must know instinctively that the water would not rise again? But the men were not convinced.

A huge bird came sailing clumsily by on creaking, gamp-like pinions: a pelican—an unexpected sight. It circled the boat, inspecting us with the disillusioned eye of an old roué, and exhibiting that dishevelledness and patchiness of the pate that makes pelicans so endearing. The men had not seen one before, and reached for their guns. They were amazed at its tameness, and bursting to shoot it. But I told them that pelicans were uneatable, and were common in the West Indies, where they were never molested. This seemed to convince them, at least for the moment.

I had never seen a pelican before in Guyana, even on the coast, and very few man-of-war birds, or of the larger fish-eating sea birds common in the West Indies, a fact that I attributed to the muddiness of the sea. I secretly hoped that this bird had a mate and might found a colony on the Essequebo River, where fish were plentiful and could easily be seen in the comparatively clear water. So I emphatically forbade the men to shoot it, saying that I should be angry if it were harmed in any way.

No sandbank suitable for camping had been seen when, finally, we came into the lee of Arisaru, winding our way through groves of water guavas, previously submerged but now growing among rocks, beaches, and gurgling shallows. Our camp site now stood on a splendid hillside terrace above great bare tables of reddish rock. We passed a mass of rusty iron, where a steel pontoon for the goldfields had been wrecked, negotiated a hundred yards of raging currents, and at last disembarked upon one of these vast red-veined rock slabs, deliciously cool underfoot in the late afternoon.

I had the men enlarge the clearing so that there was plenty of room for two more tents on either side of my own, in case my bosses arrived, and room besides in which to walk around and think. The site was magnificent, commanding the narrows and the whole swing of the river southwards, with superb views over forests, islands, rocks, sandbanks, on into blue distances.

As dusk fell the air was filled with thousands of dragonflies, swooping and hawking low over the ground, as though all the dragonflies for miles around had gathered to feast on the many insects disturbed by the clearing and felling of the day. The ants in the old Kakaralli tree behind the camp were on the move again in their rustling throngs, with tiny leaf fragments held aloft. Frogs boomed in the bushes, and every now and again came the drum-strokes of the tympani frog, which seemed always to live near rapids. Kunyow had built an elaborate bathing stage for me, with a platform on piles projecting some 15 feet out over the stream, almost within reach of the nearest water guavas. From it I could look far up and down, and as I flung bucketsfull of chilly water over myself I could hear the men shouting from sheer exuberance as they swum and splashed from the rocky beaches and in the racing water a little way downstream. Basil was fishing from the stern of the boat, flinging perai, jerking discs of silver, on to the shore. Among the rocks fires glowed red in the twilight, and heavy smoke coiled up through the leaves. The air was cool, kept in constant movement by the water, the sound of which, rushing and bubbling a few yards down the slope from my tent, was a relief to the spirit.

I went to bed early. It was a bright moonlight night, and as I lay in bed I could see the track of the moon across the water, through the silhouetted black tracery of the guava bushes. I turned over, trying to sleep, and seemed to feel a steady movement. Was it the pulsation of the falls, or the motion of the earth itself, spinning on its axis? I had pulled my bed clear of the canvas roof, and I could see huge golden stars drifting slowly across the gaps in the trees.

14

The Big Chiefs

A Morpho butterfly with scintillating blue wings flew past my mosquito net and settled on a tent post. It was dawn, and I was half awake, watching the mist-muffled river in the pale light. Seen through my mosquito net outlines were softened and dissolved: the sinewy twisted guavas clung precariously to their rocks, like trees in a Chinese drawing, mist-spirals rising from them like clouds of midges on a summer's day; over the far forest, banks of white cloud stirred in the sun; there was a smell of damp things touched by warmth.

Behind the camp a line led inland, and I strolled along it in my pyjamas, for the melancholy rising trill, piercingly sweet, of a tinamou came from close at hand. Suddenly I was aware of two white objects bobbing about close to the ground in the undergrowth. I bent low and gazed intently, until I saw that the white patches, now motionless, were the breasts of two birds as big as turkeys. They had large golden wattles, and their bright round eyes were fixed upon me. They gave curious little honking cries, ran off a little way, then stopped again and looked to see if I was following. They were powis, or curassows (Crax alector), very delicious eating, with fine, rather dry white flesh. We were short of food as usual, and I had my bosses to welcome, so I fetched my gun and crept cautiously forward till I could just make them out ahead running and stopping, occasionally showing their white breasts, but most of the time difficult to see. I could not get an unimpeded view through the bushes, and I dared not run lest they fly away. The most I could do was to creep along quietly in their wake. Briefly one showed itself clearly about 30 yards away, and I quickly aimed and fired. It leaped into the air with a cry and fell on its side. Its companion at once flew up into a low branch, uttering cries of distress. It refused to fly away whilst its mate still lived, but called out plaintively, and even flew lower and nearer as I approached. I shot it, and it fell heavily, then fluttered away along the ground, obviously dying slowly. For a long distance I pursued the panting wounded bird through the thick under-growth, trying to kill it with my gun butt. It would crouch seemingly helpless under a bush, its breast heaving, and bloody foam dribbling from its beak. Then as I drew close it summoned its strength and dragged itself away for a little distance further. I thought I should never catch it, but at last I pinned it to the ground and snapped its neck—Kunyow had shown me how to break these birds' necks quickly, by holding them by the head and whirling them round and round like a toy rattle. Then I searched until I found the first bird, and killed that too.

The beauty of the dying birds, with their gentle eyes, soft glossy coats of blue-black feathers, long slender legs feather-pantalooned down to the knee, snowy breasts and buttercup yellow combs, lingered in my mind for weeks afterwards. Their fidelity to one another haunted me. I could not forget or excuse my brutal pursuit. I made a resolution never again to shoot another animal unless my need was great, and unless I was sure of killing it outright. And I have kept it with few lapses ever since.

Two miles upstream from Arisaru, the half-obscured tunnel and marking-post of an old unfinished line stood upon a 15-foot cliff of yellow clay, and here we started work. Little Rufus went scrambling up the sticky wall with a rope up which we in turn followed. Basil struck off along the riverside with his gun, and we cut in along the old path until we found its end, only a short distance in, in a marsh of stilt-rooted trees. The ground here was a confusion of hoof prints and the air fetid with the smell of pigs. The men grew restless, excited at the thought of another hunt. Then came a succession of shots: Basil had encountered the herd.

We continued on our way, cutting through the stilted wood-land, or sometimes in open savannah waist-deep in saw-edged sedges, reeds, and rushes, and ankle-deep in water, for most of the day.

'Water camudi plenty here,' said Little Rufus, pointing to some flattened growth. We skirted deep pools of onyx water with lily-pads floating on the surface and yellow flower-spikes rising from submerged bladderworts.

The weather was squally, with bright hot sunlight alternating with sudden pelting cold rain.

Then ahead we saw a line of high forest, and soon we were walking up a gentle slope of white sand under immense trees, and on into superb forests growing on level stretches of white and brown sand. The miles sped away as we enumerated, and when we were finished the eye of the sun was straight ahead through the trees, its rays lighting up the huge shafts which rose all around. It was late. We turned our backs, and racing after our elongating shadows, hurried towards the boat. Darkness had already fallen in the forest when we came out into the lower savannah area where brilliant red and golden-brown reeds waved autumnally under an intense blue sky; and it was five-thirty by the time we reached the boat.

We slid down the rope and landed amongst a shoal of silver perai and three big bristly peccaries, shot by Basil in the morn-ing. We were laden with food: powis, wild pig, fish, and an Acouri; while for a vegetable I had chopped down a Turu palm and cut out the heart: mountain cabbage, one of the world's delicacies. I could have feasted a score of men.

Basil now told me that, two hours before, my chiefs' boat had put in at our camp, just visible downstream. I was pleased that our long working hours would be so immediately noticeable.

Yet I was dismayed as we drew near the camp to see that instead of pitching their tents alongside mine, where plenty of room had been cleared for them, my visitors had placed theirs directly in front, obscuring my view. Had this been done deliberately? Brushing the thought aside I ran forward and greeted my visitors warmly—Smeed, Taylor, and Taylor's wife—saying how delighted I was to see them.

But they were far from reciprocating. I had done wrong, it appeared, in not being there when they arrived. Presumably I should have sat around all day awaiting them. Years after I can still feel the chill of that greeting, and my realisation that, far from being regarded as their host, I was merely a little appanage.

From the moment of arrival they had taken over the camp. My cook and camp boy, both of whom I paid out of my own salary, my stores and utensils, which were my personal belong-ings, had been commandeered. In any case I would have put them at my visitors' disposal—but I was upset at the way in which everything had been requisitioned without their even waiting to ask me.

But I was excited at seeing new faces, and determined to avoid any conflict by being as courteous as possible, so I said nothing. I withdrew, bathed, and changed. Then I went and sat with them under a large tarpaulin that they had had erected as a sort of sitting room. In face of considerable dourness I chatted away, telling them about the work, what had been achieved, and what remained to be done, and asking them about their own journey—without, however, mentioning my ecological ideas. Slowly, it began to dawn on me that their hostility was deliberate, a means of crushing me.

Dinner passed in silence. It was hardly over before I was facing criticism of my reading-matter. Beside scientific and technical works connected with my studies, I had on my shelf Boswell's *Life of Johnson*, Tourneur's plays, a volume on Byzantine architecture, books of criticism and poetry by authors such as Eliot and Pound, Proust's *Remembrance of Things Past*, and some of Virginia Woolf's eassys.

As he surveyed these books, Smeed began to bristle. He turned to me: 'Those are not the sort of books to take on an expedition. What do you fancy yourself as—a *dilettante*?' It was evidently the worst term of abuse in his vocabulary.

After 2½ months alone, uncomfortable, in these melancholy jungles, I was in no mood for criticism of my literary tastes. But I answered quietly:

'No, I'm just used to reading that sort of book. Mostly these are books I've wanted to read for a long while, and this trip has been a good opportunity. Surely it is not all that important how I amuse myself in my spare time?'

'Well I judge you by that stuff. Chuck it out, get something wholesome. You are supposed to be a forest officer, not a drooling ninny.'

His anger amazed me. No lesson is more salutary than encountering someone in a position of power who is resentful of tastes he does not understand. I tried to parry. 'What would you suggest—for example, what have *you* brought?'

He exploded. 'That's totally irrelevant! You have no business to question me, whereas it's my business to lick you into shape!'

'Well, you have no business to question my reading!'

'How dare you answer back!'

'Just please understand that I feel very strongly about what I read,' I was trembling slightly. 'Further I have no wish to be a routine forest officer. I have a degree in botany and wish to do research. I joined the Colonial Service on that understanding. Yet instead of being paid more for my extra qualifications I have actually been reduced in seniority and lost one year's salary increment. I'm living on my own savings. I've had enough.' I calmed myself. 'Do you know whether there has been any reply to my enquiry?'

I had had my say and thought I had also rather cleverly changed the subject. Smeed was breathing hard. For a long while he was silent. I could see that he had not done with me. Then he spoke: 'No, there's no reply. Well, what time do we start in the morning?'

'Seven o'clock. Breakfast at 6.30.'

'Good,' he was glaring. 'Then I'll turn in now. We'll talk more tomorrow.'

Taylor also rose, then his wife. 'We'll be off then, also. Goodnight,' he said. Throughout the evening neither of them had said so much as a word.

By 8 next morning work was under way, cutting inland towards the northern flank of Arisaru. Behind the tall riverside levee with its Mora forest lay a thick and unpleasant bog. I was secretly pleased to see my companions' discomfort as they sank to the knees in thick mud, or floundered and scrambled over the black rottenness of decaying logs. In places lianes grew in thick tangles, and as we cut through them, showers of irritating bark fragments fell off on to our faces and down our backs, into our eyes and nostrils. Mud, dead leaves, spiders' webs caked our sweaty bodies; over the floor of the forest snaked the buttresses of Moras and other trees; stilt roots tripped and hooked the unwary at every step, and water lay in deep stagnant pools, transparent over the rotting leaves.

We waded several small streams, and were already thoroughly soaked when we came to a deep rapid river about 60 feet wide, filled with rushing, brown, cold water from the recent rains. Smeed and Taylor eyed it nervously. They had not been very talkative, even to one another.

'Don't worry,' I said. 'No need to swim—we'll fell a tree across.'

'Can't you cut something bigger?' Taylor asked, as the axe man set to work on a slender bankside tree.

'Nothing in the right place that don't take long time,' said the axe man.

The tree fell so that half its length lay below the surface, shaking in the current, with a wave curling over it. The men walked quietly across with widely splayed feet and clasping toes —then of a sudden Little Rufus gave a shout and fell in with a mighty splash. He came up, flung the water and hair from his eyes and swam ashore a short way down. Next I walked across with the help of a long wobbly pole, with which I could only just feel the bottom. Last came the two great men, Taylor first. Half-way across he gave a sudden lurch and dropped a beautiful oriental knife he was carrying, but recovered his balance and continued safely. Smeed came last without mishap, but with a noticeably grey face and set countenance. Obviously this was more than they had bargained for.

Little Rufus, being already wet, and Levi, the other boy, were set to work diving for the knife, which was a momento of Taylor's days in Burma. Holding on to the branches of various fallen trees which could easily have trapped them, they submerged in the brown water and with their toes felt over the sandy bottom for the sharp blade. The sky was leaden grey and rain now began to fall in a steady downpour, lashing the river surface into a mist of dancing drops and filling the jungle with steam and spray. It was bitterly cold as we stood there, soaked through and with the prospect of a hard day still before us.

Eventually we abandoned the search for the knife. The line-cutters had gone ahead, and the way led out of the swamp and up a long and increasingly steep slope, strewn with boulders of smooth black dolerite and red-brown rotted ironstone, protruding like weird sculptures among the leaves.

We had gone some half a mile when the line crossed a broad confused swathe which curved down from Arisaru on our left and led away into the swamps below us—like the path of a herd of Gardarene swine plunging headlong to destruction. For a width of about 25 feet the saplings and seedlings had been torn up, the ground was trampled by an unrecognisable mass of foot prints, and the bark of some of the trees was savagely torn as if by claws. I heard the men muttering a good deal to themselves about this, and poking about and examining the marks, but did not take them seriously. Had I listened to them then I would have examined this broad path more carefully. As it was, after noting these details, I dismissed the path as the work of stampeding peccaries, perhaps followed by a jaguar, and thought no more about it.

Further along, the slope became steeper, and then abruptly it descended nearly vertically to a small stream of clear water beside which grew a cluster of crabwood trees, tall, red-barked, with huge-fingered leaves. We had to scramble down on hands and knees among the boulders, slipping on the red clay and loose lateritic beans, and clinging to tree-stems for support— then up again the other side. A series of such ridges left us exhausted. At last, 2 miles from the Essequebo and four hours after we had started, Smeed said he could go no further. I sent the men ahead except for Justin, the axe man, and stayed behind with my two chiefs.

The rain had just stopped and we sat down for a short rest. Then we began cutting our way up the slope on our left in an attempt to reach the summit ridge of Arisaru. Soaking lianes descended from the canopy in web-like tangles and coiled amongst the boulders. Silver discs shone on the wet floor whenever the huge hurrying clouds exposed the sun. The forest was gloomy, tangled, and full of scratchy-leaved bushes; the heat and humidity were intense, and we sweated and panted as we struggled up the slope. The two chiefs maintained a dour silence.

Higher up still we came to a crossroad of ridges, where three vertical-walled gulleys, on the point of capturing each other's headwaters, led away in different directions. The forest, in pockets between the boulders, was tall and filled with Greenheart trees, many of them showing that rippled bark which indicated wavy 'Bull-Forehead' grain—used for making one of the most beautiful and expensive veneers in the world, a glossy silken radiance of browns and golds, incredibly difficult to work. Here on these slopes the trees were almost inaccessible.

By looking along the three gulleys we could see, through gaps in the tallest trees, over great stretches of country, including to the south the silvery stubble of the burnt Dakama forest.

Finally, at the summit one or two gigantic rocks lay perched on a narrow ridge, whose surface of loose lateritic beans and red clay gave a very insecure foothold. But even from on top of them it was impossible to obtain any further views. A couple of charred logs led me to suspect that fire, not the poor thin soil, was the cause of much of the irregular growth on this mountainside.

In silence we descended the slope towards our line again, stumbling over the gigantic fruit of a Maho (Sterculia), and passing a place where pink and white Bombax tassels lay in profusion over the rocks. The men caught us up as we re-crossed the deep creek, in the midst of renewed heavy rain; and again unsuccessfully they dived in an attempt to retrieve Taylor's knife. I knew how much Taylor was attached to this knife, as he had owned it for many years, and I noticed how well he took its loss.

Back at camp the bloody carcasses of two caymans shot during our absence lay on the beach, and a smell of roasting greeted us. An enormous bird was sizzling on a fire on the rocks: the pelican, shot by one of Smeed's crew. Half an hour later, when his men found it too fishy-flavoured for their liking, it was thrown into the river and floated off downstream.

After tea and a bath I sat out in the open, reading, partly to keep conversation at bay. It was cold and damp, with a lemon sun shining out of ragged clouds. A big spectral bird—a gigantic sun-bittern over 3 feet tall, striped tawny-orange and brown —stalked slowly out from the bushes 10 feet away, and stopped, frozen with stiffly erect neck and bill, at the water's edge. For a long while I gazed at its brightly polished black eyes. Was it trying to deceive fish—or me? I looked again, and unperceived it had gone.

I strolled down to the men's camp and listened to their talk, feeling lonely and distressed.

'You know, Mr. Guppy,' said Jonah, 'this afternoon we was in bad danger.'

'How's that?' I asked.

'Well, you see where that big wide path come down the mountain, with everything torn up? That was made by warakabra tigers.'

I knew warakabras—the trumpeter birds, large flocks of which we frequently encountered wandering over the jungle floor. But I had only vaguely heard of warakabra tigers. 'Tigers' was a term which included nearly all wild carnivores, most of which were members of the cat family, Mustelids, or Canines, and the various forms of 'tigers' were given epithets denoting size: the largest, the jaguar, was known as the maipuri (or tapir) tiger; the next smaller, the puma, as the deer tiger, and so on. I had presumed the warakabra tiger therefore to be an ocelot or something similar. In this I was wrong—the epithet had been chosen because of the trumpeter birds' habit of going around in large flocks.

'Are they so very dangerous?' I asked.

'They are the most dangerous animal in the whole of the jungle. Yet they is very seldom seen. They hunt in large packs just like wolves, with animals of every size. The biggest is big like a wolf, and they also have little kittens with them. That is the marks we saw today, and that is how you know it is warakabra tiger. There is no other animal that makes marks like that.'

'But that looked just as if a herd of pigs had charged down the slope—perhaps a jaguar was chasing them? Surely those masses of footprints could not have been made by cats?'

'No, Sir. This was quite different. Did you see how every little tree in the path was uprooted? Pigs never do that. And all the trees was scratched, just the way a cat does, but with claws of every size, big and small. They always tears up the trees like that—a pack of these animals devours everything in front of it —they cleans out the whole jungle, just like yakman ants. They kill rats and mice, and big animals as well. It was a lucky escape. They must have pass about an hour before we— certainly not more than two or three hours. They could have kill us all.'

'Have you ever seen one?'

'No, Sir. I've been lucky. But they used to be very common Pomeroon side, where I comes from. They always live in the wildest parts of mountains, and they used to live there in the Muri [a curious upland region of bare sand dotted with tiny islands of trees], between Supenaam head and Lake Tapacoma. Many of my friends has seen them. Once I knew a man, a balata bleeder, and he and a friend were going to tap trees in the hills between Aripiako and Ituribisi creeks in the Pomeroon district. They come to a ford where there was many footmarks in the ground like a tiger had been there, but of all different sizes. The marks was several days old, but the two men decided to walk up the stream bed to cover their scent, for they was very frightened. In the night they hear a terrible noise at the ford as of snarling, and they saw the tigers by the ford, jumping and touching the water as if afraid to cross. The only things they is frighten of is water and dogs! And the next day when they go back they see the whole ground was covered with fresh tracks. And they do say that that is a ford which is always used by the warakabra tigers, because it is usually narrow enough for them to jump.'*

'Have you ever seen one—even a dead one?'

'No, but plenty of people has. They is chocolate-brown colour, with lighter spots.'

What could these animals be? Were they just a legend, the Guiana equivalent of the spotted lion of East Africa, the abominable snowman of the Himalayas? It was difficult to see what such a mass of ravening carnivores could find to eat, for their demands would be enormous. Yet indisputably since the advent of firearms the forests contained much less game than formerly—and under such circumstances predators are always the first animals to disappear. Pumas travel sometimes in small family parties, but are not known to be destructive. Caricissis, or wild hunting dogs (Icticyon venaticus), were still fairly common in the Rupununi–Illiwa region and the Pakaraima foothills, 100 miles away. They were fierce and hunted in packs or family parties, but seldom of more than four or five individuals. The local Indians were said to be terrified of them—but they were small jackal-like creatures not much bigger than corgis and of the same pale fawn colour, and had no reputation for tearing trees. Kibihis, or coatimundis (Nasua), also were reputed to hunt in parties, but though quite likely to scratch bark to pieces in their search for grubs it was hard to think of them charging down a slope, for they were largely arboreal, or

* Two years later I surveyed this region, and heard many more tales of these tigers, but I sent two men of the region off alone, unarmed, on a 50-mile walk, and they did not seem to mind going in the least.

of their being stopped by water. And they are not much bigger than large domestic cats, are very well known to the Indians, and not in the least feared—while what we had seen was a positive swathe of destruction. I looked through my books to see if I could find any descriptions. In Charles Barrington-Brown's *Canoe and Camp life in British Guiana* published in 1876 I came across the following:

> In the evening I was attracted by our two dogs, which were tied up, barking furiously, followed by a great stir in camp. Then some voices proclaimed loudly, 'The tigers are coming!' and one man called to me to come down as quickly as possible to the boats, and bring my gun. . . . To my surprise, I found the beach deserted. Where some twenty Indians had been camped, there was now not even a hammock left. . . . My men had all taken to the boat. . . . They greeted me with cries of 'Quick, sir, quick; the Warracaba tigers are coming!' There was quite a flutter of relief—when the boat was pushed off into midstream, where they all began to talk excitedly over our escape. . . . I eagerly enquired what were Warracaba tigers, and was hastily informed that they were small and exceedingly ferocious tigers, that they hunted in packs, and were not frightened by camp fires or anything except the barking of dogs. To water they have a special aversion, and will never cross a stream which is too wide for them to jump.
>
> As we stopped (on the opposite bank) a shrill scream rent the night air, proceeding from the opposite side of the river, not 200 yards above our camp, and, waking up echoes through the forest, died away as suddenly as it rose. This was answered by another cry coming from the depths of the forest, the interval between them being filled by low growls and trumpeting sounds, which smote most disagreeably on the ear. Although I knew that I was perfectly safe from any attack from these animals, whatever their nature, having the river between us, yet I felt a sort of creeping sensation of horror pass through me at the first shrill cry I heard. Gradually the cries became fainter and fainter, as the band retired from our vicinity, till they utterly died away. . . . I pictured them in my mind as a withering scourge sweeping through the forest.

. . . The call of these animals resembles that of the Warra-caba or Trumpet-bird (Psophia crepitans), and hence they have obtained the name of Warracaba tigers. The Ackawoise Indians call them 'Y'agamisheri', and say that they vary in size as well as in colour. As many as a hundred are said to have been seen in one pack. . . .

. . . They are said to frequent the mountains, but when pressed by hunger during the dry seasons, at which time their march is not impeded by streams, they descend to the low-lands, and scour them in search of food.

Barrington-Brown was a distinguished geologist, already famous for his discovery of the Kaieteur falls, and other explorations, and one would imagine him and his companion, the geologist Sawkins, of unimpeachable truthfulness. His description was by far the best I could find—yet of course, like me, he never actually *saw* a warakabra tiger.

In Vincent Roth's *Animal Life in British Giuana*, at which I next looked, there was a photograph of an animal said to be a warakabra tiger. It looked exceedingly like a jaguarondi—and was evidently even more solitary and elusive than that rarely-seen medium-sized cat. The young of the jaguarondi sometimes have pale spots—perhaps adults occasionally did also, or adults of a closely related species? Perhaps, like the yellow butterflies crossing the jungle rivers, or the lemmings of Scandinavia, the jaguarondi, or one of its forms, is subject from time to time to unaccountable mass movements or migrations?

I could think of no better answer. But Jonah was not con-vinced. To him it was a completely distinct beast from the jaguarondi or the ocelot. One or two of the men even stated flatly that they did not believe in the warakabra tiger at all—it was just an old story. Yet what had made that trail in the forest? Ah, that they could not say—it was a different matter.

Thinking to interest my two chiefs, I told them about this discussion and of our possible escape.

They listened in silence.

Then Smeed said: 'I don't see what this has to do with our work. We have more important things to consider. Fetch a representative of the men, will you? The oldest man. And tell Jonah to come too.'

After which, for half an hour Philbert and Jonah were subjected to such a cross-examination on the subject of the work
and new wages that they began to tremble and shake.

'But we can hardly change a contract we've already agreed,'
I interjected.

Smeed turned to me: 'Please do not interfere, Guppy. It is
not your business.'

'The men are my business—I've been working with them.
Not unless we terminate work now—then start again on a new
contract.' I was determined to have my say. 'That might be
more expensive than the money we save.'

Jonah struggled to speak: 'The men will be very dissatisfied,
Sir.' (Philbert nodded agreement.) 'I don't know how I can
tell them, Sir.'

Philbert spoke, in a curious wooden rasp: 'Men never work
like this. We all go.'

Taylor and Smeed glanced at one another. Then Taylor
grinned, a nervous dog-like grin, showing a lot of teeth: 'Of
course, you understand that these are only the new conditions
of employment. They will apply in future. But as Mr. Guppy
says, we will not change the present contract. For the duration
of this expedition the existing terms apply. You can tell the
men that.'

There was a sigh of relief from Jonah and Philbert. They
nodded good night, and returned to the men's camp.

After this the two chiefs brought their camp chairs back into
the shelter of the sitting room, and began chatting together.

I drew mine into the circle, but I was not included in the
conversation. I listened all the same, in what they probably
thought was awed silence. They were reminiscing about
different timbers, Taylor in terms of Burma, Smeed of the
Caribbean and Africa, each trying to be one up (though Taylor
always let his superior win). Timber and allied subjects were
evidently the only topic on which both felt safe. I reflected how
different was this absorption in one small aspect of human
activity from the outlook in which I had been reared. How
could such attitudes help the image of England abroad, or such
men perform more than limited functions in aiding the evolution of Guyana?

Then Smeed began talking about Russia—to which he had

evidently made a visit before the war. I was interested. He seemed in a more mellow frame of mind, perhaps exhausted by our hard day in the forest. My guard down, I began to ask questions. This was one subject on which he was obviously enthusiastic, so I said: 'But isn't it still an appalling tyranny—can one excuse that?'

'What on earth does that matter, when one considers what has been achieved?'

'But surely if the revolution hadn't been taken over by a horrific dictatorship, peaceful reforms could have been achieved as in other countries? I always think that was one of the greatest tragedies of modern times—it has made more problems than it has solved.'

At once his mouth snapped shut and the whites of his eyes showed all round. Trembling, he shouted at me. 'Thinking that way leads to madness! All this nonsense you talk is rubbing away at things that are finished! All pure dilettante twaddle.' And so forth for about ten minutes.

I let him continue. It wasn't that he had been drinking, for he was not a heavy drinker. No, it was something completely personal—I seemed to be a crystallisation of everything he resented.

He stopped, still glaring and shaking.

I spoke quietly: 'If you wish to talk civilly you may have my company. Otherwise you must excuse me.'

He grew white, but said not a word. Then he got up and strode away.

Throughout these exchanges Taylor had kept silent, and I began to realise that he was outraged. We exchanged glances. He was on my side. He spoke very quietly:

'I'd like you to know, Nicholas, that I think you've done very well under very difficult conditions.'

We never quarrelled again. We even later on, in a limited way, became friends. But this was not easy, for though kindly and simple he was a disappointed man, unable to take any positive position for long.

The following day the two chiefs set off for Omai in their boat. I was left to continue my work. On their return they were silent and I thought a little angry and dejected. All that I could draw from them was that they had been shown around and given lunch: but I guessed that perhaps they had begun to realise the extent to which the survival of the expedition had depended upon the kindness of my friends at the mine. I asked them whether they had arranged to repay the food I had borrowed. Both Taylors, to my surprise, blushed.

On the next day I was again accompanied by my chiefs. It sometimes took a little searching to find the points at which we had started cutting particular lines at the beginning of the expedition, and today while doing this Smeed suddenly barked out: 'Stop all this arsing around and let's get on with the job.'

Out of earshot of the others I explained that I liked politeness, and that if there were any more rudeness he would have to find someone else to lead his expedition. I also explained that we had already done half an hour's work on this line and that five minutes' delay was surely unimportant.

The line went through a succession of deep swamps with majestic forest in between. It rained nearly the whole day, and when we returned we were soaked and caked with mud. I was used to this—but I was pleased that again my bosses should have had a taste of the discomforts of my work.

The following day they departed, and I was glad to see them go. But I felt sure that Smeed would try to get even with me. Alone once more, my heart sank. There was nothing for me to do but continue and finish the expedition's task. Yet the pleasure derived from it had gone, and did not return.

15

Rain

A few days later, when we had shifted camp downstream to Mocca-Mocca Point, the expected reprimand arrived and spoke about attitudes to Life and Work, etc. There were no particular accusations, but it appeared—upon technical grounds—that unfortunately it would be impossible to grant me local leave at Christmas. I laughed to myself when I read this, and thought of the pettiness of the man who had written it. But I wanted to go to the West Indies to see some of my family, to swim and recover my spirits, and I felt I had earned my holiday. So I composed a fairly sugary conciliatory letter and at the same time wrote to Fanshawe, saying how sorry I was that I might not be able to get my leave, and how much I needed it, and could he intercede direct with Swabey, the conservator. That, I felt, might do the trick.

On the other side of the river a series of enticing little half-moon beaches edged the water, scented caverns overhung by shrubs full of pink blossoms. A few bare rocks—cold, clean, sand-washed—rose newly uncovered from the water, and led down to a line of small rapids composed of jointed slabs through which the water poured making a noise that, from the camp, sounded like a distant dynamo. Little grew on them save a few guava bushes and a thorny sapling, Fagara.

Further downstream were islands fringed with grey Awara-balli palms; and one could see clumps and stretches of them inland, waving above tangled, ropey forest, where only a few large scattered Mora trees survived from some great fire of the past, perhaps that of 1926. Everywhere one could sense the softness of the earth, the lowness of the banks. We were on the edge of the maximally flooded region that continued down past Rockstone to the barrier of the main Essequebo falls.

I lay on my bed one Sunday morning after breakfast and

read Proust, escaping from the lonely riverside to the *plage* at
Baalbec, the illuminated restaurant at Rivebelle, to Robert de
St. Loup, Mlle. de Stermaria, the sprightly Albertine and her
girl friends. At intervals I went down the notched tree trunk to
my little bathing platform of sticks and lianes, to scan the river
for signs of a boat bringing us food. And eventually I sat half-
way down, where the morning mist was thinner, and read. All
at once I saw by the peculiar speckled light and shade in the
water that a cayman had swum up, intent as ever upon eating
me. I looked at it, irritated, then continued reading. It was
about 8 feet long, and floated motionless beneath the surface
with its head concealed by the platform. I was safe, being about
6 feet above the water. By now I had begun to associate my
Proust readings with these stealthy beasts—there seemed to be
no escaping them. Even if I read in my tent they would come
to lie offshore.

I was lost—far from the jungles. Then the delicate probings
of an insect proboscis brought my mind back. Two big eyes
were looking at me unblinkingly. The beast had drawn much
nearer, indeed was almost directly under me. I shuddered,
thinking of stories of crocodiles' tails sweeping men into the
water, hastily scrambled up the platform on to the bank, and
threw sticks down on it. Chagrined, it snapped at them,
crunching some sticks of the platform as it did so, and bellowing.
Then it turned and started to swim away. As it drew clear I hit
it hard on the back with a heavy log—whereupon it dived,
surfaced again immediately, and went off swimming fast with a
curious zigzagging and rolling motion that seemed to express
terrible rage.

Far away in the mist we heard a voice calling, 'Woooo . . .
hoo, Woooo . . . hoo . . .', with a long falling cadence. We
replied and presently it drew nearer and I detected a weird
boat out in the stream. Tiny and square-ended, it was built of
loosely nailed-together pieces of old packing cases, and looked
as if it could not possibly float. Seated perilously on the edge,
paddling it with a small piece of board, was the old Negro fisherman we had last seen at Omai, wrinkled, bearded, like Father
Time himself. Inside his boat was a bundle of rags, and in one
corner lay a ragged dried fish, slightly curling at the edges.
That was all.

He stood up in the little, wildly rocking craft and tied it to the landing stage. He would not disembark, though his eyes were red and bleary from lack of sleep, but begged us to tell him the way through the rocks which he could hear just ahead. The mist still lay heavy on the water, mysterious amongst the trees, wrapping us in silence. From it came only the chirping of crickets, faint clashings of no apparent origin, and the distant rushing of the water.

Basil and Jonah waved and pointed while I found some rice and a tin of condensed milk to supplement his dried fish. Then he paddled straight out into the stream heading for the other side and was lost to sight, though we heard him hallooing once or twice to get his position from the echoes and our replying shouts.

'You know, Sir,' said Basil, after he had gone, 'dat ol' man is a very lecherous man. He is famous for bothering women.'

'I can hardly believe it.'

'Well you see, Sir, he really belong Mazaruni side, dat is where he does live, all he life. He only been here about tree years—I met he at Bartica when he come through. That was when he was on his way to Apoteri.'

This was a village inhabited by people of mixed Amerindian and Negro blood—largely balata bleeders—on the edge of the Rupununi region.

'So?'

'Well, he hear that in Apoteri there is a woman with a cunt so big he can put his head right inside—that is why he lef' Mazaruni. He says he mus' see dat before he die. So he travel about 2 months to get down to Bartica. And another 2 months goin' to Apoteri. Dat is 4 months travelling for one purpose. A man like dat really love women, don't you think, Chief?'

'I do. But did he find her?'

'Well, dat is de disappointin' thing, Sir. By the time he reach, she gone.'

'But what about the lady he was with up by Omai? Wasn't that her?'

'Oh, no, Sir. That is somebody else he just pass de time wid. But dat is why he is waiting aroun'—he tinks de oder *mus'* come back.'

'I hope she does—4 months' journey and 3 years' wait— and he looks as if he is getting a bit old.'

That evening I went to fetch a bucket of water from the
landing and took my torch with me as the night was still misty.
When I shone it on the water, two bright red spots glowed of a
sudden in a big floating log. I threw sticks at it, but it moved
closer, fascinated by the light. It was the first time a cayman had
stalked me in the dark. Finally I hit it between the eyes and it
drew off a little way, so that I could fill my bucket.

Only then did I realise the extraordinary beauty of the night.
The moon was full directly overhead, and around it were a
series of concentric circles of delicate rainbow hues. The whole
sky glowed with a pearly luminescence through which the
larger stars and planets shone softly. The gentle water lapped
milk-white against the log on which I sat. I could just discern
the dark outlines of trees behind me and even the distant shore-
line opposite. I stayed for a long time, gazing up at the moon
and at the immensities of nacreous heaven. I was filled with so
many complex and conflicting thoughts, but this enveloping
whiteness seemed to soothe them. Finally, overcome by a feeling
of complete quietness, I walked back to my tent and sank to
sleep.

I stayed in camp for about three days after this, suffering
from acute earache caused by a boil in the left ear, which I
treated with sulfathiazole powder. Perhaps I only used the earache as an excuse, because my internal tides of emotion were so
strong, as if something was bursting to come out. Liberty! I felt
chained to my work, and in my life and all its circumstances. I
had responsibilities and commitments, yet they were probably
no worse than most people's. Why then did I have this overwhelming feeling of imprisonment? All I could now dream
about was escape, and freedom to think and find my true self.
Sometimes, as I walked up and down in camp, or stood gazing
over the river, I felt like crying out: 'Oh God, why am I lost?'
But such an appeal was useless, mere rhetoric. All I could do
was shrug my shoulders and wait.

My nights were increasingly disturbed. I would wake
suddenly, sometimes sweating and in panic. What was wrong?
What were my body and mind trying to tell me? Like the tiny
sounds of the forest, heard because of the absence of other com-
peting noises, feelings, memories, images long suppressed were
making themselves manifest, and if I were only patient they

would emerge and tell me truths about myself that might otherwise never reach the light. I must be quiet and let my fantasies develop.

Mostly these days in camp were spent in working out the results of the expedition to date, or in reading Proust. Always whenever I raised my eyes I could see my cayman lying patiently amongst the fallen debris by the landing stage. When Little James lowered his bucket to draw water it would float imperceptibly nearer. Bathing was risky, and I would search carefully in all possible hiding places before stepping on to the platform each morning and evening. I could have shot it, but enough caymans had been killed by us already, and after my revulsion at shooting the powis, I simply did not want to.

Then one afternoon from upstream I heard a great splashing, and panic-stricken shouts of 'Cayman! Cayman!' Little Rufus and James came running up pointing, and I ran to the river bank and saw a beast that seemed as big as a submarine cruising a few yards off. He turned in towards me and clambered ashore on a small ledge just below my bathing stage.

Boodhoo was quite pallid with fear and gesticulated and shouted, 'Ee go bite me when I go fetch water! Shoot ee, Baas! Shoot ee!'

I still had no wish to shoot another crocodile, enormous and dangerous though this one was, so I flung sticks at it and chased it away. It roared in anger, biting at the branches which landed near it in the water, and lashed savagely with its tail. Then it dived, reappearing many yards off swimming upstream.

The next day we moved downstream again—back to our first camp. Three months before we had come there late one afternoon in despair of finding dry ground; now it was perched above us like a fortress, its bathing stage hanging absurdly 12 feet above our heads. Tree seedlings 2 feet high had shot up all over the clearing, and razor-grass sprouted in delicate-looking tufts which in another month would have consolidated into an impenetrable tangle of cutting edges.

Then, we had laid down a corduroy floor over thick soft mud; now the mud had hardened to a pavement, and the logs had rotted away. As the leaves and wood-debris were swept up centipedes 9 inches long writhed to escape, and swarms of tiny pale-grey scorpions clicked and scuttled to and fro; together with a few big crab-like ones about 6 inches long—horrible looking; but the smaller ones were much more feared.

Boodhoo caused great excitement by picking one of these up and playing with it, letting it walk along his arm.

'Don't worry, Chief,' he said. 'It ain' goin' a-harm me. I get "cut" for scorpion, and I is dey friend.'

He put the little beast down and urged it with his finger under a leaf, right in the middle of my tent. I scooped it up and put it a little distance off.

'Yes, Chief, dey is men who is cut for scorpion. You get cut also for snake. One time man came to Uitvlught and he cut several people. After de cuts is made he make a live scorpion sting in de wound. Den you has to swear never to harm a scorpion again, an' always to protect dem and be deir friend. And dey will never harm you after that.'

Evidently he had received some crude form of inoculation against scorpion venom, and in the spirit of sympathetic magic had made his vows in return; and certainly his quiet, confident handling had not alarmed the creature. But Ranger Lord, who scoffed at all such superstitions, became a little careless in imitation, and next day he was stung in the toe by one. For a whole day he was in the greatest agony, with tears streaming down his face and his breathing slow and laboured. I dressed his enormously swollen toe but he refused to let me lance it. After the stoical Amerindians his unrestrained howling, whining, and weeping was a great surprise—not that I doubted his pain. At one stage I thought I should have to give him an injection of antivenomous serum, so convinced was he that he was about to die; but my syringe was defective. Luckily, by nightfall he was easier, and in two days he was up and working again.

From this camp we sailed past Plantain Island, with its huge epiphyte and liane-hung Mora trees, amongst whose leaves cicadas sat singing, and flowering bromeliads glowed like rubies, to a point 2 miles upstream, where we had previously failed to land. Only a few yards in we plunged into a Corkwood swamp where snaking buttresses and roots interspersed with boggy pools made every footstep perilous.

R

I could hear the men grumbling and joking to themselves: 'Now its goin' to be overboard again all de time. You go for more swimming lesson, Smallie' (to Little Rufus).

But it was no longer a question of encountering seasonal floods: almost the whole area was evidently bog, waterlogged or submerged the entire year. As we progressed the Corkwood trees became increasingly majestic, their buttresses gigantic twisting walls 16 feet high, terminating below in little squiggling roots and crowned above with diminutive trunks bearing tiny top-knots of branches, like so many fat, dignified, but small-headed women. Between these tree-monsters the pools became progressively deeper, choked with black mud and decaying leaves. Piece by piece I discarded my clothing as we struggled on, until at last I was in nothing but tennis shoes and bathing trunks.

Then the Corkwoods ended on the levee of a wide, deep stream fringed with aroids, Jotoro (Dieffenbachia) and Mocca-Mocca. We peered under and amongst the trees: the level water-surface extended into the shadows of a dense forest of Arisauros, Sarebebes, and other bog trees, with no sign of dry land ahead.

We had been wading all morning, we were cold and wet, longing to be out of this muddy, choked forest and back in camp warming ourselves beside the fires. Finding no way forward, the men began drifting back towards the boat. But I could not have them taking upon themselves the decision to abandon work. So I sent word back to prepare to swim, and leaving my clothes in a bundle in a branch, struck out into the deeps. The water was dark, damson-coloured and sour tasting as it splashed into my mouth. My legs brushed against the prickly Mocca-Mocca stems, and against nameless foul-feeling objects in the depths.

> Yea, slimy things did crawl with legs
> Upon the slimy sea.

Inside me a voice was crying 'This is a nightmare! You are degraded, like a worm. You were never meant to crawl through fearful jungles bathed in sweat, plastered with mud and twigs, tortured by insects, or to swim in black water choked with vileness, far from everything you love.'

I was tired, longing for the trip to end. I had no resistance left to cope with the unpleasant fancies that now rushed into my brain. The jungle in which I had formerly delighted and found my chief interest had changed colour, as if illuminated by a new light. From being impersonal it had become alien.

When I was stronger reason would tell me that I knew everything that the jungle held and had no cause for such fear and revulsion. But my faith in what I was doing had been undermined both by acquaintance with my bosses and by critical examination of the results likely to accrue from the methods we were using. I tried to tell myself that this was a wonderful experience, that my private studies had been of value; that my attempt to develop an understanding of human societies by analogy with the forests had given me an insight into what had previously been bewildering—that I should look upon this not only as a time of testing, but as one of the most important formative periods of my life. But it would take a long time for me to shake off the melancholy which had now descended on me. I was lonely, bound to a job I hated—and would be, it seemed, for years to come. My life consisted of finding expedients to make the days pass swiftly, of retirement inwards, of reading. Smeed had probably summed me up correctly—I was not the person for this work.

It was a long horrible swim through the thick soupy water. But after some 60 yards I found that I could just touch the bottom, so I swam on again and a little further I was able to walk. Looking back I could dimly discern the heads of the men bobbing along after me. Then a high bank rose out of the water, and beyond it a level landscape packed with small trees. The line seemed interminable, but towards its end came reward—a woodland of very big trees of Cyrilla antillana, a species that I had previously known only as a small shrub.

Here at last our three and a half miles were completed, our statistical requirements satisfied. We turned back, running through the glades, plunging through the creeks, balancing our way along tacoubas—I tired, thinking of tea and a bath, while the men enlivened themselves with talk of wives and women, rumshops, gambling, and the varied gaieties which civilisation would offer in a few days more—the world of shops and cinemas and streets only a hundred miles below us. They were growing

restive and independent, making plans. But I did not want to
think of it, to face it.

On our way downstream next morning we rounded a bend—
and there was familiar Gluck Island some 4 miles ahead, bright
green with the sun on it, whilst we were rolling on dark water
under ominous clouds. Reattempting our first line ever of the
expedition, we slashed in through the dense liane tangle over
the top of which we had pulled our boat three months before,
slipped between the trunks of Kakarallis and Ituri Wallabas
whose upper branches we had then cut. Even now the ground
was wet, and we had hardly gone 400 yards before we were
stopped by a large and broad itabu. Tall walls of Mora and
Kakaralli rose perpendicularly at its sides; the clay of its banks
shelved so steeply into Stygian water that there was room but
for a tuft or two of sedges. A sunfish splashed; there was no other
sign of life. Then, as we turned to go, in quick succession came
two thunderous claps, and broad silver rings spread over the
surface far down the lake. We jumped, startled; and I recalled
to Jonah that we had heard something like this before, in Inner
Tipuru Lake.

Felling a small tree out into the itabu to mark where our line
reached the bank, we returned to the boat and proceeded down
river to search for the entrance. Slowly the river expanded into
that huge stretch of green waters that had once seemed the
threshold of a new land of adventure and discovery. We sailed
close in to the high rounded masses of lianes, whose floating
half-hanging draperies completely screened the banks and
might easily hide the mouth of the itabu, allowing its water
to escape beneath or through their branches.

At last Little Rufus pointed to a tiny ripple stretching from a
twig. A minute gap showed, and pushing through we found
ourselves in a sluggish channel about 10 feet wide. Long, thin,
diseased-looking Awaraballi palms leaned shaggily out from the
banks. We 'junked' a few to clear our way, then wandered zigzag through the swampy land, searching our way towards the
lake. We turned right and left, chopped through logs, came to
dead ends, returned, and went up alternative channels. It was
hot, fetid, a welter of greenery, in which I was swept and lashed
by passing branches, dazzled by the sun's noon searchlight

glaring up reflected from the water. Sometimes we disturbed a turtle, floating just below the surface with its feet hanging down. Rapidly, looking like a giant water-beetle, it would sink down into the depths. Darters rose and flapped among the tree-tops; kingfishers curvetted in their headlong flight. When we had all but given up, round the very last corner there stretched our black ribbon of water with its felled-tree marker.

As always when I came into these inlets I felt a sense of foreboding. The olive-green water, black and silver where sunlight sparkled on it, brooded into the distance between curved silent precipices of sad green, its darkness staring up at the hard blue and white sky. It was as if on our entry some great activity had been suspended, while with beating hearts a multitude of watchers lay hidden. In the black mud at the lake bottom bacteria and blue-green algae multiplied in gelatinous lumps, food for browsing catfish. In the sunlit upper waters green and yellow algae and transparent infusoria floated or sculled along in their myriads, with slender cilia and flagella, making a thin soup in which moved elegant cichlids, savage perai, electric eels. Arawhannas, garfish, swam near the surface; skaters waltzed upon the water's tense skin. On the reddish mud-banks, often yellow with the chromoplasts of billions of diatoms, lay caymans and iguanas; and growing from the mud on penetrating roots were giant trees—each tree a city, carrying an uncountable population of mammals, birds, reptiles, amphibians, insects, crustaceans, ferns, lichens, mosses, algae, bacteria, viruses. All this life was seething here—yet of it not even some tiny face did we glimpse among the foliage. Perhaps when we had gone, with a mighty sigh, all these held breaths would be exhaled, and movement start again: while at night. . . . But I shuddered at what this place would be like at night.

To our left there was a resounding crack, and a ring spread slowly:

'Dat *ain*' no cayman!', said Basil—'big fish!'

'Manatee,' said Levi.

'Loch Ness Monster,' drawled Little Rufus.

We waited, but nothing more happened. Then just as we were about to return I saw rising out of the water a great black back some 18 inches broad, rolling swiftly over away from me —like a porpoise, but covered with an armour-plating of enormous scales. On and on it rolled, then a wide blunt tail emerged and slapped the water, and the huge fish sank in a fountain of spray with a noise like a depth-charge exploding. A few seconds more, and it rose again in a mighty bubbling swirl about 100 feet further on: an arapaima, the world's largest fresh-water fish!

It was only a few years since this fish was first recorded in the Essequebo, as well as the Rupununi River, on its spread from Amazonia; now it had almost reached Rockstone, its furthest north yet. In a short while, doubtless, it would have descended the falls and be seen at Bartica.

Several times more as we traversed the lake I saw these fish rise to the surface, and judging from the sequence of splashes, there must have been three or four patrolling up and down. One rose only about 3 feet away from me, when the launch was travelling fast.

'Shoot him, Chief,' called Basil—for we needed food—but I was unprepared. Its blackish scale-armoured back was 12–15 inches broad, suggesting from my memory of the shape a fish about 9 feet long. Specimens are said to have been caught 12 feet long and weighing 500 pounds.

It seemed that the fish all came straight up from the bottom, somersaulting just before reaching the surface, for no ripple ever appeared before their backs broke into view, and their heads were never revealed, though occasionally we caught a glimpse of the dorsal fin, and even of the tiny rounded tail. One thing was evident—the great creatures' immense strength: for when they struck the surface the noise was like the report of a cannon. Determined to catch one, we tied up at the end of our line, while Basil cut a Yarri-Yarri rod and baited a gigantic hook with turtle meat, which he proceeded to swish up and down, and I stood ready with the gun. Once he got a fierce tug, and the meat was taken; but that was all. After half an hour all he had caught was one perai.

We came out into the hot sunshine of the river, and saw nimbus masses piling up to windward. I hoped they would pass so that we should be able to start cutting across the neck of Tipuru peninsular on the opposite bank. But just as we had tied up and had made an opening amongst the spiny palms there, rain descended in grey blankets. The drops struck the water like machine-gun bullets, so hard that spray stood a yard high while the surface of the river looked like a sheet of lead upon which thousands of hammers were falling. It was impossible to see more than 10 feet.

We let down the awning flaps and sat packed in the tiny shelter of the boat, holding the wet curtains taut in the gale. It was dark and close, but intensely chilly inside, filled with coiling tobacco smoke. The men sat silently or smoked, partly to pass the time, partly to keep warm, their eyes gleaming, and occasionally a broken tooth showing as a small white dot in the obscurity. Irritating as flies, bundles of Basil's odorous dried fish swung before my nose with every movement of the boat.

After an hour of this I got Basil to start the engine, and we made our way upstream. As the camp at last came into sight the rain ceased, the sun broke through the clouds, and water, sky and dripping foliage shone jewel-like in the clarified air. But by this time it was too late to start a line.

Two weeks before, when I had been laid up with earache, the surveying party had found an abandoned railway line near a place called Butakari Point. I had never expected that anything of this would remain, but I knew something of its history. The firm of Sprostons, which had built the Mackenzie to Rockstone railway and had operated steam launches on the upper Essequebo in the days of the gold rushes, worried by the steady decline in traffic as the gold and diamond booms passed, had built this railway in 1925 hoping to compensate for their other losses by extracting wood from far inland. But 1926 was the colony's great year of drought and fires and the forests which they had planned to work were destroyed, while a competitor called Willems had started up nearer the coast. In despair, the following year they had abandoned their concession, uprooted the rails, and left the region for good.

The railway had worked forests previously tapped by floating logs down the Urumaru Creek, Waiarima Creek, and the Great Tipuru River—three vaguely marked rivers which entered the Essequebo in the uncertain, swiftly changing region around Tipuru inlet. We had been unable to find any of these at the beginning of the expedition. Perhaps with the river lower we might be able to locate one of them and trace it inland. Then on another day we would follow the railway and so penetrate from another direction that once-rich forest region and discover its present condition.

Finding these forests became the last of the expedition's objects. In quest of them we went up Tipuru inlet far beyond any possible river opening, turned, and followed the bank slowly back towards the mouth and out on to the main river, scrutinising as we went every twig or leaf hanging into the water for a ripple, pushing into and examining every indentation of the vegetation.

Through an inconspicuous gap in the inlet's blind far end, and past a small circular pond of great depth, lay Inner Tipuru Lake, and here we searched again for the two rivers. But we found only the blank quaking of flowery leafy lianes floating upon water 10 or 12 feet deep even now, from under which, in a little cul-de-sac of vegetation, there issued a gentle current which might have been the Waiarima. Then a little further a swamp of Barabara and Kakurio trees stood where the Great Tipuru River should have rolled yards broad. Subtle differences in the vegetation, a few broken bottles, and a few cut stumps, indicated an old camp site here. We cast off and tried again further downstream. At last, almost opposite Gluck Island, the Great Tipuru River showed. We forced our way with cutlasses and poles through a small gap in the riverside luxuriance, and emerged into a dark-watered channel fringed with aroids and acacia-like trees. Awaraballi palms leaned out over the water, nodding their grisly plumed heads.

There was little current and the channel soon narrowed. It ran parallel with the main river, behind a long levee built up evidently in only the few short years since our map was made, as was shown by the fact that no sooner did we reach the point at which the old mouth was marked, than it turned inland. So choked was it with fallen trees—again and again we had had to chop through them—that we realised that it would take us several days to go even 2 or 3 miles inland. So we gave up and returned upstream to Tipuru inlet, hoping to find a place from which to cut towards those distant forests.

We landed on a muddy beach much walked by caymans, waded through a swamp until stopped by the almost inevitable water path, returned to the boat, cruised around until we found the entrance, ascended, landed, and again began cutting westwards, struggling waist-deep in mud and brown water full of rotting logs and prickly palm stems, until we emerged on to the higher land of the far levee—at which moment massive rain descended and completed the job of soaking us. Under a few hastily-gathered bunches of palm leaves, which broke the force of the rain but did not keep us dry, we huddled, shivering; then, when the rain ceased, we moved on down a long gentle slope into a burnt area unlike any I had seen before. The enormous charred logs of a once mighty forest could just be seen lying like primitive monsters beneath mounds of blackened twigs, which formed a continuous springy mattress 6–8 feet high over everything. This charcoal forest—evidently the result of several successive fires each destroying the regrowth of the last— covered a low-lying expanse of white sand, with limpid water knee-deep in the hollows. Showing forlornly wherever they could penetrate were plants of the latest generation: a few palms and Cyrillas, and soft-wooded, dichotomously branching Douanier Rousseau trees with large thick leaves.

We walked slowly over the twigs in constant fear of breaking our ankles, under a watery sky with ragged grey clouds trailing their fingers in the tree-tops. Occasional yellow gleams of sunlight illuminated the dripping Hadean scene, and always behind us the amethyst clouds were piling higher, scowling and blackening as if preparing to launch tons of water upon us, and destroy us with floods and lightnings of unimaginable ferocity.

At the far side of the white sand area the land tilted upwards, and we raced forward through tall Wallaba and Greenheart forests until at last we reached the end of the line in an upland of red lateritic earth scalloped out into precipitous gulleys and ridges. Here were the lost forests we were looking for—for scattered on the ground, where they had been abandoned forty years before, were the evidences of old timber workings— magnificent squared logs of Greenheart, now iron-hard with all their sapwood rotted off.

All together, we turned to hurry back to the boat. Kunyow led the way, and I kept close behind. The line was full of twisting roots and cut ends of saplings, of lianes, fallen logs, and sudden pot-holes, so that our feet had to move up down and sideways as much as backwards and forwards, in a sort of ballet. Everything depended upon quickness of vision, anticipation, precise balance and placing of the feet—every move had to be made consciously. But by running, then walking, alternating with a jog-trot, we made good speed.

Then the threatened rain began, and it became increasingly difficult to see where we were going. The whole forest was in an uproar. Through the steam and spray I could only just discern Kunyow a few feet ahead. The rest of the men had been left far behind. Suddenly I ran into a large spike of wood protruding horizontally from a branch, which struck me on the bone of the nose just beside my left eye. I was flung backwards to the ground, an inch of flesh torn on my bruised and bleeding nose. For a minute I crawled about in pain, with my hand cupped over my eye. Fortunately there was plenty of water running down my face with which to wash myself; and even more fortunately, I had hit the branch in the one place where it could do least harm: a quarter of an inch to one side, and I would have lost my vision.

After some half hour spent sitting against a tree, I could just see a blur through the eye, the bleeding had stopped, and I was able to run on.

A stumbling footstep, a misjudgement with the cutlass, a fall on to a pointed stake—then the loneliness of lying in the forest with no help at hand. These are the real dangers of jungle life, far more real than the dangers of snakes, jaguars, or perai; and from them many more lonely pork-knockers have disappeared forever.

As I ran on I gradually stripped off my wet clothes until I was running almost naked in the downpour. At first I found it difficult to see where I was going with only one useful eye, but my vision gradually improved—and it was almost normal again when I came out into the open burnt areas, where the rain thundered down out of the livid sky.

At last I reached the *Tacouba Express*. From the centre of my bundle of clothes I pulled a comparatively dry cotton vest, and, brushing the water off my hair and face and body, I put it on. At once I felt much better. Warmer for one thing, and because of my vest's absorbency, dry. I sat up and began to take an interest once again in my surroundings. A few feet off a small cayman showed, floating under the shelter of some bushes. I watched it intently as, with suspicious eyes, it drew slowly

nearer, keeping in the shadows. Then seized with doubts, it
sank up to the eyes and swam softly away.

Half an hour later the men arrived, and we set off to camp
through the continuing rain. My books, for which I always
feared, were dry, for Boodhoo had spread towels over them. But
spray whirled about under the tarpaulin, and it was almost
dark, so heavy were the clouds. I combined dinner with tea
and, as I ate, quantities of winged ants flew around the light
and fell into the food, amongst them the enormously fat queens
of the Cushes or leaf cutters.

Then, though it was still early I went to bed, in the hope of
keeping fairly dry and warm. But my blankets were damp, and
water ran down the sides of my mosquito net. Occasionally,
with a heavy gust of wind, spray penetrated it and fell on my
face.

The rain continued all night and late into the following day.
Then it started again, and went on steadily for almost a week.
Before long the ultimate misery was reached: clothes, pyjamas,
towels, bed, all were soaked. Attempts to dry clothes over a fire
resulted in their getting burnt; and when I had a fire lighted in
my tent, the wood was so wet that I was nearly smoked out, and
the discomfort was if anything greater than being wet and cold.

In such conditions there was no point in staying in camp. We
had few lines left and I determined to finish them while the
forests were still passable. In the morning I would plunge into
the river from my bathing platform—because at that hour the
river water was warmer than the air. Then I would soak my
damp clothes and pull them on wet, sometimes even while I was
still in the water, because it was so awful putting them on to a
comparatively dry body up above. From then onwards it was
important to keep moving lest I caught a chill. And on returning to camp I would strip completely and go to bed, for it was
better to be naked and comparatively warm than to stand
around in wet garments.

On one of these nights I had a strange dream—perhaps the
same dream that had woken me before, but this time I remembered it (if that can be the word) after the terrible jolting shock
that had awoken me and left me lying in fright. How can I
describe this dream? It was of memories formed before my brain
knew words, when I was in a state of abject fear, suffocation,

desperation and total enclosure and imprisonment. I was help-less, unable to move—yet now conscious, still experiencing this state through my skin, my hair, my toes, my face. Oppression—I must get *free*! Then as if awakening to yet a higher level of consciousness, I knew what was happening: I was being born. My mother had been in labour 24 hours and an unborn child during such a slow birth must experience terrors we know not of, suffer from oxygen-deprivation, from exhaustion, from God knows what else, because it has no way of describing what is then stamped on the brain before it has words or vision, and which the memory later probably tries to suppress. But I knew now what was happening to me, and why perhaps I needed liberty so much, and had so great a horror of enclosure and small spaces.

This dream was one of the revelations of my life, and some-how it set me free, because it enabled me to understand myself better. I pondered on it; and in the days ahead I recovered a lot of my gaiety, despite the weather and other conditions we were working under, and the gloomy prospects offered by my career.

Sunday came, and I was nearly at the end of the sixth volume of Proust, *The Sweet Cheat Gone (Albertine Disparue)*—which I found exceedingly heavy going, for I had enough self-mortification in my own life without wishing to share Proust's. I sat reading all morning on a long log that sloped down into the river. Above me an overhanging bush gave a pleasant shade, and I was well soaked in dimethylphthalate.

With relief I closed the volume at last, and looked up—and there, actually crawling out of the water towards me along the log, was yet another cayman. It was too much. With a cry I pulled my feet up. It opened its jaws—and I flung the Proust straight into its pink and gaping mouth. With an awful choking noise that was perhaps an interrupted bellow the beast col-lapsed, slithered off the log into the water, and swam away as fast as its crippled frame could carry it. I wondered whether, in its different way, it found that volume any more digestible than I.

A few minutes later when I began on Proust's final volume I chose a safer spot on the edge of the bank itself, a clear 20 feet above the river. Yet even here I was attractive to these monsters, for by far the largest I had ever seen now approached, saw me, changed direction, and came swimming towards me, perhaps drawn by the sight of my legs dangling over the bank.

I detest causing pain, and I had made a resolution never to shoot again unless there was a real need for food and I was sure of an outright kill. Yet I find it hard to explain the irrational horror these caymen inspired in me—their shape, their sly habits, their panic-stricken scuttling when surprised on land, all aroused an uncontrollable loathing. Further, I had been pestered for weeks past by their stalking of me whenever I went to bathe or read. I had had enough of them. Suddenly at sight of this huge specimen my hatred boiled up and I felt an inexcusable urge to destroy it.

As it approached I made Boodhoo go out over the water on a leaning tree where he was perfectly safe, but where he might act as a lure, while I fetched my gun. The enormous beast was only some 10 feet away from him when I fired—and struck it on the nose, blowing half away. It leaped up vertically, then dived and swam off under water. Half an hour later shouts summoned me some hundred yards upstream, to where, lying on my stomach on an overhanging bank, I could see it directly beneath me on a beach. It was fully 17 feet long. I clambered out on a tree, feeling sorry now at having unnecessarily wounded it, but still determined to kill it. But before I could take aim it got up, gave a bellow, and lumbered into the water.

The men, busy with their laundry, were now in a state of alarm. Not an hour had gone before yet another monster, almost submerged, approached some who were bathing. While they ran up begging me to shoot it, it remained where it was with an expression of blatant innocence in its eyes. I shot it in the eye at a distance of 30 yards with a charge of BB shot, the largest I had. It shook itself from head to foot, turned on its back and sank, blood spurting from its wound.

Big Rufus cried, 'Dat is a direc' shot!' And Little Rufus did a cartwheel.

A little later it floated up. Again I shot it, and it rushed forward into some branches trailing in the water, turned sideways and floated belly up, supported by them. It showed no signs of life and began to drift away, seemingly in imminent danger of sinking; so we jumped into the boat and paddled hastily to secure it.

It lay relaxed in the water, iridescent on the belly where the sunlight struck its pearly white scales. I held one of the front claws and Leno and Everard each one of the back feet, while with great daring Lord passed a noose over its jaws and gradually drew it back along the head and neck, conscious of the treacherous capacity of these reptiles for playing possum.

Lord and I leaned over the narrow gunwale, slowly adjusting the rope to encircle the belly.

Suddenly the jaws snapped to with a clap like a gun going off: the huge beast seemed to stand on its head—its tail, convulsed into an arc, lashing sideways and to and fro in great swings that could have killed any of us; it gave a low strangled roar, and while we all cowered back on the far side of the boat scarcely breathing, plunged down deep and out of sight. Fortunately the rope had come free, or at least one of us would have gone overboard.

We paddled ashore, and watched the water. Half an hour later it floated up. This time it was really dead. So we hauled it out of the water and measured it. It was just 12 feet from tip of nose to tip of tail. Suddenly I felt disgusted with myself at having shot it, despite the acclamation of my fellows. I had failed in my resolution.

Whilst we had been so engaged, Hamilton's launch had arrived almost unnoticed bringing our pilot, Captain Skeet, and his bowman, Milton Jones. Now, as I prepared to photograph the cayman, Skeet appeared as if from nowhere, shook hands, picked up my gun and to my astonishment planted his foot on the dead beast, threw out his chest, and called loudly for photographs to be taken.

Motheaten but pugnacious, the rolling-eyed old apparition had lost none of his flamboyance, and I was pleased to see him. He reminded me suddenly of what I could still hardly believe—that the outside world lay only two days away. He was the right man for my mood: of a sudden he increased my eagerness to return, even though I knew it would require a lot of readjustment.

16

Civilisation

The last day of the expedition came. While the men under Jothan surveyed the one remaining line I sailed upstream with Justin, Joseph, and Basil.

We cruised along close to the left bank, observing numerous big domes of rock newly emerged from the falling waters, until at one point a long tongue of grey rock lolled from the forest. As we drew close a fat powerful cayman some 15 feet long scuttled out of the forest and with loathsome reptilian fluster hustled down the rock and swam off. On the bank above a couple of tent poles, an empty tin, and a piece of sacking showed where our old fisherman had spent the night after leaving us. The whole place stank so powerfully that it made us suspicious. Scarcely able to breathe, we searched to discover the cause and found the mangled remains of a dried fish which the cayman had been eating. Retching, we rushed back to the boat and pushed off.

Next we went to the Trinity Isles to look at their sandbanks. Most sandbanks behave like underwater sand dunes, rolling along urged by the current and more or less keeping together as a streamlined, ripple-marked unit, which may break up, fuse with some other sandbank, or stabilise in quiet waters and build up into an island.

Many islands in the river had apparently originated in this way, and still had sandbanks attached to them as low tails, and sometimes as heads as well. But the peculiarity of these particular sandbanks was that, though extending as long yellow tails downstream from the forested green of the islands, they were some 5 feet *higher*. Furthermore, the Trinity Isles themselves were composed of very fine silt, such as one would not expect to be deposited under the same conditions as sand, and which now bore dense forest, including high Mora trees. At first I thought that the finer silt might have been deposited on older areas, as they became colonised by trees, while sand had gradually been swept around to the rear and piled up high by back swirls; but now I saw that there was no mixture of sand and silt at the junction between forested island and bank, which one would expect in such a case. Instead there was an abrupt transition. My surmise was that the islands were fragments of former river-side levees, in the lee of which sand collected when they were submerged—the greater height of the sandbanks being due to the fact that they were still being built up in the calm water behind the trees, while the silt islands themselves were probably being eroded, though the trees on them checked the current sufficiently for this process to be slow, and to prevent sand brought down from upstream from penetrating in amongst them.

On the large sandbank where the sand looked smoothest we found several turtle-egg caches by prodding with sticks, whilst overhead screaming terns and skimmers dive-attacked us, wheeling close past our heads—the latter, with their projecting underbeaks and long slender wings, like reconstructed ptero-dactyls. Search as we might though, we found no birds' eggs, and saw only one young one, a fully fledged ternlet: a beautiful sandy-speckled bird with gentle eyes, almost ready to fly, which rose at my feet and walked away a few paces. I picked it up and carried it for a little while. Then I put it down, and it ran away into the water and swam buoyantly just out of reach. For fear that it would be attacked by perai I stood off a good distance away until I saw that it had come safely ashore.

Back at the entrance to the day's line we tied up to a tree and lay chatting and fishing for little striped cichlids and sunfish, waiting for the men to return, while Basil told me about his plans after we had reached Bartica. It appeared that he and the old fisherman had talked, had become friends and partners, and that as a result for several weeks past he had boned, cleaned and sun-dried or smoked all the fish he had caught—those odorous bunches that swung now from the launch's ceiling. I had been on the point of complaining about them, and asking why they were never eaten. Now I remained silent. There was apparently a ready sale for such dried fish at the coast, and also at Bartica and Mackenzie. All the more accessible waters of British

Guiana were already over-fished, so Basil planned to buy a large net and to return with the fisherman to work these almost virgin stretches. His eyes dilated in anticipation as he described the enormous catches he would make.

Suddenly he pulled out a little cardboard box and showed it to me. It was filled with the dozens of big caymans' teeth which he had been collecting to sell as charms against snake bites. Not only would a snake not bite a man who carried one, but it would actually turn aside and flee! Furthermore, should it make a mistake, a little of the cayman's tooth scraped into the wound would counteract all ill-effects. Now Basil explained that he intended to mount the teeth in gold—he needed about $60 to buy the gold with (apart from $100 needed for the net). But like all entrepreneurs he was short of capital—he spent all he earned on his wife and children. Where could he find some? Fortunately the line-cutters began to come back just then, for in another moment I might have offered to finance him, and I had no money even to begin to acquire my own freedom.

We returned to camp, our work completed on the very day planned, and busied ourselves with packing, still hardly able to believe that on the morrow we should be returning to the half-forgotten world of shops and houses and other people.

Before dawn I got up, shaved, and dressed in my smartest dry clothes—a blue Aertex shirt, grey flannel trousers and white tennis shoes, all reserved for the occasion. It was a cold, wet morning, the still black trees and their dangling lianes dripped with moisture, and dew lay in a white sheet over the ground. At the men's camp fires glowed, tea was brewed, everyone was astir. Soon bundles were being passed down into the boat, along a frieze of men silhouetted against the white cocoon of mist that lay thick on the river. On the bank we left behind some forlorn dew-soaked cardboard boxes, a few tins, and a pile of newly-made Bartaballi paddles ordered by the Forest Department, for which there was no room on board.

As we pushed off the first apricot flush was in the sky. In midstream an enormous cayman swam slowly past, surveying us with red-glowing eyes. His nose was damaged—and I felt a strong pang of regret at having caused him pain. He vanished behind us in the mist, his lopsided nose bobbing along like a cork.

s

Blue drained into the waters—and ahead floated the emerald
of Gluck Island. The chameleon-river was totally calm, resting
between illusions, the light upon it like a skin, shimmering in
blue, green and pink iridescences that broke brown beneath
our bow. Then the surface glittered like a shoal of fish with dark
calm spots. The wavelets sprang higher and a cross-diamond
pattern of minute striations appeared, only to flatten into oily
undulations behind the shelter of a promontory.

With the sun higher, a sapphire and diamond sparkle began;
white-crested waves raced along and slapped against us, con-
trasting with the duller olive brown of shadowed water. We
drew abeam of Gluck Island, and saw that it was rimmed with
yellow sandbanks. The grey and brown dilapidation of Rockstone appeared ahead, and we landed for a moment to tell
Hamilton's men of our departure, so that mail could be re-
addressed and our paddles collected. A few derelicts leaned
over the railings of the jetty or sat upon the broken steps of the
surviving houses. A wrinkled old woman with one or two yellow
and green teeth cracked a joke which gave rise to non-commital
grunts from the men and an uproar of cackles from her. Our
mossy-faced old fisherman friend nodded his grey head at me,
shook me by the hand with a horny claw and begged me to
photograph him and send him a copy.

I had the feeling that I should never see the place again, that
a chapter of life was closing. These curious derelict houses and
people seemed already to have become abstractions, symbolic
to me of a twilight state of living. They sank behind as we
sailed on into a limbo that was not yet quite the past. The
pictures would fade, the memories dissolve, the words be
forgotten: the scents at night, and moonlight flooding the water;
early morning opalescence and diamond mid-day heat; yellow
afternoons and baroque sunsets—for a while my dreams would
be full of them, and of the gaping mouths of haimaras, the
rolling backs of arapaimas, of blue and red kingfishers flashing
down endless waterways, of wild pigs stampeding through
teeming jungles, their strong smell drowning my nostrils. The
rivers would rise and fall, change their courses and disappear—
endlessly time would shape the land. I could reason about all
this, but its emotional impact upon my lonely self had been
overwhelming. For a brief while I had lived this life, and now

it was over. But it would tinge my years to come with lingering emotions.

I had lost many of my former ideas about human beings, and about how to live. Perhaps more than any other result of the expedition I treasured the new values I was beginning to think out. The Indians, initially so remote and nebulous, now seemed more solid, and much nearer to me, than many who from background should have been. I had become so familiar with the jungle that at a pinch I could have survived in it, given a cutlass and file, and perhaps a few fish hooks (though I could have made those). I could recognise and name more of the trees and their properties than most of the men; could run almost as they through the forest; follow a trail; walk along a tacouba; light a fire; build a shelter; make bows and arrows; and make a wood-skin canoe. I was still not as strong as they, so I could not portage heavy loads for long distances, as they could. But I had felt in better health than in all my previous life during those three months.

Thus I mused, sitting on my rubber tyre on the roof of the boat, whilst the green jungle walls slid past with increasing speed. Milton Jones now stood at the bow shifting his balance and throwing his weight on to his paddle every now and then. We were driving through narrow winding channels, and above the engine could be heard the pounding roar of cataracts, glimpsed as sparkling foam on either side.

Rounding a point, we were swept sideways with straining engine towards towering domed rocks, in the lee of which a canoe rocked on the dark water with a squared log beside it. Above, a glorious golden tree showered its flowers into the pools, while on a small ledge, totally unaware of us, a solitary naked Indian, poised like a statue of red clay with drawn bow and arrow, gazed down into the water for the rust-coloured paku fish. Then he was lost to view, the channel widened, and we found ourselves sweeping along a broad reach between fantastic rock masses—spheres, hemispheres, sugar-loaves, pyramids, reclining figures, weird distortions, all finished to a smooth, massive perfection. Wherever there was a foothold blazed the chrome yellow of flowering Iteballi trees, the feathery green of guavas.

The rapids were far more dangerous now than when we had
s*

ascended, for the water level had fallen some 20 feet, exposing rocks before covered and making the channels narrower and more tortuous; and above all we were now going downstream, racing the engine in order to keep control, and travelling many times faster. Then, our speed against the current might have been 1 to 3 miles an hour; now it was more like 20–30, and an accident would have been correspondingly more serious. The force of the water could be gauged by the way in which even quite big pieces of wood swirled about, were sucked under in whirlpools, or shot up suddenly into the air.

I sat on the roof photographing the scene, and although nearly thrown off from time to time by the swerves and shudderings of the boat, I had no sense of danger. I trusted Skeet— there was nothing to be gained by doing otherwise.

And Skeet was working hard. His keen old eyes constantly swept the water ahead. Yet the rain had caused landslips, the movement of boulders, the wind had blown down many riverside trees—there were dead trees riding downstream with us, or stuck, twitching, at various points. The very channels might have changed. Before we started there had been some muttering amongst the men about Skeet's failing strength, and that he was forgetting the best routes. But now they were silent. Occasionally he shouted to me, but I could scarcely hear his voice above the turmoil. Then he beckoned and waved so purposefully that I scrambled back and inclined my ear close to him.

'There is a certain channel, Sah, in de *wors'* part ahead. If we could shoot through without unloading it save one or two hours. Do you wish me to try?'

'Go ahead,' I said. 'If you think we can get through.'

'It's very dangerous, Sir, if de water too low.'

A moment later we changed direction, and went racing down a long steep chute of water with jagged rocks to the left. To the right another great rush of water came in at an angle—a welter of white foam juggling, wobbling, and flying up in fountains, flashing rainbows in the sunlight. One hundred and fifty yards of curving, sliding water—and then ahead appeared a barrier of little black rock-teeth! Skeet and Jones simultaneously gave loud shouts of alarm and threw their weights on the steering paddles. The boat keeled over with a lurch that flung me on my back and nearly into the water, a wave swept through amidships, practically carrying Boodhoo away—and before we really knew what had happened we had turned and were slowly fighting our way up the foaming water slope on the right. Skeet was grey as a ghost—another instant and we would have been ripped open.

Now the mad rush had ceased: the boat was motionless, the rocks stood still, the water moved past terrifyingly fast. We paddled to help the engine and prayed that it would not fail. Imperceptibly at first we climbed the slope, clinging to bushes as we went. Then we were unloading among silvery guavas on to smooth stones and rocks thickly pilose with dried Podostemon-aceae fruit. To my surprise, beyond a grove of twisted trees I recognised the entrance to the portage we had used on our way up. It was this we had tried to shoot! In that hillside grove the men, then up to their necks in water, had hauled the boat on the second morning of the expedition.

Now, only half-loaded and with a skeleton crew, the boat was sent round by another route, whilst the rest of us carried the baggage along the cool earth path with its lushly grown Sela-ginellas and feathery mosses, its slow fluttering Heliconia butterflies, its scent of damp earth, vegetation, and pulverised water, its strange subterranean tremor from the throbbing of the falls.

On the other side of the portage instead of huge waves there were now great sloping tables of reddish-streaked rocks and a few trickles of water. Everywhere on wiry stalks the little pepper-pot fruit-capsules of the Podostemonaceae waved above their dried encrusting thalli, shaking seeds over the rocks, wait-ing for the waters to rise to produce the new generation. Over-head amongst the flaming orange-and-yellow inflorescences of a Rubiaceous bush, a humming-bird gave a high piping whistle, fluttered, and returned to its twig. Above it, a tree bore large saucers of close-compressed white flowers with a sweet scent. A tiny 8-foot-high mangrove tree on tall stilt roots—perhaps the highest up the river—indicated that we were back on waters still occasionally tidal. A trickle of yellow butterflies was crossing between two islands downstream, tiny specks of life bobbing about in the air. A darter sat on a rock in midstream near them, and I watched him dive into the fiercely racing white foam—then many yards downstream his head emerged like a water snake above the current, and with body still submerged he swam to another rock and climbed ashore.

Then the boat was shooting between far away rocks upstream, with little tufts of white where the bowman strove with his paddle. A moment later it turned broadside on below us, managed to get across the current, and drew up on the sand close by, the men aboard pale and excited.

We reloaded and sailed on.

We passed through one, then another cloud of butterflies. Then the river was a level plain of water with only a few lingering foam-piles to show for the falls. Familiar place-names were uttered by the men—Winiperu, Moroballi, Monkey Jump (where a new quarry now gashed the hillside). The sun was high—it was past noon. The water vibrated with a million points of light, the forest was dead black-green and sullen on either side, a mile away. The clouds which had piled high all day suddenly massed, and drenched us in a torrent that swept across the water and over us before we had time to take cover.

Then the sun broke through again, the world sparkled—and far away across the water a glitter of tin roofs was Bartica. Soon we could see red houses; the stelling came into sight, tall cabbage palms waved above the police station. We tied up and stepped ashore. The familiar strong personalities of the men dissolved and broke, became nondescript in the tide of other faces. The trip was over.

There remained the unloading of the boat, the checking and packing away of equipment, the paying of the men, the greeting of old acquaintances.

The place was bewildering: Chinese and East Indian traders shouted and displayed their wares; baskets of fruit of all colours lay beside the road and piled on the stelling, guarded by squatting vendors. Opposite my hotel the Futui tree, which had been in flower when I went away, was now in full green feathery leaf.

When the day's work was over I strolled along the once familiar sawdust trails between the soft, heart-shaped arum leaves, a little way to a quiet beach where I sat on a log, gazed over the water, and collected my thoughts. Among my letters had been one from Smeed, saying that it had been found possible to grant me my leave. So do we learn the uses of hypocrisy.

How beautiful the river lay in the evening!

I turned back to the town, brilliant with electric lights, and thought, 'Tonight I shall have dinner in an hotel and sleep in a proper bed. But I shall never be my old self again.'

17

Postscript

'Aw heck! If it ain't Nick!'

It was Aggie—her voice, like a macaw's, coming from a parked car as I strolled in the dusk with a friend down Main Street, Georgetown, a few days later. I shook hands with the vibrating button-eyed creature.

'Well, Aggie, how's tricks?'

'Jesus, man, why aren't you in the bush?'

'I've just got back. They seem to find me more useful at present in town.'

'A chap like you ought to be *kept* in the bush.'

'Well, I'm going back for a few days soon. Shall I give your love to the crocodiles—or might they prefer to forget you?'

'The same old Nick. Always ready with a nasty crack.'

'You started it.'

She was looking murderous, so I said goodbye and walked off. The car started up behind me quietly, and some instinct made me step into a doorway as it shot past swerving violently, with Aggie's hand grabbing at the wheel, her other fist outstretched to strike me.

'Get you next time!' she shouted.

And she did indeed manage to land a blow on me at a dance a few weeks later, as well as threaten me with a knife. I had been too slow for her, and she imagined I was having all sorts of other love affairs. If only it had been true! For in the last analysis it was lack of love that spoiled my years in Guyana. Even Sheila von Battenburg I never met again—the only girl I might have loved.

After the expedition I spent Christmas and the New Year in Tobago and Trinidad, and recovered a little of my *joie de vivre* on their beaches, watching the pelicans and the man-o'-war birds fishing, chatting with simple extroverted people, swimming in fizzy blue water, dancing calypsos with voluptuous and apparently boneless girls. Guyana seemed a sullen nightmare, the tomb of all my hopes. When I closed my eyes I could see the steely river at Bartica, feel the dread pangs of loneliness at the thought of returning.

Fanshawe, Swabey, Taylor, even Smeed expressed admiration when I delivered my report. It was the first time that such a scientific approach to a survey had been made in the department. The expedition had lasted from September 2nd to December 1st, 1949. It had cut 45 lines totalling 134 miles, and had counted every large tree in 1,571 acres out of a total area of 186,126 acres (292 square miles). This gave a 0.85 per cent survey at a cost of $9.79 per square mile. We had seen 900 species of woody plants, over 250 of them being trees above 12 inches in diameter. And we had collected 148 plant specimens, including 15 woody species never seen before in Guyana, some of which might be new to science.

At the riverside our area was about 100 feet above mean sea level, and in the middle of the true Rain Forest zone where no month in the year has less than 4 inches of rain (save in disastrous fire years like 1926); where the daily temperature averages 78°F (68–91°F); and where the humidity at the riverside fluctuates between 77.3 per cent at midday and 96.7 per cent at 6 a.m.—though in particular places rich in filmy ferns the air was probably saturated much of the time. In this area, enormously rich in useful trees, each thousand acres contained approximately 5,030 Soft Wallaba trees, 2,580 Greenheart, 2,460 Ituri Wallaba, 1,450 Common Kakaralli, 1,410 Mora, 1,180 Wamara, 1,110 Dakama trees, and thousands of others, including Morabukea, Korokoro, Smooth-leaf Kakaralli, Yaruru, Sand Baromalli, Ite palms, Broad-leafed Kakaralli, Sarabebeballi, Wirimiri, Purpleheart, Balata, Crabwood, Letterwood.

These are bare statistics, which give no idea of the majesty of the forests I had seen. Would they soon be exploited, and left in hideous ruins as had been those nearer civilisation? Or would they last intact for a few years more to give solace to those who value nature and what solitude can give?

Even when my report had been read the esteem of my colleagues was not enough to repair my disillusionment. Until

Smeed was promoted away, life never really smiled, except on my long solitary journeys into the interior, the most beautiful being that to the Wai-Wais, and until finally, after four years, I was able to strike away from the Colonial Service. I spent my next two years doing research at the New York Botanical Garden, returning twice to South America for expeditions, one of them to advise *Life Magazine*. Then after that I began to work on those things that I alone could do, and eliminate what others could do equally well.

Not everyone can use his skills without oppressing his fellow men. But I had to try. I wanted to delineate the similarities as well as the differences between people: I felt that there were continents waiting to be explored as unknown as any in past history—continents of the mind, as the different classes and races of mankind begin to discover each other. Perhaps we should all marry or at least love someone of a different breed? In miscegenation lie the best hopes of the world.

Index

This index will provide added precision for anyone who wishes to use the book as a source of information. For instance "acacia-like trees" on p. 250 are defined herein as *Macrolobium acaciaefolium*.